Drums of Rebellion

Kenya in Chaos

by

J. Gordon Mumford

Published by:
Zebra Publishing House
413 - 3 Rialto Court
New Westminster, BC
Canada - V3M 6P2
Tel: 604-520-1487; Fax: 604-520-1497
E-mail zebrapage@shaw.ca

ISBN 0-9736297-1-1
Printed and bound in Canada
Copyright 2005

Cover photograph: Fortified Kikuyu home guard post near Fort Hall, 1953, © J. Gordon Mumford.

Layout and Design by Zebra Page Design.
Printing by Benwell-Atkins, Vancouver, BC.

Canadian Cataloguing in Publication Data

Mumford, J. Gordon, 1925-

    Drums of rebellion: Kenya in chaos / by J. Gordon Mumford.

    Sequel to: White man's drum.

    Includes bibliographical references.

ISBN 0-9736297-1-1

    1. Mumford, J. Gordon, 1925-

    2. Kenya—History—Mau Mau Emergency, 1952-1960.

    3. Kenya—Description and travel

    4. East African Posts and Telecommunications Administration—Biography.

    I. Title

DT433.576.M84A3 2005   967.62'03'092   C2005-901872-0

To Barbara: We have shared good times and bad. Without your help, encouragement, support and expertise, my books would never have been written. You are my life.

I would also like to thank my friend Alan Brooks, who was the UNDP representative at the EAP&T Central Training School in Mbagathi, Kenya, for his encouragement and assistance.

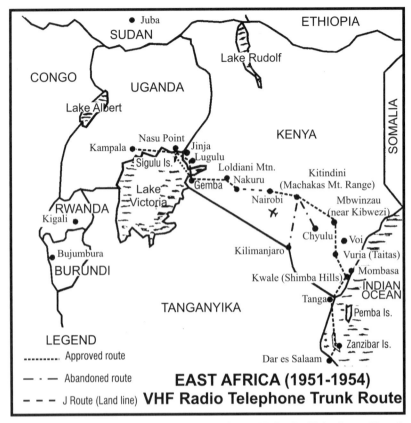

Figure 1. Map of East Africa showing the VHF Radio Telephone Trunk Route. This prototype, developed by the Marconi Company, was first installed in East Africa in the early 1950s. The system was then used in North and South America and elsewhere.

Legend for Maps

Contents

Introduction

Drums of Rebellion is the second book of a trilogy set against the background of Africa in tumult and the Kikuyu rebellion. To the five young men, the lure of the word *safari* had been irresistible. They had fought in the Second World War, and missed the adrenalin rush that had been their constant companion in wartime. Unsettled and bored in England, they had come to East Africa looking for fresh adventures.

Split into two teams, they were assigned to a four year project that involved the survey and installation of a viable route for a modern VHF (very high frequency) radio-repeater multi-channel telecomms. system across East Africa. The project ranged from Kampala in Uganda, through Kenya to Dar es Salaam in Tanganyika via Zanzibar.

They worked under canvas on safari for months at a time, encountering inhospitable country, wild animals, and extreme weather conditions. Halfway into the project, they faced more excitement than they had bargained for. The Kikuyu tribe in Kenya's Central Province rebelled against British rule (*Mau Mau*), and the crew found themselves working in the midst of a savage civil war.

The author was one of the men involved, and his books present an informal history of East Africa in the post war years. The trilogy focuses on the building of VHF radio-repeater routes in 1951-1954, describing life on safari in East Africa, and providing an insight into the experiences and adventures of an expatriate in Africa in crisis. These are not luxurious big game hunting safaris, but working safaris in the bush and back country of East Africa.

***

The following information is provided for readers interested in the technical side of the project and the reasons for its implementation. Prior to 1949, telephone and telecommunications, including long distance telephone and telegraph systems, relied on single or multiple pair telephone wires strung on telegraph poles. These overhead wires were vulnerable to breakages by elephants and giraffe, and to theft by local tribesmen who cut the copper wire to make bangles.

There was a serious technical problem with overhead telephone line pairs: the characteristic frequency response limited the line to audio frequencies. The overhead pair of lines was capable of carrying only one or two audio (speech) channels at a time, dependent on the type of line. Balanced lines, such as J-routes, could be used; only one route, Nairobi-Nakuru (100 miles, 12 channels), existed in Kenya in 1949.

Worldwide, the demand for better communications systems was increasing in both modern and developing countries. This inevitably led to research and development of multi-channel radio repeater telecomms. techniques and systems. That demand, and the pressing need for a multi-channel telephone system capable of catering for the needs of a variety of individual and business subscribers, led Marconi engineers to develop and install a prototype of a modern VHF radio communications repeater link system to be used between Nairobi and Nakuru in Kenya. It was successfully tested in Kenya in 1947-49, and used the VHF frequency band for use on backbone telephone routes. Frequencies ranged from 180 to 210 MHz (Megahertz).

The test sites and repeater stations were located on mountaintops because VHF transmissions travel in a straight line (line of sight), and, unlike lower frequencies, are not reflected by the ionospheric layer surrounding the planet. For effective communication the two ends of the communication link must be in sight of each other. To maximize the distance between terminals the survey crews had to select the highest possible sites, usually on mountaintops.

The success of this twenty-four channel prototype system developed by the Marconi engineers led to the use of VHF radio repeater equipment and systems all over the world, including the radio backbone routes across North and South America. The routes have largely been replaced by microwave radio repeater systems worldwide. These systems link into satellites using broadband equipment for television and telecommunications that carries over nine hundred channels.

The radio repeater project from Uganda, to Kenya, Zanzibar and Dar es Salaam was a pioneering one, paralleling the development of the railroad from Mombasa (Kenya) to Lake Victoria and Uganda. Although referred to as the *Lunatic Line* when it was first proposed, the railroad opened up East Africa to economic development. Likewise, the VHF radio telecommunications system provided the people with access to communications, not only with the rest of the world, but to their own towns and cities. It was truly an essential element in nation building and deserves its place in the history of East Africa.

Chapter 1
The Uprising

The Declaration of Emergency

How quickly our euphoria had dissipated! Elated by our successful climb of Kilimanjaro, Geoff and I had arrived back at the hotel, wearing the wreaths of flowers that our guides had placed around our necks. When the hotel manager told us the latest news, however, our jubilation soon turned to anger and despair. While we had been on the mountain, civil unrest in Kenya had turned ugly, and the Governor had declared a State of Emergency.

"Aye, it's true," sighed the manager, handing me a copy of the local newspaper. "It's all in the East African Standard." Taking it, I glanced at the date, October 21, 1952, three days ago.

Probably the proclamation should not have come as a surprise, but it did. Somehow the starkness of the headlines stunned me. There had been indications of trouble before we left, including random killings on the Kikuyu Reserves and rumours of mass oathing ceremonies. The most serious incident, however, had been the recent murder of Senior Chief Waruhiu. The final step had now been taken, and the war against *Mau Mau* was on. There would be no turning back.

The hotel bar was filled with angry white settlers, discussing the latest events. *Yes, Mau Mau has already cast its evil spell over the population. How many lives will be lost in the coming conflict?* Both white residents and Africans suspected of being loyal to the government have been murdered, while cattle belonging to white farmers in the Central Province have been hamstrung and killed.

Now as I wait in the Moshi terminal for the country bus to Arusha, my thoughts go back to my recent climb. Joan and I had met Geoff and his family while we were holidaying in Malindi. When Geoff heard that I was going to climb Kilimanjaro, he wanted to come with me. He is on his way back to Rhodesia now, but in my mind, I can picture the two of us climbing the mountain, the scree at 16,000 feet, and the struggle to reach the icebound crater rim. We had reached the peak, and signed the book at Gilman's Point, adding our names to the long list of climbers stretching back into the early nineteen-twenties.

I am the only white man in the bus terminal, but it doesn't bother me, because I am used to working on my own in remote areas. Besides, I'm in Tanganyika, and the people belong to the Wachagga tribe. *I wonder what it will feel like when I'm surrounded by Kikuyu in Kenya's Central Province? Will it be different now that there is a state of emergency?*

Thinking back to last night in the hotel bar, I remember the hatred displayed by most of the old settlers. It's hard to blame them for their bitterness. After all, they've seen cattle hamstrung, crops destroyed, and houses set afire by marauding gangs. Lured to Africa by the British government's offers of cheap land and labour, many found themselves living on isolated farms, forced to scratch the dirt for a living. Now they stand to lose their homes, livelihoods and even their lives. It's a no-win situation.

The newspapers have reported that gangs are taking narcotic drugs before they go on crazed killing sprees. There may be some fanatics, but the Africans that I know and work with are not like that. Even in the troubled areas of the Central Province, most Kikuyu are loyal to the government and oppose the large scale oathing taking place on the Kikuyu Reserves. As I think about the situation, I shake my head. *Brothers are fighting their brothers, Kikuyu are fighting Kikuyu. God what a mess. What lies ahead?* We will soon find out.

There is a commotion as the bus arrives, and I'm carried aboard by the surge of the throng. The bus is crowded, and it's standing room only. Most of the people are going to the Arusha market, and with luck, I'll be able to get a seat there for the rest of the trip.

✳✳✳

When the bus stops at Arusha, the colourful mass of humanity pushes and shoves as people struggle to disembark. Not many people board the bus here, and I move to an empty seat next to a window. An older man, a Wachagga, takes the seat next to me.

"*Aiyee, bwana,*" he says, "*unakwenda Nairobi*—are you going to Nairobi?"

"*Ndiyo,*" I reply. "*Ninakaa uko*—yes, I live there."

As we talk, my companion tells me about his *shamba* in the Namanga River district where he farms with his wife and children, then listens with interest when I tell him about climbing Kilimanjaro. At Namanga

River, he leaves the bus, and I watch him go, his battered old hat bobbing among the departing passengers. He waves his hand and disappears from sight as the bus moves off on its journey to Nairobi.

Settling back in my seat, I watch the thick bush of the countryside bordering the Amboseli National Park and the Ingito Hills disappear in the dust plume of our bus. Ahead lie the flat Kapiti plains and Nairobi.

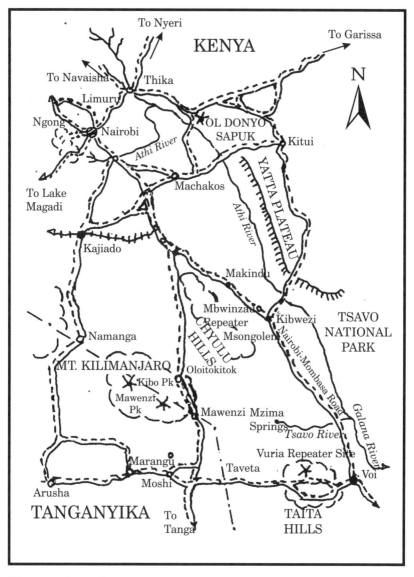

Figure 2. Map showing the route from Moshi to Nairobi.

Kajiado looms up out of the plains, somewhere between Magadi and Konza, where the railroad local line joins the main Nairobi-Mombasa railroad. The small whistle stop consists of a ramshackle station and a few huts located in the middle of nowhere. It's a lonely and lost place in the flat, dried-up plains, and soon vanishes in the heat haze.

As we approach Athi River, I can see the Aberdare mountain range in the distance. Nairobi is still half-hidden in the foothills, but the glint of sunlight off the high buildings betrays its presence. It's only a few miles now, and I'm eager to get home and see Joan.

An Armed and Tense City

There's a suppressed tension in the air when I alight at the country bus depot in Harding Street. Security patrols with weapons in plain view are everywhere, carefully scrutinizing the disembarking African passengers who scurry away down the side streets. As the lone white man in a throng of black people, I feel conspicuous. The eyes of a patrolling police inspector in charge of a group of African *askaris* (policemen) watches me quizzically as I collect my baggage. Leaving the station, I walk up Harding Street to the New Stanley Hotel.

It's the afternoon of Sunday, October 26, and the "State of Emergency" is only five days old. I feel apprehensive, the way I did when war was declared in Britain in 1939. The sight of small groups of white people in the hotel lobby and the sound of their animated conversations reinforces this feeling. People cluster together and seem more aware of one another. There's a feeling of camaraderie, of "us" against "them," but this time it's whites against blacks, and the war is a fight for our existence against the unknown force called *Mau Mau*.

Expecting my call, Joan answers the phone quickly. "I'm at the New Stanley," I tell her. "I've just got in." For some reason, I laugh nervously; maybe it's the tension and excitement. "I'll be in front of the hotel, on the corner," I add. After exchanging a few more words, I replace the receiver and walk outside to wait.

✳✳✳

Delamere Avenue is a familiar sight. The beautiful, broad avenue is edged with jacaranda trees and palms that separate the roadway from the parking bays on either side. It is an avenue fit for the first Charter City in the Commonwealth.

It was two years ago, on March 30, 1950, that the Duke of Gloucester had given the mayor the Royal Charter. I remember the parade that day, and the colourful floats that depicted scenes from Kenya's past. One float had shown Sergeant Ellis who, in 1896, had pitched his tent in the swamp that was to become Nairobi, while Gailey & Roberts' float depicted a prehistoric monster. Behind the floats marched Masai warriors, followed by modern army units with armoured cars and Bren gun carriers.

At Harding Street, the parade turned right, passing Lord Delamere's statue in the centre of the roundabout near the New Stanley Hotel, opposite where I am standing now. *Yes*, I think, *Joan and I watched the parade from the offices of Kaplan & Stratton in Corner House on Harding Street.* Joan left that firm a year later to take up her present secretarial position with Archer & Wilcock, another law firm.

Across the street, I can see the Mutual Building where she works now. It is quite an imposing building, solid and functional, built of brick and concrete with supporting columns over the sidewalk. My reverie is broken by the arrival of our Austin, as Joan draws up to the curb beside me.

✳✳✳

"So, you made it," Joan says, as I slip into the passenger seat. "I knew you would." Her voice is matter-of-fact as she lets in the clutch and moves off down the parking lane, then turns onto the main road. After our initial greetings, she doesn't speak again, and I sense there's something on her mind.

"Billy okay?" I ask.

"Yes," she says, then after a pause, she adds, "I saw him a few days ago. He's joined the KPR (Kenya Police Reserve). He's up at Gilgil this weekend, some sort of training camp."

Figure 3. Float showing Sgt. Ellis, Nairobi's first European resident.

"Lucky devil," I mutter. "Now the emergency has been declared, everyone will be joining something or other. I'd like to join the Kenya Regiment."

"Oh, you men!" Joan sounds exasperated. "You're like bloody kids, scrambling about in the bush. You've been in one war," she exclaims angrily. "Isn't that enough?"

"Yes, I guess you're right," I sigh. "It's just that this is so near to home. The Declaration has brought things out into the open, and it is easy to get caught up in the anger and excitement. Kenya is our home now, and it's being threatened. I feel that something has to be done to help. Things seem to be going from bad to worse."

As I settle in my seat, I think about the first time that I saw Billy Roche. It was like an old-time melodrama. It was late August, and I'd returned from *safari* a day early. Joan and Billy were on the point of going out to the movies. Doug Price, our landlord, kept me talking by the truck while his wife rushed back to the guest house to tell Joan to get Billy out of there.

Doug and his wife had assumed the worst, not realizing that Joan had already written to tell me about Billy. Now the red-headed Irishman is a close family friend and visits us often. He works for his brother, a building contractor with an office in Westlands, and we've met Paddy and Mary, his brother and sister-in-law.

I can still remember how annoyed Joan was with the Prices. I don't think their relationship was ever the same after that. Shortly after that incident, we were assigned a government-owned apartment in Daphton Court in Riverside Drive, Kileleshwa. I know that Joan was glad that we finally had our own place and were able to move. After all, we'd been living in various residential hotels and guesthouses for over four years while we'd waited to be assigned to government housing.

The Sunday traffic is light in downtown Nairobi. Just before the railway crossing, we turn right into Saddler Street from Delamere Avenue, and then speed up past the army football stadium near the junction of Saddler Street and Government Road. On our right is the stately old Norfolk Hotel. Joan nods her head towards the stadium, as she asks, "Did you hear that the Lancashire Fusiliers were airlifted into Nairobi this week?"

"I heard that army troops were being flown in, but that's about all. Did the newspapers say where they've been stationed?"

"We've not heard much, except that they're based at Kahawa in the army camp with the KAR (King's African Rifles). Most of them are being used in the Rift Valley, because the European farms there are under threat of attack from gangs hiding in the forest reserves in the Aberdares." She pauses for a moment before adding, "The army have set up checkpoints on the main roads out of Nairobi as well as in the

Kikuyu Reserves. They're searching all suspicious vehicles for guns and ammunition."

Just ahead are the gateposts of Daphton Court, a three-storey complex of twelve apartments on Riverside Drive. The iron gate is open, lying back against the hedge. Joan slows the car, turns into the drive and parks in the *makuti* (thatch)-roofed garage. We're home. It's been an eventful month, and tomorrow I go back to work.

The Survey Office

"Aye," says Mac. "We're putting the finishing touches to the Nakuru-Kampala survey." He glances at the small group gathered around the table in his office, and then turns back towards the map. "There," he says, pointing to a mountain peak on the Mau escarpment, "Loldiani! It's on a knife-edge at ten thousand feet. The hills and high land below the ridge will cut out any adverse effects of reflected waves from Gemba, and," he adds, "it has a clear optical path."

It is Monday, October 27, and we're in the shack on Whitehouse Road that houses Mac's office. Emergency or no emergency, the survey for the backbone routes must go on. These routes are vital for security, as well as for general communications, because repeaters can be safeguarded, whereas overhead telephone wires are easily cut.

Mac's face breaks into a smile. "Mumford," he says, "the site is located in a thick bamboo forest on the top of Loldiani Mountain, about a mile from the end of a logging track. Your job will be to cut a road wide enough to get the Land Rover through the bamboo to the site. Once the top site is operational, the track can be widened to take a truck."

Unrolling a large-scale, contour survey map of the Eldama Ravine and *Maji Mzuri* (Sweet Water) area, he spreads it out on the table. With his finger, he traces a line leading from the small village of Maji Mzuri, where there's a sawmill along a logging track. Used mainly by loggers, the track ends just above the nine-thousand-foot contour level, but a dotted red line has been pencilled in from the end of the track to the bamboo-covered peak of the mountain.

Mac strokes his beard thoughtfully, unconsciously tugging at the short, trimmed point. "There's an old survey beacon dating back to the 1930s on the top," he says, "but the ground around it is overgrown with bush and bamboo. That'll have to be cleared."

"What about labour?" I ask. "Do I recruit them locally?"

Mac shakes his head. "No, we can't trust them, not with all the *Mau Mau* oath-taking ceremonies and unrest among the Kikuyu. We're giving you fifteen hand-picked workmen from Nairobi. They're good men, been with us for years, so they're trustworthy. You'll have to make a base camp at the end of the logging road in the forest where the bamboo begins, and cut the track to the top from there."

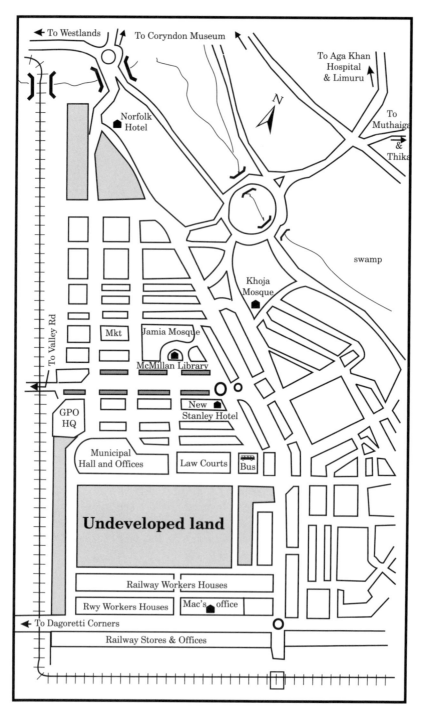

Figure 4. Map of Nairobi, showing location of Mac's office.

We talk on, clearing up the details of transport and timing before dispersing. My deadline for departure from Nairobi to Loldiani is Wednesday, November 3, in a week's time. Eric and Bungy will leave for Gemba two weeks later on November 19. A large, four-wheel-drive, ex-army truck has been put at my disposal for transporting the workmen and the mast sections, plus camping and radio test equipment. A Land Rover is to be used for everyday running on the track through the bamboo and for the occasional trip to Londiani, the nearest town. Meanwhile, Eric will help Bungy Williams set up the Gemba site on a mountain in South Nyanza on the shores of Lake Victoria. Bungy will stay there, but Eric will join me at Londiani. I'll pick him up at the local hotel on November 25.

En Route to Maji Mzuri

Joan drops me off outside the post office headquarters in Delamere Avenue at seven-thirty on her way to work. Watching the car disappear into Nairobi's rush hour traffic, I have a momentary feeling of regret because I have to leave. But safari is a part of my job, and, as I turn away, I shrug my shoulders at the inevitability of all that it entails. Walking into the yard, I pass the truck that we had loaded yesterday, and dump my safari gear into the back of the Land Rover. The labourers are already aboard the truck, and have made themselves comfortable in the back amongst the tents, road building tools, and other paraphernalia necessary for an extended safari in the bush.

When I approach the vehicle, the chatter dies down. "*Tunakwenda sasa*—are we going now, bwana?" a lone voice calls.

Looking up, I grin. "*Ndiyo* (yes)," I say. Then, climbing onto the truck's running board, I talk to Kamau. An older man, this driver is a stranger to me, and subconsciously I memorize his features. He's a small man, with alert eyes and high cheekbones. The gashes in his ear lobes indicate that he still clings to the older, tribal traditions.

"*Fuata ghari yangu*—follow my vehicle," I say. "Do you know Maji Mzuri?" As I pause momentarily, Kamau nods, and then I continue, "We'll take the Lake Baringo turn-off and go via *Campi ya Moto* (Hot Camp). If we get separated, I'll stop and wait for you at Maji Mzuri. I want both vehicles to travel together through the forest track from that point because the gradients are steep and our base camp site is difficult to find."

Turning my head, I talk to Njeroge, the elderly *neopara* (foreman) in charge of the labourers, who is sitting next to Kamau. "*Umepata kila kitu yako*—have you got everything for your labour gang?" I ask.

"*Ndiyo, bwana,*" he says. "My men are all here, and ready to go. I checked the safari equipment and tools when I arrived this morning."

Pleased, I nod. I've known Njeroge for some time now, and trust his judgment. He's a mild-mannered, gentle soul, and liked by his men. "Right," I say, "we'll be off then. I'll lead the way in the Land Rover."

We leave in convoy, turning right out of the post office yard into Saddler Street and down to Whitehouse Road. Checking in the mirror, I can see the truck close behind as I pass the Railway Club and climb South Hill heading towards Dagoretti Corner.

Alone in the Land Rover, I let my thoughts wander to the events of the last two weeks. The Lancashire Fusiliers, with their patrols and Bren gun carriers, are now a familiar sight in Nairobi. More than a hundred alleged *Mau Mau* leaders, as well as many other suspects, have been arrested and detained in police and army raids. *The raids seem to have had an effect as the streets are quiet, but for how long?*

Heading west under a cloudless sky, we leave the suburbs of Nairobi and climb steadily through the hilly, rolling country of the Kikuyu Reserve on the Naivasha main road. The road surface is asphalt, the only section of tarred road outside the townships in Kenya, but it is plagued by lack of funding for maintenance. Potholes and worn edges to the road are only too apparent. "Damn," I mutter to myself a I strike a particularly bad potholed stretch, "Bloody potholes."

Cresting the slopes of the foothills leading to the Rift escarpment, I glance back at the distant city of Nairobi. It lies nestled in a hollow on the edge of the foothills where the Kapiti game plains stretch down to the Tanganyikan border. Now, only occasional reflections of sunlight from glass windows betray its presence.

Kamau and the lumbering, heavily laden truck are some way behind me, and, on reaching the top of the Rift Valley escarpment I pull into the viewpoint on the brink, and wait for them to catch up.

This spot is a favourite with Nairobi residents, and the view never fails to impress. The paved road built by Italian prisoners-of-war during World War II is cut into the steep cliff, and swings down from the lip of the escarpment to the floor of the Great Rift Valley two thousand feet below. At a point where the road flattens out, the Italians built a small church of quarried stone to mark the completion of the road.

✳✳✳

Now as our two vehicles travel along the floor of the Rift Valley a short distance apart, there is an air of peace in the countryside that is not apparent in Nairobi. Apart from occasional army checkpoints, nothing seems to have changed. Mount Longonot, an extinct volcano, still slumbers in the dried-up, rolling plains of scrub grass and wait-a-bit thorn trees. Naivasha Township and the lake, bordered with fever trees, are behind us. High up on the rift, Gilgil town overlooks Lake

Elmenteita on the yellow valley floor below. Rimmed by thousands of flamingos, the lake glistens like a blue jewel in a red setting.

The sight of the lake reminds me of Billy. *He's stationed here in the Gilgil police transport section.* He's now a mechanic in the police reserve. Billy is very good with engines and cars, and frequently helped me with repairs to the Austin.

Thinking about it, I wonder if the fact that Billy had joined the Kenya Police Reserve influenced my decision to volunteer as a Special Police Officer. *God knows that I'd tried hard enough to join the Kenya Regiment.* I shake my head. *No, I don't think it was that. The Special Police are something like the Home Guard in Britain during the last war. At night, we patrol the residential areas to guard against terrorists.* Whenever I'm not on safari, I will be on the regular roster of the Kileleshwa unit.

***

The Baringo turn-off is just ahead, beyond the Thomson Falls turn-off and close to the eastern suburbs of Nakuru, a large farm-marketing centre in the White Highlands. Signalling to Kamau, I turn onto the dirt road leading to Lake Baringo, heading north up the Rift Valley. As I bump and jolt along in the Land Rover, I glance in the rear view mirror and smile with satisfaction. The open-bodied truck is still behind me, but keeping back a short distance to avoid my dust.

Menengai, an extinct volcano, lies on my left. It forms a part of the western side of the Rift Valley as it twists and veers to the north. The thorn trees and scrub on the valley floor seem endless. The coarse, dried-up grass on the flat plains, which are sandwiched between the towering escarpments of Laikipia and the western White Highlands, is scorched yellow by the heat of the sun. Now, as the vehicles leave the rough bush track to Lake Baringo and head into the forested foothills of the western escarpment, the small settlement of Campi ya Moto is behind us. The truck carrying my labour force falls back on the steep gradients, and, as I pull ahead in the Land Rover, the gap between the vehicles widens. Passing Eldama Ravine, roughly two thousand feet above the valley floor, the Land Rover bumps over the uneven surface of the winding road.

"Maji Mzuri is ten or twelve miles west of Eldama Ravine," Mac had said. "You can't miss it because there's a big sawmill by the side of the Timborua Road. If you go too far, you'll hit Equator, a small township on the railroad line to Uganda."

True enough, Maji Mzuri lies exactly where he said. Rounding a blind bend in the road, I can see the small settlement and sawmill on my left. The sawmill dominates the cluster of buildings nestling amongst the dense forests at the northern end of the Mau Escarpment. Easing the Land Rover to the side of the road, I stop and wait for the truck to catch up.

While I wait, I take stock of my surroundings and check the logging trail on the large-scale survey map. Mac has marked the trail in red. *Yes*, I think as I put the map on the seat beside me, *it looks simple enough*. There's a large bush track running alongside the sawmill and heading southwest. Taking out my compass, I check its direction. *That's the track all right. I'll be fine as long as I head west and don't take the sidetracks*. The roar of the truck's engine interrupts my thoughts as it rounds the bend and stops beside me in a cloud of dust.

Showing Kamau the route on the map, I say, "We'll head west on that logging road. It should take us to the edge of the bamboo forest near the peak. We'll make our base camp there." Pausing, I add, "I'll lead the way. You may need to use four-wheel drive, because the slopes may be steep in places."

Kamau nods. "*Ndiyo, bwana,*" he says. "*Nitaenda taratibu*—I will go carefully."

Glancing at my watch, I say, "*Sasa saa kumi*—it is the tenth hour now," referring to the tenth hour of daylight. I use the Swahili method to tell the time because this is what Kamau understands. Translated into English, *saa kumi machana* (the tenth hour) is four o'clock in the afternoon. On the equator, days are roughly equal in length throughout the year, with twelve hours of daylight and twelve of night. Seven o'clock is the first hour of daylight—*machana*, or of night—*usiku*.

Pausing momentarily, I look up. The sun is still high in the west. "We should reach there in about an hour," I say. "We'll have time to make camp before dark."

Climbing back into the Land Rover, I drive along the track into the forest followed by the truck. Here, the trees are large and tall, good timbers, not straggling and stunted, like the trees on the plains. It is close to five o'clock when we reach the bamboo at the nine-thousand-foot mark. The logging road curves round at this point and heads back into the forest and on to the Njoro to Londiani road. Where the track ends and the bamboo begins is roughly a thousand feet below the top of Loldiani. This is where we will make the base camp.

The Loldiani Base Camp

Raising their voices in a chant, the labourers use their *pangas* (machetes), to clear the glade of its long grass and underbrush. The chant rapidly degenerates into a babble of Kikuyu chatter when the men begin unloading the tents from the truck, and erect them.

"*Weka hema yangu uko*—put my tent over there," I say, pointing to a level piece of ground sheltered by a shady tree. Struggling with the cumbersome canvas and poles, the men, working under my supervision, lay the groundsheet, and erect the large tent. It has an extended fly-sheet that serves as a veranda, and a bell attachment. They place my *chop* box (containing my provisions) and the large, wooden camp bed alongside one side of the tent, while the boxes with the radio transmitters go into the bell section.

"Your people have worked well, Njeroge," I say to the *neopara* (foreman). Looking around, I can see the base camp taking shape. The labourers have put their tents on the opposite side of the glade, and they've already lit their cooking fires. The truck stands to one side of these tents. Njeroge and Kamau, the driver, will sleep in the back of it, under the canvas tarpaulin cover.

The Land Rover is parked next to my tent, while my personal baggage has been unloaded and placed inside the tent. The two Yardley Wavis motor generators are still in the truck because they won't be needed until the top campsite is ready.

Night has fallen now, and the light from several fires flickers in the glade, illuminating the labourers' faces as they sit by their fires, and casts silhouettes onto the tents. The intermittent hum of conversation carries across to me, where I, too, sit in a camp chair by my fire, watching my supper of potatoes and a can of stew cook. A labourer had gathered firewood from the forest and stacked some nearby.

Behind me, there are occasional rustling noises from the bush, and an involuntary shiver runs up my spine. Here in the middle of this dense forest on the tip of the Mau escarpment, I feel alone, alone and vulnerable. The laughter and chatter of my Kikuyu workers, sitting

Figure 5. My tent at the base camp on Loldiani, the start of the road.

around their fires about thirty or forty feet away, is somewhat reassuring, but what protection do I actually have if these superstitious people have taken a *Mau Mau* oath?

Superstitious! How can I talk of superstition when I, too, fear the dark and remain on tenterhooks, like an animal alone in a forest alert for the sound of a predator at night. *Remember Mbwinzau and the leopard*, I say to myself, *you were scared that night.*

What would happen if a Mau Mau gang attacks our small encampment? Would these men come to my aid, or would they join in the slaughter? There is no way to tell these days. It would take a brave man to break a *Mau Mau* oath after swearing to kill all whites and take their land, especially knowing that they, themselves, will be killed if they do not carry out the oath.

"Yes," I mutter to myself, unconsciously touching the Enfield point-thirty-eight revolver strapped to my belt. "That's why I bought this handgun. I've got six bullets in the chamber and another twenty-five spread round the belt." My nine-point-five millimetre Mannlicher-Schroner rifle is too cumbersome for fighting at close quarters. I glance back at the tent entrance. The rifle is under my bed, hidden in blankets.

As I think about Nairobi, my thoughts wander. It's like an armed camp these days. Most of the white residents carry guns. I've bought Joan a small Podnic automatic. She carries it in her handbag, and sleeps with it under her pillow when I'm away.

∗∗∗

I sleep fitfully that first night in the base camp, and keep my revolver under the pillow. The feel of the serrated handgrip is comforting. The safety catch is on but it will take just the flick of a finger to release it. Only the noises of crickets and the occasional breaking of twigs disturb the night, as an inquisitive animal halts, smells the presence of man, then turns and wanders off. The camp is sleeping, and I turn over in my camp bed and fall asleep.

There's a mist hanging over the trees when I undo the tent flap and step outside to wash my face and hands in the canvas washstand. The dry wood stacked by the tents revives the cooking fires as the camp comes alive and another day starts in the bush.

It is mid-morning before Njeroge and I can leave the base camp to survey the track through the bamboo. It's taken time to organize the work groups into three teams. An advance party armed with *pangas* and axes will be followed by a clearing crew, while a third group will use *jembes* (hoes) to remove the more obstinate stumps that the others leave behind. The labourers have already started clearing the track up the lower section of the ridge where we are camped. They will follow the marks that Njeroge and I blaze on the bamboo.

For a moment, I watch the men clearing the bush. Turning to Njeroge, I nod towards the man that he has chosen to lead the crews in our absence. "Think he can manage the crew, and follow our trail as we mark it?"

"*Ndiyo, anajua kazi*—he knows the work, bwana. His name is Karanja. He and I work well together."

Satisfied, I set off, followed by Njeroge; periodically we slash the bamboo with our *pangas* to mark the path. Worming our way slowly up the rising land, we crisscross the ridge to reduce the gradient, and allow the Land Rover, and eventually the truck, the easiest path. There is only one direction that we can go, and that is uphill. Following the slopes and gradients, we mark a track that winds its way around rocky outcrops in the closely packed bamboo. Periodically, I check and re-check our southwesterly course with the compass at every detour.

I am thankful for the protection of the ex-army boots and leggings that I wear. Splintered bamboo spikes are no match for the thick leather. Still, I tread cautiously as we work our way over fallen bamboo, being careful not to stumble through the haphazard layers of rotting shafts wedged between the growing shoots. Clambering about in bamboo can be dangerous, because you could get a serious injury if you fall onto an old broken stump or a freshly splintered one.

It's noon when we reach the summit. Stepping into the small overgrown clearing, we see the survey beacon. Looking like an hourglass, it's an ungainly structure about forty feet high, consisting of four long poles stuck into the ground. About two-thirds of the way up where the poles cross, they are bound together with galvanized wire. Just above and below the centre of this hourglass, triangular pieces of corrugated iron are nailed, all with the apex pointing towards the centre. The whole structure stands out above the surrounding bamboo, so that the beacon can easily be seen from a distance.

Njeroge is puzzled by this contraption. Scratching his head, he says, "*Hii kitu namna gani*—what sort of thing is this?" Approaching the structure, he touches the poles. "*Kwa nini wazungu tumia hii*—what do white men use this for?" he says quizzically.

Smiling with amusement, I explain that this structure is taller than the surrounding bamboo so that surveyors can see and recognize its strange shape from a distance, usually from another mountain. The surveyors can take a visual bearing so they can locate its position and use it to make maps. Then I show him a map that I have of the area and forest.

Njeroge nods slowly as he examines the map. "Ah," he says, "the *wazungu* (white men) are strange people. Sometimes they do crazy things, but now I can understand how they make maps."

Having blazed a trail for the Land Rover track to the top, we retrace our footsteps to the base camp using our own marks. Nearing the camp, we can hear the sound of *pangas* slashing the bamboo and the voices of the labourers. "They're still hard at it, Njeroge," I say as we approach the men. "Karanja is doing a good job." They've roughly cleared a two-hundred-yard strip from the camp.

The *neopara* smiles. "They are good men, bwana," he says, "All have been with me for many years."

The Bamboo Forest

It's over two weeks since we started cutting the track through the bamboo—eighteen days to be exact—and we've reached the top. The old foreman is very likeable, but he is quite useless when it comes to controlling the labourers. Karanja, the number-two-man, and I have had to do the job for him.

Fortunately, I have always enjoyed doing hard manual work such as hacking away at the bush. Stripped to the waist, I work alongside the labourers, swinging an axe or a *panga* into a thick stalk of bamboo, and then watching it fall with a crash. It satisfies me to be able to show my men that I can work as hard as they can, if not harder. I also find that it encourages my workers to greater efforts, because they don't want to be outdone.

Figure 6. Gordon sitting on beacon.

As they work, the men often sing in Kikuyu, a tribal language that I don't know, swinging their *jembes* or *pangas* in rhythm. When they chant in Swahili, I sometimes join in. One man will chant a line, and then the rest of us join in with the chorus.

Now, as I watch the labourers clearing the undergrowth from the test site on the rounded peak of Loldiani, I feel pleased. I have completed a Land Rover track through the bamboo to the top, and I have met my deadlines. True, the track still has to be widened and it will have to be dug into the slope in places, but I can now use the Land Rover to transport the main tent and my equipment to the test site.

Standing by the beacon, I think about how the *panga* felt in my hands when I cut into the bamboo, and remember how the labourers had laughed when I got showered with stinking water. I had not realized at the time that the old, cracked piece of bamboo was filled with stagnant water.

✳✳✳

It has been a busy day. Late yesterday evening, the track had reached the summit. Today, we've been transferring the camp equipment and the main tent from the base camp to the test site, which took most of the morning. The Land Rover has proved invaluable for ferrying the loads up the track. Looking beyond the campfire towards the surrounding forest, I can see the silhouette of the beacon and mast standing out against the clear night sky. It is quiet; there is not even a chirp from the crickets or the rustle of leaves to tell of the passage of small rodents. Shivering, I turn back to the warmth and comfort of the fire.

We had quite a struggle to raise the mast, but we got it up, all sixty feet of it, and lashed it securely to the beacon. There are long, steel stay wires supporting the upper and lower sections, keeping the mast and the Yagi beam antennae steady. All the antennae are lined up on the Gemba site, and this test site is now fully operational. My small radio communications transceiver has its own omni directional antenna hoisted on a bamboo pole attached to the veranda tent pole.

When I tried to get up a steep slope with a forty-four gallon drum of fresh water aboard, despite my muttering and cursing, the Land Rover just couldn't make it. The drum was too heavy, and the ground was soft and uneven. The wheels were slipping and sliding, and the straining engine stalled.

Njeroge was nearby at the time, and he came over with a group of labourers to help. He squatted down on his haunches next to me while I inspected the underside of the Land Rover and the churned-up ground. "*Ona* (see), Njeroge," I said, pointing to the springs. "They're bent flat. They'll break if we go much further with a load like this. Tell your men to off-load the drum, but to be careful. I don't want it rolling downhill into the bush."

"*Aiyee, ni kweli*—true," he exclaims. "They will take care. They can also roll the drum up to the top, because it's not far."

Somehow the labourers managed it—there were five of them—and now the drum of water is standing upright outside my tent. Njeroge has a strange sense of distance. He had said "not far," but it must have been at least half a mile. Apart from the mishap with the drum, the Land Rover has performed well. We used it to carry everything up the steep slopes, except the heavy steel sections of masts, which the labourers carried. All my food supplies and personal effects are here with me in the tent, while the two Yardley Wavis motor generators with their fuel are stored in a small tent nearby.

Now that the rough track is completed, the work crews have started widening the track so trucks can use it. The big ex-army truck will be the first vehicle to test it. However, there's plenty of work to be done before that can happen. We don't have bulldozers available for road building out here in the bush, and have to rely on manual labour. Njeroge's crew will be busy working on the road alignment, drainage, surfacing and widening the tight curves. That will involve cutting into the slopes, and throwing the earth out onto the road.

✳✳✳

"Gemba, this is Loldiani. Do you read?" I release the radio transmit button and listen intently, but there is no reply, only the background hiss from the receiver. I call again, call several times, but there is still no reply. It is six-thirty in the evening of November 22nd, and I'm sitting by the camp table under the tent veranda. The Aladdin lamp hanging from the ridgepole casts its light over the table and the radio transceiver. When I reach out to switch the radio to standby, my weight shifts on the camp chair and it squeaks.

"Ah, well," I sigh, muttering to myself. "I guess they can't be on site yet." Moodily, I gaze into the flames of the campfire. It's lonely up here, away from the chatter and noise of the base camp. I get up, stretch my arms, and then walk over to the fire where my supper is cooking in various pots and pans. *Well*, I think, *Eric should be here in a few days. It will be nice to have someone to talk to.*

It's my third night on top of Loldiani when I finally make contact with Gemba. I'd switched the radio transceiver onto standby on the calling frequency while I ate, and have just finished dinner when Eric's voice comes booming through. "Loldiani, do you read? This is Gemba."

At the sound of his voice, a feeling of relief comes over me. Hurriedly, I put my soiled plate into the washing-up bucket, and pick up the microphone. Settling back in my chair, I press the transmit button. "Reading you *strength five*, Eric, loud and clear. This is Loldiani. Over."

"Good to hear you, Gord. We're up the top now, and ready for testing. What's it like at your end? Over."

"Wait one moment," I reply, "I'll switch on the test transmitters." Hurrying to the bell of the tent, I switch the transmitters on, check the output on the Elliott recorder, and return to the microphone. "Both on and transmissions steady on both channels," I say.

I can hear voices in the background as Eric and Bungy talk, but it's unintelligible. Then, as Eric speaks into the mike, his voice returns at full strength. "Yes, that's fine. We're getting a good signal here. We may

Figure 7. On a particularly steep section, we lightened the load on the Land Rover by off-loading the forty-four-gallon water drum.

as well start the test cycle tonight, instead of waiting for morning. It will give the equipment time to settle down."

Now that I've made contact with the outside world, it doesn't seem so lonely, and it is with a sense of satisfaction and accomplishment that I sit by the fire. The Gemba-Loldiani tests have begun. Njeroge and Karanja can supervise the work crew for a day or two. Once Eric gets here on the twenty-fifth, I will have more time to oversee the base camp and the roadworks operations.

At ten thousand feet above sea level, there are no mosquitoes, but it does get cold at night, even though it's less than a degree south of the equator. The ground mist disperses once the sun rises, and it's warm and pleasant. But when I got up this morning, there was ice on the water buckets outside the tent. Now, sitting close to the fire, I can feel the heat penetrating the long trousers that I put on this evening. From the small store tent thirty feet beyond my tent, I can hear the muffled, rhythmic beat of the generator. Stretching my arms, I yawn, letting my thoughts wander in a haphazard fashion. I half doze in my chair, watching faces form in the flames.

✳✳✳

Chapter 2
Mau Mau Attack

Londiani Township

Yesterday, Eric had contacted me from Gemba on the morning radio schedule, and I'd arranged to meet him this morning with the Land Rover. "Aye, Gord," he'd said. "I'll be leaving here about noon and should reach Londiani late tonight. Bungy's got the Podson in the base camp, but Mac wants the International back in Nairobi. They'll drop me off on the way, and I'll stay the night there." We talked on a while, and, before breaking off the contact, I'd arranged to meet him at the hotel.

Njeroge, the work gang *neopara*, had come up to give his daily report, and listened intently to the end of our conversation. "Bwana Scales," he said. "*Anakaa wapi*—where is he?"

I smiled at the old man, "*Mbali sana*—very far away. Gemba is a mountain on the shores of Lake Victoria in South Nyanza."

He nodded solemnly. "*Aiyee, kweli*—very far," he said, and then shook his head. "*Watu uko, washenzi, Wajulua*—the people there are savages; they're Julua."

I laughed, amused at the animosity between the Julua and the Kikuyu, the two major tribes. Then I told him that he was to look after the top camp tomorrow because I was going to Londiani in the morning to collect Bwana Scales from the hotel. Karanja, his second in command, would be in charge of the road gangs.

✳✳✳

It is early morning, November 25, and the sun is barely an hour old. After heating the water on the Primus, I've made myself a cup of coffee. There's a nip in the air, and, as I slowly drink, the coffee warms me. Putting the cup down, I walk over to the Land Rover. Since we cut the track through the bamboo, the Land Rover has been kept at the top site close to my tent while the four-by-four ex-army truck is still down in the base camp. The engine is cold when I switch on the ignition, and it starts hesitantly.

The work crews are busy as I drive down the track and on past the silent base camp to join the logging road. Londiani Township is roughly ten miles to the southwest as the crow flies, but it must be fifteen or twenty miles by this dirt road that winds its way through the valleys and ridges of the forested highlands.

The bamboo forest and the base camp are behind me now. Flanked by tall trees, the track wanders through the forest to the small township, not far from Mau summit on the edge of the Mau forest. The sky is blocked out by a thick canopy of tangled branches and leaves high above the forest floor, joining and intertwining over the track. It's like passing through a dimly lit tunnel, against which the noise of the Land Rover's engine reflects, echoes, and intensifies.

The forest thins and the undergrowth thickens as the track nears the bush country. Tall trees soon give way to stunted ones, and then the land opens out into plains where grazing cattle and fences are the first indications of habitation. Just ahead on the left is a signpost where a rough track leads off into the bush. As I get nearer, I learn that this land belongs to a Mr. Black, and in the distance I can see the farmhouse

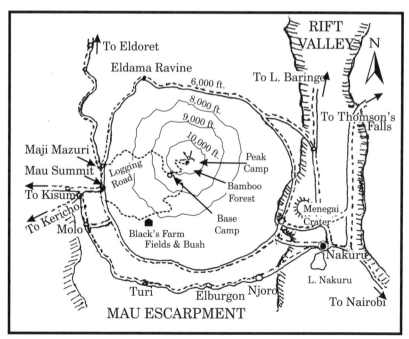

Figure 8. Map showing Loldiani Repeater Site and Black's farm.

on a small, flat-topped hill. A high barbed-wire fence surrounds the house. Two watchtowers are erected on diagonally opposite corners and outside the fence lay military-style rolls of barbed wire. Farmer Black is evidently security conscious, and I wonder if he's had cattle attacked and hamstrung.

I turn my attention back to the track ahead as it runs along the property fence. Leading onto the Nakuru-Londiani township road, the track is a typical potholed farm road. It's been more than three weeks since I've heard any news, and I have a feeling that something more important than cattle maiming and thefts is taking place. There will be newspapers in Londiani, and I'll have lots of time to catch up with the news. It will be another three weeks or more before the tests finish between the two sites, and Eric and I will be camped on top of Loldiani for at least that period.

The Hotel

The hotel sign has seen better days, but the gardens are well kept. Pulling up on the driveway at the main entrance, I look at it critically. It's not a luxury hotel, just a standard, upcountry residential inn whose long wooden walls are painted green. Equipped with a dining room and bar, the hotel offers good, substantial food. There are a few guest rooms in the main building, but most visitors prefer the individual *bandas* (thatched huts). The *bandas* are on a hillside, set back from the main building where shrubs of bougainvillea and frangipani grow in profusion, and canna lilies are as thick as weeds.

Eric is sitting on the veranda that runs along the front of the main building, with his wide-brimmed, black hat resting on the back of his head. When he sees the Land Rover stop in front of the entrance, a grin spreads across his face. "Hi, Gord," he calls, as he gets up. "You've made it. About bloody time."

"What d'you mean, about time," I say, grinning back at him. I'm glad to see him, and hear his complaining. "You've had it easy, sitting in a hotel, being fed, with a nice comfortable bed to sleep in. Just wait till you're up on Loldiani. That'll toughen you up. You're getting soft, Eric. You can bloody well buy me a coffee. I've been up since dawn while you were still sleeping."

We sit at a table on the veranda, and I order coffee from the African steward. The talk inevitably turns to the escalating emergency situation. "I don't suppose you've heard the latest news," Eric says quizzically.

Shaking my head, I say, "No, but as you know, I've been on my own with a gang of workers cutting through the bamboo for the last three weeks. I've had no news since I left Nairobi. Has anything startling happened?"

"Yeah," he says, "things are beginning to hum now. It seems that the bloody *Mau Mau* have got their second wind since Jomo and his cronies were arrested and sent to Lokitaung." He pauses, his face thoughtful as he stirs his coffee, then he continues, "It was fairly quiet for a while following the declaration of emergency, but now the gangs in the forests are becoming active and are raiding farms. According to the police reports, they wait for the farmer to leave, and then they ransack his house, destroying everything inside. At first, they were mainly after firearms, but now they're murdering Europeans!"

"Why, only last Sunday...." He stops in mid-sentence and looks up. "It is Thursday today, isn't it?"

"Yes," I say, "the twenty-fifth."

He nods in satisfaction, "Then, as I was saying, last Sunday some poor bastard copped it on the Kinangop. It was a young farmer named Eric Bowyer. He didn't stand a chance. He was attacked when his servants let a *Mau Mau* gang into the house. They slashed him to death with pangas. He was disembowelled and mutilated."

Eric pauses to sip his coffee, and then continues. "On Tuesday night, the Meiklejohn farm was attacked. Again the gang had the help of the Kikuyu servants. They all burst into the lounge where the family was and killed Meiklejohn, slashing him badly and almost severing one arm. His wife was injured, and left for dead. After ransacking the house, the gang left. She managed to struggle into her car and drove for help." Eric's voice trails off and we sit in silence for a moment.

"Yeah," I reply with bitterness in my voice, "and I bet they've had their servants for years. These old farmers treat their servants well, and the servants' families generally live on the farm. Christ," I say, "what makes men turn into vicious animals like that? I can't understand it."

"Huh," Eric snorts, "I doubt whether any European can." His voice softens, "It's the oaths, I guess," he says.

I nod, "It has to be. The Kikuyu have always taken oaths, but I understand that these forest oaths break all their old traditions and go against their moral beliefs. They started out with relatively mild oaths, but now they are going to extremes of bestiality as they rise in rank in the *Mau Mau* organization. The Naivasha screening team released the Batuni platoon oaths—I suppose you've seen copies of them because they were going round all the offices. They compiled them from confessions they got."

"Yeah," Eric growls, "the *Mau Mau* are bloody animals. No. Animals don't stoop so low." He pauses and then goes on. "Christ, their rituals are obscene." Eric's voice breaks off; then, after a moment's silence, he says, "They're subhuman. They've been degraded to the stage where

Figure 9. Njeroge, the neopara.

they are lost souls, not men." He gets up from his chair as we finish our coffee. "Let's go, Gord," he says. "We've got more supplies to buy, and I've got to pay my hotel bill. I've got today's paper, but I'll ask the reception desk to let us have some old newspapers when I'm booking out. When we're back in camp, you can catch up on all the news."

It's nearly noon before we leave the small town to return to the mountaintop site. The Land Rover is loaded with provisions from the local *duka* (shop), along with Eric's battered suitcase and small holdall bag.

"The track is looking good," says Eric as we pass the labourers working on it. He nods towards Njeroge, the *neopara*. "How'd you find the *mzee* (old man)?"

"He's a nice old soul," I reply, "but he doesn't really know how to handle the men. His assistant, Karanja, actually does his job." I laugh, and then say, "I like him, but he's too old and easy-going."

The Long Night

It is peaceful and quiet on our own in the top campsite. Dinner is over, and the campfire flares as Eric prods the burning wood. The bamboo forest shields us from any noise or clamour from the base camp; only the constant throb of the Yardley Wavis engine breaks the silence. This is the second night that Eric has been here, and we've now both settled back into the routines of the camp and testing. It's nice to have company, and the two of us are just sitting round the fire, talking.

Eric smiles sardonically, "The men were all hand-picked from Nairobi, weren't they? Security-wise, I mean."

"Yeah, that's the way Mac wanted it. He said that people in this area had probably taken oaths, so they could not be trusted."

"Well, I hope he's right about these men. We're like sitting ducks up here." Eric shrugs his shoulders, and adds, "There's nothing much we can do about it either. What's the old jingle: *Put your trust in the hand of the Lord, and he'll lead you safely through the forest?* I wouldn't like to bet on that."

We continue to talk on into the evening until, feeling drowsy, we leave the warmth of the fire, extinguish the lamps, and go to bed.

✳✳✳

Suddenly, a distant explosion jolts us wide awake. "Christ," Eric yells, "that sounds like a bloody grenade." We can now hear the sounds of automatic fire, mixed with occasional grenade blasts, rolling across the forest.

Hurriedly dressing, I open the tent flaps, and, gripping my rifle, run to the survey beacon in order to look around. Eric is close behind me, despite his artificial leg. I can hear him panting from the exertion as his feet pound the ground. "See anything from up there?" he calls, as I climb up to the central crosspieces.

"Only the flashes of explosions over the bamboo. It must be happening close to the edge of the forest," I shout down to him as he starts to climb up the tower. He joins me on the centre crosspiece, and together we watch and listen to the noise of rifle shots and the flashes of distant, sporadic explosions borne across the still night air from the southwest of us.

"I reckon the shooting's coming from the direction of Black's farm," I say. "You know, that fortified farm where the timber track enters the forest. We passed it on our way in from Londiani."

The reality of *Mau Mau*, which had seemed so distant from us, is no longer an impersonal thing. It is here in the forest, just a couple of miles away as the crow flies. My heart pounds with anger and frustration. "Christ, Eric," I mutter, "What the hell can we do? We can't even radio for assistance. There's no one on our frequency, only Bungy in Gemba, and he can't do anything. Anyway, he's not even listening for a call from us at this time of night."

Eric nods, "We can't do a goddamned thing to help the poor bastards. We've only one bloody rifle and a revolver! Even if we could get there, the chances are we'd be cut down in the crossfire between the *Mau Mau* gang and the farm defenders." Eric snorts, as he adds, "Or it's more likely that we'd be killed by an army patrol ambush."

Figure 10: View of the tent and beacon

Gazing at the distant flashes, he swears in frustration "Bloody *Mau Mau*. Where's the goddamned army? That racket should waken the dead in the township. All we can do is watch and wait. I just hope the Black family can hold out until the security forces get there."

I nod. There's an empty feeling in my stomach as I reply, "Yeah, you're right about the Land Rover. They'd hear us coming, and simply take us out."

Helpless, we watch from the survey tower as fresh bursts of fire reach us from the fighting below. "Their phone lines will have been cut for sure," I say. "That's the first thing that goes. We didn't see any flares, but the farmer probably fired off his signal rockets while we were in the tent. The police and army units in Londiani must have seen them, Eric. They must have." I bite my lip, clutching the rough poles as we continue to watch in silence.

After half an hour, the noises from the fighting die down, and now the quiet of the night is broken only by the steady rhythm of the motor generator that supplies power to the test transmitters. We wait a few more minutes on the survey tower, and then wander back to the tent, undecided about what to do.

It is cold as we sit under the veranda of the tent, and we wrap blankets round our shoulders. "That's it, Eric," I say. My throat aches as I speak, and I swallow hard to keep my voice steady. "The farm's either been overrun or the gang has been driven off by the arrival of army patrols. What with the watchtowers and all that barbed wire surrounding it, the farm seemed prepared for trouble. The gang is probably out there in the forest now being pursued by an army patrol."

Eric nods, "Yes, I think you're right. If they're pushed this way, they could try to come through the bloody bamboo, but that's hard going. Hopefully, they'll keep to the forest tracks. That's easier than the bamboo, particularly at night when they've got an army patrol with tracker dogs breathing down their necks."

"Yeah," I say, my eyes fixed on the far end of the clearing where the freshly cut track emerges. "That generator's making too much noise. I think we should shut it down, because it could attract attention to us. It's just too damned easy to get up here now we've made that track."

We switch off the motor, and shovel earth over the burning embers of our fire. An uncanny stillness descends on the camp. The site is bathed in moonlight, and the surrounding bamboo is silhouetted clearly against the night sky. In the shadows, the bamboo forest is dark, pitch dark, mysterious, and unnerving. Occasionally, the silence is broken by a creak or rustling noise as something moves in the forest and disturbs the dry leaves, or by a sharp crack as a fallen bamboo shaft snaps.

As we sit watching for movement on the edges of the clearing, I shiver and draw the blanket closer. My imagination is starting to run riot. *Is that a terrorist moving in the bamboo, or is it an animal? How would I know?* I take hold of myself, and banish these thoughts. As we continue to watch, we talk in low tones.

"Aye," says Eric, his tone bitter. "All we've got is that bolt-action rifle of yours, a revolver, and a couple of pangas. They'd be a fat lot of good against a gang of twenty or thirty bloody fanatics high on *bhang* (drugs). The gang would swamp us before we could get off a shot or two. Now, if we had a couple of Sten guns, that would be a different story."

Sighing, I look down at the rifle lying across my knees. My hand strokes the wooden stock, my fingers instinctively feeling

Figure 11. Eric on the beacon.

the steel bolt that ejects the empty bullet case as I slam another bullet into the breech. "You're right. Shooting animals is one thing, but shooting at drug- and blood-crazed men is another. We might get one or two, but that's about all." My shoulders relax as I slump in the chair, easing the tension in my neck. "Maybe we should take turns on guard against a surprise attack."

Eric's voice is weary. "There are only two of us. These men live in the forest and know it intimately. They're probably trained in guerrilla combat as well. A lot of Kikuyu are ex-servicemen. They served in Europe and Burma during the war. He pauses for a moment and continues. Probably the gang leaders themselves are ex-servicemen. You can bet they'll have trained some of these bastards in guerrilla warfare."

Shaking his head, he says, "No, there's no point in sitting up all night doing guard duty. To be effective, we'd either have to hide in the bamboo or on the survey tower, and watch the clearing and bush for movement." Pointing to the black shadows etching the edge of the clearing, he continues, "Do you really think you could detect a man crawling from the bamboo through that grass?"

"No, I doubt it, Eric," I say, admitting that the task is impractical. "They're not complete fools, and they'd take out any sentry first." Laughing softly, I add, "We're looking at the worst case scenario. Chances are that the army has already captured them, or that they'll bypass us in the night. Maybe we should just sit tight for two or three hours. If they're coming at all, they will be past us and the base camp well before then."

Eric nods. "Yes, that's true. At the moment, it is all conjecture anyway. All we know for sure is that there has been some sort of an attack, either on the Black's or on a neighbouring farm. Assuming that the army patrol got there, the gang has either been arrested or they're being pursued by the patrol. If the patrol has dogs, the gang could be hard pressed or they could just have vanished into the bush. Whatever's happened, the next few hours could be critical."

About two or three in the morning, we finally go to bed. The loaded rifle is on the ground between the two camp beds so that either Eric or I can reach it, while the revolver, its safety catch on, lies under my pillow. Drained by tensions, I listen to various sounds in the night. Occasionally aroused by a noise, I sit up, waiting, my revolver in my hand. Then, as the sound fades, I lay back, my muscles relaxing. Exhausted, I close my eyes, drifting off into a troubled sleep in the small hours of the morning.

The Army Patrol

Awakened by the early morning sunlight, I slip out of my bed, bleary-eyed but thankful to see the dawn. About an hour later, Eric and I are sitting under the tent veranda, drinking coffee, while a frying pan with eggs and bacon cooks on the Primus stove, the fat spitting and spluttering.

Suddenly three men, armed with Sten guns and rifles and wearing British army fatigues, appear on the track from the base camp. Instinctively, I feel that they're bringing bad news; what else could they bring at such a time. They halt momentarily, their weapons at the ready, and then move towards us.

As they approach, we stand up. One of the men hails us, and from his accent I know that he is from the north of England. Recognizing the dull gold fusilier badge on their bush hats, I realize that they are Lancashire Fusiliers. The meeting is brief, and they decline our invitation to share our breakfast.

"A terrorist gang attacked Black's farm last night," the corporal, a man in his mid-twenties, says. "They were able to hold off the attackers until we arrived. Black and his family are okay, but some of his men have been injured. We tracked the gang to your labour camp during the night."

Stunned by this revelation, Eric and I can only listen in disbelief as the corporal continues. "Aye, man, you're bloody lucky we were close on their asses," he says. "You wouldn't have stood a bloody chance if they'd come for you. That gang was well-armed." Pausing, the corporal scratches his head. "Anyway, what the hell are you two doing out here in this bloody, godforsaken place?"

"We're a government radio survey team," I reply, "and we're testing the VHF signal strengths between here and Gemba on the shores of Lake Victoria."

The corporal nods, "That figures. There's a Posts and Tels truck in the base camp. Well, we've clobbered your labour. The bastards were harbouring those bloody terrorists. We found weapons and bloodstained clothing hidden in the tents and the bush. The gang left them behind in their haste to get away. Some of the gang are wounded, and our men are hunting them down now."

"You've taken all our labourers off to jail?" I ask. My mind is still trying to grapple with the fact that our labour gang was involved in the raid, and with the realization that we had narrowly avoided death. I shudder at the thought, and glance at Eric. He, too, looks shaken.

"Yes, too bloody true," the corporal laughs, his voice harsh. "We called our headquarters in Londiani, and they sent a prison truck out. Your men have all been taken to the nearest screening and interrogation centre. They told us you were camped up here, so we came to investigate. We thought you might have bought it. Are you in radio contact with your department?"

"Once we get our motor generator started, we will be," Eric says. "With all the noise and shooting going on last night, we shut down the generator, just in case there were *Mau Mau* wandering around. We've got to resume testing again, and we're also going to need more labourers to finish the bloody track."

"You plan on staying up here then?" asks the corporal.

"Yes," I say, "unless our department withdraws us. We are supposed to continue testing for another two or three weeks with both Gemba and the Nakuru terminal. We also have to widen the track through the bamboo so we can bring the truck up from the base camp."

"It's a strange, bloody department you work for," the corporal says, shaking his head. "At least, they should've sent a guard with you." He pauses, and then adds, "Especially when it's a well-known *Mau Mau* hotbed like this area. Well, we've got to rejoin our unit." Wishing us luck, the corporal and the two privates go back down the track.

We watch them cross the clearing and disappear as the bamboo closes around them. "Aye," sighs Eric, glancing at the partially cooked eggs and bacon, "We'd better finish breakfast and get the tests restarted." He breathes deeply, and then says, "Oh, what the bloody hell! Bungy will be wondering what's happened, that's for sure." He bends down and turns up the heat, watching as the congealed mess begins to bubble and spit fat.

***

Breakfast is over. As I pull hard on the lanyard, the Yardley Wavis engine coughs, belching a small puff of smoke. It splutters, and then starts on the second pull, settling into the typical rhythmic note of a two-stroke engine. Satisfied, I walk across the clearing to the main tent.

When I enter the tent, Eric is huddled over the transmitters in the bell section. With the power restored, he's just finished checking and tuning the test transmitter output signal strengths. "Yeah," he says, "the output's okay. Give Bungy a call on the radio."

Bungy must have been waiting on the watch frequency, because he answers my first call. I smile when I hear his voice. "Hi, Gord," he says. "What's happening over there? I lost your signal around midnight. Over."

Pressing the transmit button on the microphone, I tell him about the *Mau Mau* attack on the nearby farm, and about the gang having been tracked to our base camp. "We had no real option but to switch off the engine," I say. "It was making too much noise. As we were stuck in the middle of a bloody bamboo forest with *Mau Mau* around, it seemed wise not to advertise our presence." I pause briefly, and then add, "An army patrol came up the track soon after dawn. They've taken all our labourers into detention for screening and interrogation, because the security patrol pursuing the gang found weapons and bloodstained clothing in the base camp. Apparently our men had sheltered the terrorists, and, for all we know, some of them may even have taken part in the raid."

"Christ," Bungy's voice reflects his concern. "What's happening now? Have the army patrol or police headquarters contacted the department? You're going to need more men for the road, won't you, apart from security?"

A voice breaks into our conversation, overriding Bungy's transmission.

"Wait one, Bungy," I reply, "We've got a breaker. Perhaps it's the Nakuru carrier terminal. Come in, breaker," I say. "Go ahead. Over."

"Nakuru Terminal calling Loldiani. Geoff here, reading you *strength five*. The police and army security contacted us first thing this morning, so we've been monitoring your frequency here in the carrier room. Glad to hear you and Eric are okay, Gord. It's been quite a night. We're sending a driver and more labourers from our Nakuru staff to you this morning. They'll include Wakamba and Kipsikis tribesmen and some trusted Kikuyu loyalists. Hopefully, there should be no further problems. Their *neopara* is an ex-sergeant major from the KAR and a bloody good man.

The truck will go via Eldama Ravine and should arrive at your base camp about noon today. Did you get that? Over."

After talking a little longer, I sign off with Nakuru Terminal and Bungy. We'll talk to Bungy again tonight as scheduled.

The distant throb of the motor generator and the steady clank of the Elliott recorder arm, striking and marking the slowly unwinding roll of recording paper, are getting on my nerves. It doesn't appear to faze Eric who is sitting on the tent veranda, placidly reading a novel, absorbed in another world. I wonder about the differences in our personalities. Maybe it's the loss of his leg during the war that keeps him chained to the tent, but he is as energetic as the rest of us when we're on the move. I envy him his detachment because I am impulsive and emotional by nature.

It will be another two or three hours before the truck from Nakuru reaches the base camp. Restless and driven by curiosity, I leave Eric in camp and wander down the deserted and silent track to the abandoned camp.

A Scene of Desolation

The sun shines fitfully on the track through a gap in the overhanging bamboo fronds. It is peaceful, washed clean of the menace of the night. It's almost as if nothing had happened, except that now the track is no longer filled with the sounds of *pangas* cutting bamboo, or the chatter of the labourers. And old Njeroge is no longer here, encouraging the men to further efforts.

I wonder where they've been taken. The screening camps and interrogation centres are not pleasant places, but pale into insignificance compared to the hideous rituals, torture and crimes that are being committed by the *Mau Mau*. I shrug my shoulders, recognizing the facts. The labourers harboured the forest gang, they supplied food and shelter, and maybe they participated in the fighting. Now they must face the consequences.

As I walk on down the track, I note the fresh *panga* marks where the men widened the track yesterday. Soon, other hands will be here, and the air will reverberate with the chatter of many tongues—Wakamba and Kipsikis, mixed with some Kikuyu and Somali.

On reaching the base camp, a scene of desolation greets me. Tents are ripped and flattened, probably in the chaos when the troops encircled them. The men—*Mau Mau* and labourers—inextricably mixed and indistinguishable from one another, tried to escape into the surrounding bush. In the dark of night, it would have been no easy task to separate the innocent from the guilty. But in the eyes of the law, however, there are no innocents in this case because all who help terrorists have violated the law. The truck remains untouched, standing alone and aloof from the upset cooking pots, burnt-out fires and personal paraphernalia discarded by the searching troops who have taken away the incriminating evidence, including any bodies.

As I sit on a log near the remains of the burnt-out embers of a cooking fire, I think about the memorandum that was circulated around the office just before I left. It was a lurid list, detailing *Mau Mau* rituals and atrocities committed against their own people and white settlers. These included reports about torture, decapitation and mutilation, and bodies being bound up in sacks and dropped into wells. Some victims had been held down while their heads were sawed off slowly with *pangas*, pregnant women had been split open along the stomach, and some Africans loyal to the government had their ears cut off, to identify them in the future.

Nearby there is an old tattered shirt, torn and abandoned, and I wonder who owns it. My thoughts turn to Njeroge. *Surely that old, kind, gentle man could not do those things*. Saddened and sickened by the thought, I rationalize his involvement. Maybe he had been forced to take the oath, and could not bring himself to break it.

According to acknowledged authorities on Kikuyu customs and tribal society, such as Dr. Leakey, a leading archaeologist and expert on the Kikuyu language, superstition and witchcraft are deeply rooted in the Kikuyu people. In their minds, an oath is binding, and they are convinced that they will die if they break it. A basic tenet of these oaths is to kill all white people, as well as any dissenters in their own race. If the army platoon had not arrived so quickly last night, it is very possible that Eric and I would now be dead, and our death would have been both slow and cruel.

Waiyaki, the Neopara

When I finally hear the distant roar of a truck, it has gone noon. With its engine growling in low gear, the heavily loaded truck moves laboriously up the steep slope of the timber trail. As it rounds the final curve, the familiar dark green departmental colours and insignia proclaim its identity. A *mzungu* (white man) is driving, and there's an African in the passenger seat. The truck pulls up beside me with a squeal of brakes.

"I'm Jerry, Jerry Coates, from the Nakuru Transport Section," says the driver, as he climbs out and shakes hands. "You must be Gordon. I've met your mate, Eric. He's got an artificial leg, hasn't he?"

"Yes," I say. "He's looking after things up on the repeater test site. We've started testing again."

"Yeah," he says, as he looks around at the trampled and rumpled tents. "We'll have to sort out all this *taka taka* (mess), and get the labour organized. I've brought new tents and camping gear as well as tools, but you've probably still got some in your truck."

"There are some in the back, but we'll have to take inventory," I say, then add with a laugh, "You know what the *wallahs* in the Stores Department are like."

"Office types are all the same," he says. Turning to the men standing in the back of the truck, he calls loudly, "*Toka nje, iko kazi*—get out, there's work to be done."

A tall, broad shouldered African approaches us, and stands to one side awaiting orders. By his bearing, he must be the *neopara*, an ex-military man. Jerry confirms this when he introduces us. "Waiyaki," he says, "this is Bwana Mumford. He will be in overall charge of widening the road to the repeater site, and you'll report to him with your men." Turning to me, he says, "Waiyaki is our *neopara*; you can rely on him. You won't have trouble with these men; they're all hand-picked."

Waiyaki is impressive. He organizes the men into small groups. Some clear the base camp, pack up torn tents, and store them aboard our truck, while Waiyaki takes inventory. Meanwhile, other groups erect the new tents under the shade of the trees.

Jerry, satisfied with the way the base camp is taking shape, leaves him to complete the work and walks with me up to the top site. On the way, he takes the opportunity to inspect the track. "Aye," he says, when we reach the steeper sections, "It's a great Land Rover track, but we'll have to straighten out some of these bends and reduce the gradient."

As we carry on up the track, he goes over the details, "When the site is approved, the building section will need to transport truckloads of quarried stone to the top. When that time comes, we'll need to put in culverts and surface the road with stone or even macadamize some sections. In the meantime, our men will widen the rough alignment so that we can get a four-by-four truck to the top. At a guess, it will take about three weeks. How long do you think you'll be testing?"

"Oh, a good three or four weeks in all. The Loldiani-Gemba link will take two or three weeks, and then we'll spend at least a week testing the signal strength into Nakuru terminal. I don't expect a problem there as it is close, and at the moment our signal booms into the carrier room."

Jerry nods, "So Geoff tells me. Think we'll be able to contact him over the communications link? I'd like to tell him we've arrived and everything is on schedule. I'll leave for Nakuru about four o'clock in our truck. My driver Kariuki will stay with you, and, when my men have finished widening the track, he can drive them to Nakuru in your truck. Then he'll drive your truck back here because you'll need it for all your equipment and the generators."

It is still early in the afternoon when we reach the clearing, and Eric, seeing us coming, has put the kettle on. Over coffee, talk naturally turns to the raid on Black's farm and the loss of our labour.

Shortly after talking to Nakuru over the radio communications link, Jerry leaves for the base camp. I walk down with him because I want to talk to Waiyaki. Tomorrow, Waiyaki and his crew will begin clearing and widening the road. Organized into small groups, the men will realign the grade and lengthen the sweep of the curves, digging into the hillside and throwing the rocks and rubble onto the outer slopes.

The afternoon is drawing on, and now the work force is gathering wood for their campfires. Jerry takes a last look round the base camp. "Yes," he says, "It looks fine, Gord. Waiyaki and his men are settled in the base camp, so there should be no problems. I may have to transport some culverts and piping out for one or two places, but that's nothing to worry about."

Jerry climbs into the truck and starts the ignition. As the truck moves slowly forward, he shouts over the roar of the engine, "I've arranged for a daily call schedule for you with Geoff in the carrier room. Let us know if you need anything."

I watch as Jerry and his truck disappear round the bend in the forest road. It is the end of a tiring day. I turn to the *neopara*, Waiyaki, who is

Figure 12. The Fordson (4x4), with all chains on, at the top of Loldiani Mountain

standing beside me. "*Asante sana*—many thanks, Waiyaki. You have done well today," I say, and then add, "Tomorrow, start your men on the road early. You are in charge of the work groups, and I will check with you each day. Bwana Scales and I have work to do on the test site, so I can't be here with you all the time. If there's a problem, or you want material, come and see me on the top site. We are in radio communication with Nakuru."

The sun is sinking in the west as I walk back up the track through the bamboo. It's Saturday today, but on safari there are no days off. Sunday will be just another workday. Testing and work on the track continue every day, with no exceptions.

Heading Home

Tomorrow is December 16. Three weeks have rolled by since the raid, three weeks of continuous testing with both the Gemba-Londiani and Nakuru-Loldiani links giving solid, commercial-level radio signals. Now that the end of this safari is in sight, I feel a weight lifting from my shoulders. During this time, Waiyaki and his men have widened the track through the bamboo, and the heavy four-by-four truck has made it to the top. True, the road will have to be resurfaced and drainage systems put in once the site has been officially approved, but that is in the future.

We break camp in the morning and head home. A few days ago, Kariuki took the roadworks crew and Waiyaki back to Nakuru in our truck as agreed with Jerry, the transport manager. This afternoon, he returned, bringing ten men as we requested. These men will help with dismantling the tent, antenna masts, engines, and packing up all the paraphernalia we used for the test site, plus the camping gear and road building tools.

The roadwork was completed ahead of schedule and during that time I had got to know Waiyaki. During the day, I often spent several hours lending a hand with the roadworks and wandering from group to group with him. He told me he had fought in the Second World War and reached the rank of sergeant major in the King's African Rifles, while serving in India.

Now, sitting by the campfire for the last time on Loldiani with Eric, my eyes take in the familiar hourglass shape of the survey tower, silhouetted against the clear night sky. It reminds me of the night when Black's farm was attacked. It seems a long time since then, but it is really only a few weeks ago that we watched the flashes of explosions above the bamboo to our southwest. Turning to Eric, I nod towards the survey tower. "Remember the raid, Eric?" I ask.

"Yeah," he says, his voice soft as if speaking to himself. "We were lucky."

"I wonder what happened to the old *neopara*, Njeroge. I worked with him for two or three weeks, and I thought I knew him. He was such a gentle old soul; I didn't think he could harm a fly."

Eric nods. "It just goes to show that you can never really trust these or any other people for that matter, not when life or death are concerned. You've only got to read the articles in the newspaper about the murders of Bowyer and the Meiklejohns. Their own Kikuyu domestic servants were involved; you can't get much closer than that."

"Yeah, I guess you're right." I shrug my shoulders in resignation. "Njeroge was probably forced to take the oath against his will. But, forced or voluntary, it doesn't seem to matter."

"Yeah," Eric says, "the influence that these oaths have on the Kikuyu people is too powerful to break. It's a major weapon that the *Mau Mau* use against their own people to bend them to their will and creed. *Drive the Europeans out; kill the bloody lot.*"

"What I don't understand, Eric, is why didn't they kill me and take my weapons. They had every chance. It would have been so easy, because I was here on my own. They could have done it at any time they wanted."

Eric looks into the fire, his elbows on his knees, leaning forward as he sits in the camp chair. It is a moment before he answers. "I don't know, Gord. I really don't know. Maybe they were biding their time, or perhaps you were too useful to them. Because they work for us, they can travel around the countryside and act as couriers for their central command—troop movements, operational orders, and so forth. I don't think their leaders are stupid, although I have my doubts about the men who carry out their commands. They can't sink any lower."

We lapse into silence. There's beer on the camp table near us, the last of our supply. "Come on, Gord," Eric says. "Let's think of something more cheerful. It will be Christmas in a little over a week." He opens the bottle of Tusker and pours some into my glass. "Here's to tomorrow. With luck we'll be home tomorrow night."

I laugh as we talk of happier things, of the Mombasa coast and Malindi, Watamu Beach, and other resorts so popular with Kenya settlers in the holiday season. The night is strangely silent with the motor generator and the recording equipment switched off. Kariuki and some of the labourers are sleeping in the truck while the others sleep in small tents nearby. They have long since retired for the night, and only the burning embers of their cooking fires still glow in the dark. The effects of the beer and the lateness of the hour take their toll. We, too, seek our camp beds, and, throwing a log on the fire to keep it burning, we stumble into the tent. I smile to myself when I hear Eric snore, then I turn over, hugging the blanket and sheet around me. My hand instinctively touches the butt of my revolver under my pillow; reassured, I, too, fall into a deep sleep.

✻✻✻

We're up when the sun breaks through the morning mist rising off the ground. The labourers are already astir; it is cold in the early morning, and they are wrapped in blankets as they tend the cooking fires. The smell of frying bacon and eggs, our staple morning meal, arouses my taste buds. Our bread is stale, and Eric is frying it in the remnants of the fat in the frying pan on the Primus stove. The bread is still palatable when it's fried with margarine. We sit by the table in the tent veranda, enjoying our breakfast.

The sun is two hours over the horizon and its rays are beginning to warm the ground when breakfast is over and the work of dismantling the camp begins. By mid-morning, the camp is cleared and the tents, Yardley Wavis engines, and equipment are stored aboard the truck, while the radio transmitters and recorders have been packed in the Land Rover. Then, with a last quick look round the site, we leave the clearing.

The Land Rover with two of the labourers aboard is in the lead; I am driving and Eric is in the passenger seat. The truck, with Kariuki driving, follows; it is fully laden with camping gear and equipment, as well as the remaining labourers. Eric hangs on to the side door as I drive the Land Rover down the bumpy track through the bamboo to the timber mill road. I wait for a moment to make sure the heavily laden truck is behind me, and then we set off for Maji Mzuri and the road to Nakuru.

✻✻✻

It is noon and Eldama Ravine has long gone as we speed down the escarpment into the floor of the Rift Valley. Eric yawns and stretches his arms, shifting his feet in the process. "God, I'm stiff," he says. "I'll take the truck over from Kariuki when we get to Nakuru. No sense in leaving it there. It's needed in headquarters."

"Yeah," I nod and add, "That's what I was thinking." I look at my watch. "We will be in Nakuru by two. After we drop Kariuki and the labourers there, we can get an early start on our way home. When we get to Nairobi, we'll leave the truck in the post office yard, and I'll take you home. You're now in Langata, aren't you?"

"Yes, just past the Kisembe turn-off." Pausing, he tilts his hat back on his head. "Aye, I'll be glad to get home. I guess you'll be feeling that way, too. You must have been away about six weeks now."

"About that." I hesitate a moment and then say, "I left November 3, and it's December 16 now, so it's just over six weeks." I smile, and then add, "There's been longer safaris, but I'm kind of mixed up. Although I love the life in the bush, I'm always glad to get back to Joan and Nairobi.

I guess it's the contrast, what with the clubs and friends." I laugh and glance quickly over at Eric. "Trouble is, Eric, I'm not in Nairobi very long before I get bored and want to be out again."

Eric grunts, and settles back in his seat. "Your trouble is that you're a bloody bushman, a goddamned nomad. Someday, you'll have to settle down." Closing his eyes, Eric dozes in his seat.

Yes, I think as I drive on down the dirt road, automatically dodging the potholes. *He's probably right.*

✳✳✳

We arrive on schedule in Nakuru, and, after unloading the tents and personal effects of the labourers from the truck, Eric climbs into the cab vacated by Kariuki. Jerry stands by the truck talking animatedly to him as I stroll over to the Land Rover and get into the driver's seat. Glancing back, I see Jerry step away from the side of the truck. Eric waves his arm, signalling me, and, starting the engine, I engage the clutch. Followed by the truck, the Land Rover moves forward out of the yard, and into the main street of the sleepy little market town. The open road is in front of us, and, as I glance back through the rear mirror of the Land Rover, I can see Eric following a hundred yards or so behind me. I look at my watch. It is four o'clock. Depending on the condition of the Nakuru-Nairobi road, the state of which varies with maintenance, we should be home in the early evening.

The truck and Land Rover, keeping in convoy, leave the outskirts of Nakuru, passing Lake Nakuru on the right, and on into the Rift Valley. The sun is sinking below the western wall of the Rift as we approach Lake Naivasha and the small township on its northern shore. Dusk is almost upon us and I'm hungry; we haven't eaten since breakfast. I stop and talk to Eric when he pulls the truck in behind the Land Rover.

Eric grins when I suggest stopping for dinner. "Yeah," he says, "we might as well. It's almost six, and we can get a good meal at the Bell Inn."

Driving slowly through the small town past the solitary police post, we park our vehicles in the hotel grounds and enter the restaurant. Dinner is mulligatawny soup, followed by roast lamb, mashed potatoes and assorted vegetables, served by a steward dressed traditionally in a *kanzu* (white, ankle-length robe) with a red sash and fez. "Ah," says Eric, helping himself to a generous portion of meat, "this beats your cans of stew in Loldiani, or the tough game meat you shot on Gemba." He chuckles, "Remember Mac's teeth? I don't think he'll ever forget you, Gord. Every time he brushes his false teeth he's reminded of you."

"That's his excuse," I say, laughing, and add, "It was his own damn fault. He's getting old, is our Mac, and he got pyorrhoea poisoning."

Back on the road, Eric is pushing the truck hard as we travel in convoy. After leaving Naivasha, our vehicles cross the railroad tracks,

Figure 13. Aerial view of Mount Longenot, an extinct volcano.

and then top the long rise past Mount Longonot, an extinct volcano east of the lake. The escarpment, further along the valley floor, slows Eric down because he has to engage low gear up the steep slopes to the crest, two thousand feet above the valley. In convoy, we pass through the Kikuyu Reserve. With the lights of Nairobi now showing below us, I feel a surge of excitement. There, somewhere in the lights is home, barely fifteen or twenty miles away.

We stayed an hour at Naivasha, but, thinking back on the meal, it was worth it. Now it's eight-thirty in the evening, and, after leaving the truck in the post office yard, I've just taken Eric to Langata. As he disappears inside the guesthouse, I exit the long dirt drive edged with tall eucalyptus trees and shrubs. Back on the Langata Road, I head home through the suburbs via Kileleshwa.

The quarried granite gateposts of Daphton Court appear ahead in the Land Rover's headlights. I drive through the open gateway and follow the drive. Our car is in the thatched-roof garage, and the lights are on in our ground floor apartment. Joan's at home.

✳✳✳

Chapter 3
Farm Radio Networks

The Thika Farms

"Ah, yes, Mumford." Mac's voice is low and reflective, his face thoughtful, as he leans over the table to study a map of the Central Province. Looking up at me, he says, "We've an urgent job on our hands. How'd you like to be attached to the Kenya Regiment for three or four months?" His blue grey eyes bore into mine with a hint of amusement. "The project is to install VHF emergency radio systems to link farms and any advanced army units operating in high risk areas to the local police control centres. Initially, you'll be working in the Aberdares and Mount Kenya areas."

It is January 2, 1953. New Year's Eve has come and gone in a bang of revelry, dancing, and horn blowing at Parklands, the sports club to which Joan, Billy, and I belong. Now I'm back down to earth, and prick up my ears with interest. After all, I'd gone to a lot of trouble volunteering to serve in the Kenya Regiment, only to have the department block my application. Now I have a chance to make a real contribution in this mini-war. I cannot conceal the surge of enthusiasm in my voice as I accept the offer. "Yes," I say, "it sounds great, Mac."

Mac laughs and nods, "Yeah, I thought you would." He turns to the young Kenya Regiment corporal standing on the opposite side of the table, and introduces us. "This is Terry Holmes. He'll work with you for a couple of weeks to learn the ropes, and then you'll split up and operate separately." Turning back to the map, he points to the small, black-headed pins, which denote the areas of operation. "In this way," he continues, "we can halve the time required to cover the farms needing emergency communications."

***

Terry sits beside me with the survey map on his knees as I drive the Dodge truck up the Thika Road to Ruiru, a small settlement roughly fifteen to twenty miles north of Nairobi. The outline of Ol Doinyo Sapuk looms on the horizon to the northeast, while due east the long range of the Machakos Hills stretches south, merging with the plains. Ahead, on the right-hand side of the all-weather road lies Ruiru, set on a rise in

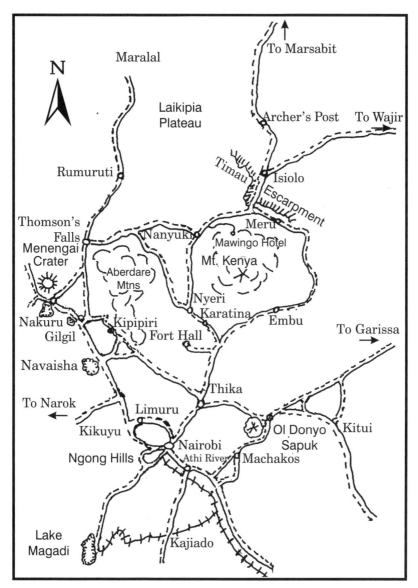

Figure 14. General location of white farming area (Mt. Kenya and Aberdares) and the Kikuyu Reserve.

the land on the opposite side of a deep valley. The settlement consists of a few houses that stand amidst yellow-barked acacia trees and blue gums, intermingled with the inevitable bougainvillea and frangipani shrubs.

It is the hot season, but, unlike the coast, the weather in the Central Province is not humid and sticky, but pleasantly warm, with the temperature rarely over eighty degrees Fahrenheit. As the truck thunders across the wooden bridge in the bottom of the valley, the partially dried-up stream has only a trickle of water. Fed by the Aberdare range in the west, these dried-up valleys become rivers in the rainy season, spreading out over the plains. Papyrus, its spindly triangular stalks capped with fluffy, spherical fronds, towers ten to fifteen feet above the swampy ground. As we pull up the steep slope on the opposite side of the valley, the full extent of the papyrus and rushes stretching up into the foothills of the Aberdares is revealed.

Terry nods towards the papyrus. "You could hide a whole army of *Mau Mau* in there," he says. "They use valleys like this because they are easy communication routes between the forest gangs and their central command in Nairobi. If we're ever going to break the links between the two, we'll have to cut wide gaps in that bloody stuff. At the moment, it's just too easy for them to slip through undetected."

"Yeah," I say, and then add, "The security forces are probably too busy right now but it's inevitable. Places like this bridge are ideal for cutting gaps in the papyrus. I guess it's all a matter of priorities."

Carver's Farm

We have crested the valley and are almost upon the outskirts of Ruiru when Terry spots the turn-off. The faded, wooden signboard is almost lost amongst the weeds and several similar signs at the roadside. "Carver's farm," Terry yells. His oval face is animated as he points to a rough dirt track leading away into the bush on our right. As we turn onto the track, the truck bounces hard over a pothole. The galvanized pipe sections we're carrying set up a din against the metal sides of the open-backed truck.

The track serves as a feeder road to several farms in the area. About a mile further along we come to another turn-off. A lone signboard with Carver's name with an arrow indicates the direction. Turning the truck, I follow this track south, driving through rugged, ridged country covered in thick dried-up bush and thorn trees. Suddenly, the front left-hand tire blows, and the truck swerves.

"Shit," I mutter to Terry, as I brake hard, bringing the vehicle to a stop. "That's the bloody tire gone." Using the Tanganyika jack, we remove the tire, and are in the process of changing the wheel, when the nearby crack of a pistol shot startles us. Pausing, we listen but there are no further sounds, only the chirping of birds and hum of insects. We look at each other, not sure what to make of the situation.

"Is somebody practising with a handgun? Surely not," says Terry.

Instinctively, I feel the butt of my revolver in its holster. I've left my rifle at home, locked in a cupboard. There will be no need to shoot game for labour here, because this is farmland. Besides, the revolver is a better weapon for close-in fighting. "No, I don't think so," I say, then add, "Maybe someone is taking an odd potshot at an animal, but it doesn't sound like a rifle. Maybe it's the farmer. Let's get the bloody spare wheel on while we can."

We are still struggling with the wheel when we hear the clip-clop of a horse's hoofs approaching on the track. Then a heavily built, elderly man on horseback rounds the bend. Seeing us, he draws up.

"Ah," he says, pointing at the Posts and Tels logo on the cab door. "You must be the two men that the D.O. was telling me about. You're putting radios into farmhouses." He dismounts from the horse, and shakes our hands. "I'm Carver," he says, "I've been expecting you."

"We heard a shot a few minutes ago," I say, glancing down at the revolver hanging from his belt. "Was that you?"

Carver nods and grins. "Shot a baboon in the bush, a big bastard. He's the leader of the pack that's been raiding my *mealies* (corn). I'd followed him into thick bush, but he came for me, so I killed him with the revolver." He pats the gun in its holster, and then adds, "A rifle's no use in bush like that. It gets tangled up, and you don't have time to aim. And if you wound a baboon, then you've got to watch out because he can tear you to pieces."

Shaking my head in admiration, I say, "You must be a crack shot." Laughing, I add, "I'd be lucky to even hit the bloody thing. I don't ever intend tangling with baboon. I understand that the whole troop can turn on you."

Carver smiles, "I've been brought up with firearms." Pointing to the east and the long, bush-covered ridge we'd been following, he says, "But come up to the house; it's just beyond this ridge. The dirt track curves round the end and bends back like a 'U'. Follow it for about a mile. You can't miss the farmhouse."

As we tighten the wheel nuts on the spare, he says, "I'll see you back at the farm. I'm taking a short-cut." Mounting his horse, he rides off through the bush, following a hidden track.

"Hey," says Terry, grinning as he brushes his fair, wavy hair back from his forehead. "Now, that's a real Kenya cowboy. Look at him ride that horse straight up the ridge."

As Carver disappears from sight over the ridge, I have to agree. "Yeah, that's true. He's got to be good to be able to shoot a baboon with a handgun, and get away with it."

It's mid-morning when we reach the house, and noon before we finish installing the radio equipment. We threaded together two twenty-foot sections of two-inch galvanized pipe, and then clamped them to the end wall of the low, ranch-style farmhouse to form a mast. A beam antenna was then bolted to the top of the pipe, with the beam pointing in the direction of the Thika Police control headquarters. The cable from the antenna disappeared under the eaves to run down the inside wall to a radio transceiver that is plugged into a wall socket. Carver's electrical supply comes from his own generator.

Sitting back in a wooden chair beside the transceiver, I press the transmit button on the microphone and call police headquarters. "Thika Control, this is Carver's farm. Do you read? Over."

Releasing the transmit button, I wait. It is a moment before they reply and a voice booms through the loudspeaker. "Carver's farm. This is Thika Control. We are reading you *strength five*. Go ahead."

We talk to the control at the police station for several minutes, testing the signal and adjusting the antenna direction for maximum signal strength, before we sign off. Satisfied, Terry and I explain the communication procedures to Carver.

As we pack up our tools, he invites us to stay for lunch. "Aye," he says, "I've told my *mpishi* (cook) that there's an extra two for lunch, so you'll have to stay." Pleased, we accept his offer.

Over lunch, we learn something of his life. He was born in England, but his family emigrated to America before the turn of the century, and he was raised on a farm in the American west. Now well into his seventies, he's tough and hardened by life. Strong and active, he lives alone on his farm, raising cattle for market and growing corn as feed.

"I've been all round the world," he says. Laughing, he adds, "Yeah, I was even a sheriff back in the States. I served in the US Cavalry during the First World War. That's where I learned to shoot with a pistol and rifle." He pauses a moment, and his rugged face brightens into a smile, "Ah, that's long before you two lads were even thought of, let alone born."

We are served a heavy meal that is more like a dinner than a lunch. There's roast beef, mashed potatoes, Yorkshire pudding, gravy, and several vegetables, followed by a steamed pudding. Carver has a good appetite and eats well, pausing every now and then to talk. I think he's lonely and delighted to have company because he plies us with questions.

Carver and I find a common bond in our Merchant Navy service. He had sailed in deep-sea vessels before finally settling down in Kenya sometime between the two wars. Terry listens in silence as Carver and I exchange stories of merchant ships and foreign ports. Terry was born in the colony, and was just a kid during the Second World War. Come to that so was I, because I was just seventeen when I joined up in 1942.

It's after one o'clock in the afternoon when we finally tear ourselves away from his tales of years gone by and leave. The farm is partly hidden in the dust thrown up by the truck as we gather speed on the farm road, then round the ridge near where we first met Carver, I glance at Terry, "Well, what d'you think of him?"

"Ah," sighs Terry. "He's quite a character, even if some of his tales are suspect. What a past! Sheriff and cavalryman, then a seaman before jumping ship in Mombasa to go farming in Kenya!"

He pauses a moment, then continues, "Shooting a baboon with a revolver, now that's something. But then, I guess Kenya's past is full of characters and remittance men, men like Colonel Grogan who walked from Cape to Cairo around the turn of the century, to win a woman's hand in marriage. There was also Karamoja Bell of elephant hunting fame and John Boyes, the self-styled King of the Kikuyu, to name just a few. But you know about them; it's a part of our history."

The Blue Posts Hotel

The Harris' farm, located on the outskirts of Thika, is next. The farmhouse stands in the middle of acres of coffee, line upon line of neatly set out green shrubs. Following the same procedure used in Carver's farm, we assemble the equipment, mast, and antenna, and then contact Thika Control to test the link. It is dusk when we leave for our base in the Blue Posts Hotel.

Built on the confluence of the Chania and Thika Rivers, the hotel is picturesque. The gardens and dining room overlook the Chania Falls on one side of the hotel, while the Thika River runs behind the hotel to join the Chania on the sharply narrowing headland in the hotel grounds.

The sun has set behind the Aberdares and Terry and I are sitting on the veranda discussing our plans for the following day, and already a general plan is taking shape. "We've enough equipment aboard the truck for five days," I say, then add, "Fortunately the farms are not widely spaced, so we should be able to average two farms a day in this area. We'll return to Nairobi for more supplies at the end of the week."

Terry grins. "Sounds great. What farms are we booked to do tomorrow?"

"We've got Juja farm on the lower slopes of Ol Doinyo Sapuk, then the White Fathers' mission station near Thika." I smile, adding, " At this rate, we should be able to get home most weekends, but it will depend which area we are tackling. We may be out longer in the Nanyuki

Figure 15. The Blue Posts Hotel at Thika.

and Timau areas, because the farms are farther apart. The same applies to Thomson's Falls and Kipipiri in the Aberdares. But we'll see."

The dinner gong sounds, interrupting our conversation, and we go into the dining room. "Hmm, this is living, Terry," I say, as we eat. "I think that I'm beginning to like this kind of safari work. We don't have to live in tents and rough it out in the bush like I usually do on the VHF surveys. There's also no need to survive on a subsistence allowance of five shillings a day, eating canned food and whatever meat I can shoot." Laughing softly, I add, "And we'll be able to go home most weekends for the next three months or so."

It is Friday night, and we've completed the last farm installation on our list. The Dodge truck is light, empty except for two or three Yardley Wavis generators that were not required. Most farms have their own generators that they use to run their lights and electrical appliances, although there are some exceptions.

Entering the outskirts of Nairobi, we pass the Thika Road House, and I slow the truck as the dirt road dips sharply down into the upper end of the Mathari valley. I curse as the wheels jar violently against the corrugations on the dirt surface of the bridge as the speed drops, setting up a nerve-racking rumble.

After negotiating the bridge at the bottom of the valley, the truck pulls up the steep slope to the intersection of the Muthaiga and Thika Road, and onto a smooth tarred road leading to Nairobi's elite residential area. The noise ceases abruptly, and I sigh with relief, but not for long.

As I turn the truck into the Eastleigh area running parallel with the airport, the rumble and jarring resumes.

I grip the wheel tightly as the truck bounces and jars over a series of potholes. "Christ," I grumble, "You can tell we're in Eastleigh by the state of the bloody road."

Terry grins, "Aye, he says, "it's the back end of Nairobi, but Mathari Valley is worse. That's the arse end."

"You can say that again," I reply, concentrating on the road ahead. "Back in 1949, I used to work in the control tower on the military side of the Eastleigh airport. Whenever we went on shift, I used the Mathari route. What a shantytown that is! This area may be poor with a large Asian population, but, compared to Mathari, it's upper class."

For a while we drive on in silence, occupied with our own thoughts. Then I say to Terry, "You live in Karen, don't you?"

"Yeah," he replies, " I live with my parents. Head for Dagoretti Corner, and I'll direct you from the Karen *dukas*; it's not far from there. It's quicker that way than going through Langata."

As we turn off into Racecourse Road, the truck jolts over the bridge spanning the Nairobi River. Usually, the river is only a stream, but during the rainy season, when there are cloudbursts up in the hills, the river has been known to flood the neighbourhood. We pass by Doonholm Road that leads to Kariokor and other African locations. Both Kariokor and the Mathari Valley are shantytowns, constructed from plastic sheets, bits of wood and corrugated iron, and are known derisively as the *Factori ya Mau Mau* by both the local Africans and Europeans.

The truck speeds on through a series of squalid streets to Whitehouse Road, passing the railroad station near the intersection of Government and Whitehouse Roads. Lining the west side of the road are drab wooden houses with rotting verandas, raised on concrete blocks and topped by corrugated iron sheets, all that remain of the original housing for railway workers built at the turn of the century.

Cresting the ridge, the neighbourhood changes again, because we are now entering South Hill, a better class white residential area that includes the prestigious Nairobi Club and the Nairobi Golf Course. Across from the golf course, on the other side of Ngong Road, the large parcel of land belonging to the French Mission stretches into the distance, bound by Kabete on the west, Kileleshwa on the north, and the Kikuyu Reserve on the southwest.

As we drive along the Ngong Road to Dagoretti Corner, dusk is falling. Seeing a familiar bungalow among the corrugated roofs of the European-occupied bungalows lining the road, I grin. Pointing to the rundown house, I say, "Look over there, Terry. See that house? I stayed there as a paying guest soon after I came to Kenya early in 1949. It belonged to Pelham-Mather. Do you know him?"

"No," says Terry, shaking his head. "No, I don't think so."

"He used to be in government service in the days of the Indian Raj, but he came to Kenya after the Second World War. I'm not sure what he does now." After a brief pause I continue. "It's strange how a man's face sticks in your mind. He was a man in his early forties, about six-foot tall and slim, with slicked back, light gingery hair, and a thin moustache. His accent was that of an educated man. I stayed there for about three months, and then found another place. My wife was still in England at that time, and I needed an address here so that I could bring her out—it was a government regulation."

I pause a moment, then continue. "It's been several years since I last saw him, but I've often wondered what happened to him. I had the impression that he was a remittance man who was down on his luck and had been abandoned by his wealthy English family." I shake my head. "This country seems to attract the black sheep, like so many of the colonies and ex-colonies. I think that his first name was Harold, and I can't help feeling sorry for him."

Night has fallen. Turning left into Karen Road at Dagoretti Corner, I drive across flat, bush-covered land towards the Ngong Hills. The lights of the town of Karen, the service station, and *dukas* appear ahead. Terry directs me to his home, roughly a mile from the shops, and, when we arrive there, he invites me in.

"Thanks, Terry," I say, "but I have to get home." I glance at my watch. "It's six-thirty, and, if I hurry, I should be home in time for dinner. Before I left, I told Joan that I would try to be home tonight. By the way, the department works on Saturday mornings. I'll take the truck back tomorrow, and we'll load it up for an early start on Monday."

By the time I get home, it's gone seven-thirty. Joan hears the truck draw up, and comes to the door. As I walk towards her, I can see her slight form silhouetted against the hall light. "Everything okay?" she queries. "I thought you might have had trouble on the road, and I was getting worried. Odede is keeping your dinner warm."

Glad to be home, I hug her to me. She's light in my arms. Like her mother, she's small—about five feet two. "We were a little late finishing off the last farm," I say, adding, "I had to take Terry home. He lives over in Karen with his parents."

When I enter the dining room, Odede's broad grin stretches across his face. "*Jambo, bwana,*" he says, "*habari ya* safari—what's the news about the safari?"

Laughing, I reply, "*Tumemaliza kazi yenu*—we have finished our work in Thika, but I'll be off again on Monday."

A Murder Close to Home

After dinner when Odede has retired to his quarters, Joan tells me the latest news. "I saw Gloria, Bungy's wife, in the street the other day. She told me that the wife of one of the men in the post office personnel section was murdered. They lived in Ruaraka, near the brewery, a little way off the Thika Road. Her servants killed her with *pangas* in the kitchen. I had seen the report of this attack in the newspaper, but I hadn't connected it with your department."

For a moment, I sit there, silently turning the news over in my mind. *I know Neilson, the personnel manager, but I don't know his staff. There's very little contact between the office staff and the* safari *crews. When we do have dealings with the accounts section, we usually deal with old Sittar, the Asian head clerk.*

My voice feels heavy in my throat, as I reply, "No, it doesn't seem that you can trust anyone these days." I pause, and then continue, "Look at my road gang on Loldiani, and the raid on Black's farm. I thought that those men were hand-picked and trustworthy; but now they're all in the detention camps. We know that Odede is not a Kikuyu. He's a Maragoli from a village outside Kisumu. The Maragoli tribe doesn't seem to be affected by oath taking, so he should be all right. It's people who live in remote areas that are in real danger. That's why we're setting up emergency radio links between the farms and the security forces."

Joan nods. "There's so many reports about attacks on the farms these days, and of houses being ransacked when the owners are away. It's almost a daily occurrence. This week, the *East African Standard* carried a report of a raid on the Squaires' house in Nyeri, along with photographs. The gang smashed everything they could lay their hands on, and stole their guns. And that's just one attack."

✳✳✳

When I arrive at the office in the morning, the place is abuzz with the news of the Ruaraka murder. Evidently the two Kikuyu servants had fled, taking the firearms that had been kept in a cupboard, and presumably they joined the gangs in the forests. The crime was not discovered until the children came home from school that afternoon. As I hear the details, I shake my head and mutter, "Christ, what a thing for young kids to see. Their mother dead on the kitchen floor and the house ransacked."

Terry has joined me, and has also heard the news. Turning to him, I say, "Well, we'd better load up the truck. There are another ten farms in the Nanyuki and Nyeri areas to do next week. We'll stay at the White Rhino Hotel in Nyeri, before moving on to Nanyuki." I smile at Terry half-heartedly. "Let's get off early on Monday. It'll take us three or four hours, depending on the road through Fort Hall in the Kikuyu Reserve. You know what the roads are like."

"Yeah," Terry says, "typical Kenya bush roads—dirt, dust, corrugations and potholes. And don't forget the mud during the rainy seasons," he adds with a grin.

Farms of Mount Kenya

Fascinated, I watch Laura Poolman, Henry's sister, as she tends the injured buffalo calf, bathing the open suppurating sores, cleaning out the pus, and applying ointment to the wounds. "Henry had no option," she says, her voice low with concern for the calf. "He had to do it, had to shoot its mother. He was mending a fence on the forest edge two days ago when the buffalo charged him. Fortunately he had his rifle with him; he takes it everywhere these days."

Laura looks up from her task and I find myself looking into two dark brown eyes framed in an elfin face. Her hair is dark and shiny black, like Joan's. *But Joan's a city girl, and a skilful Nairobi hairdresser arranges her hair into a fashionable French roll.*

"He had to shoot it; it was either kill or be killed." Laura pauses, and then says, "He just couldn't leave the young one. It's only a few weeks old and still needs its mother's milk."

"Yes, there was no other choice," I agree, and with a nod towards the calf, continue, "Look, he knows you want to help. He probably thinks you're his mother."

Laura smiles. "That's because he knows I have milk for him." She strokes the calf's head as it drinks greedily, sucking noisily on the rubber teat of the bottle she's holding.

Hearing footsteps, I half-turn as a voice calls, "Hi, Sis, have you finished feeding Brutus?" It's Henry, with Terry in tow.

Laura smiles as she answers, "Yes, he's almost emptied the bottle." She turns to me and adds, "That's the name Henry's given the calf, poor little thing."

"Thought I'd show Gord and Terry around the farm. Want to come?" Henry and his sister are looking after the farm while their parents visit relatives in Rumuruti.

She nods, "I'll put the calf back in the barn." She turns away, followed by the small buffalo. We watch her go with Brutus trotting behind her, still trying to nuzzle the hand that holds the bottle.

Henry laughs as he watches his sister. "She loves that little calf," he says. "In fact she's always been dotty about animals. The dik-dik and our dog follow her everywhere." From the tone of his voice, I can sense the affection Henry feels for his sister. She's about eighteen, and he must be roughly two years older. The bond between them is close. *It reminds me of my sister and me, only Eileen was the older one. We were close, too, but Eileen died four years ago with her second baby.* We turn and in a group follow Henry out into the fields.

***

The threshing machine cuts a wide swath in the wheat field as Henry proudly demonstrates its functions and capabilities. Its whirring blades move slowly forward at a walking pace, neatly cutting the tall stalks, and separating the wheat seeds. The piles of discarded stalks will be collected later and used for cattle fodder.

It's almost five o'clock when Terry and I leave the Poolman farm for Nyeri. As we pull away, Henry and his sister wave from the veranda steps. Unlike Black's farm, there are no barbed wire enclosures. Built of mud-and-wattle with a neatly thatched roof, the farmhouse stands defiant against the world around it. The house with its wide veranda on the southern side looks picturesque as it sits on the hillside, overlooking the distant plains in the valley below. On the other side of the valley, like a backdrop, is the rising range of the Aberdares.

There is a new addition to the farm, however, and I grin as I look back. The forty-foot mast with its antenna juts out above the roof on the gable end of the farmhouse, with its beam pointing towards Nyeri to the southeast. As the truck rounds a bend in the road, a fold in the land hides the farm with Henry and his sister.

The truck coasts down a dip as we pass the collection of thatched rondavels where the farm workers and their families live. A small group

Figure 16. Threshing machine on Poolman's farm.

of African children wave to us as the truck thunders by. I smile and raise my hand in salute.

It is the last we see of the farm, just one of a small enclave of farms clustered on a plateau and edged by dense forest high in the foothills of Mount Kenya. The all-weather road winds its way down the forested foothills as it drops into the valley separating the Aberdares from Mount Kenya.

Thatched roofs. The thought sticks in my mind as I drive, concentrating on the potholed surface of the road. Then, without shifting my gaze on the road ahead, I ask Terry what he thinks about them.

"Death traps," he says.

"Yeah," I nod my head, "I agree. There are so many farmhouses hereabouts with that type of roof, at least from what I've seen so far. They look nice, but a bottle of gasoline and a burning rag slung on the roof, or on one of those wooden verandas, and the whole lot goes up in flames."

"It's a case of materials and cost, I suppose." Terry pauses, his face thoughtful, then continues. "The options are corrugated iron sheets, or Mangalore tiles. Thatching is cheap and readily available. I don't suppose it ever occurred to people when they built the majority of these farmhouses years ago, that someday they would have to contend with terrorists."

"I'm surprised the Poolmans haven't erected defensive barbed wire fences with staked rolls of barbed wire outside it." I say, and then add. "Their location is bad because it's so close to the forests."

Terry sighs wearily, "I agree, and you'd think they would. It would spoil their view, but what's the use of a view if you're dead?"

Dusk is falling when we reach the outskirts of Nyeri and head back to the White Rhino Inn. We had booked in there at noon today, and eaten a hurried lunch at the inn before going to the Poolman farm to install the radio equipment.

By the time I reach the inn, night has fallen. The security lights are on, and the entire parking area is brightly lit. I park the truck at the far end, and Terry and I climb out. "*Jambo, bwana,*" the solitary security guard calls to us as we check the load under the heavy tarpaulin. Dressed in dark blue clothing with a *rungu* (club) under his arm and a panga in a sheath strapped to his waist, the guard is almost invisible. When he steps out of the shadows, grinning broadly, his white teeth stand out against the dark skin.

"*Unachunga ghari hapa*—do you look after the cars here?" I say with a smile.

"*Ndiyo, bwana,*" he replies. We talk briefly, and then Terry and I make our way to the reception office in the main entrance hall.

The White Rhino Inn is a small residential hotel tucked away on a quiet road near the forest. With its whitewashed, mud-and-wattle walls and high vaulted thatched roof, the building blends into the countryside. Set back from the road in its own grounds, the inn is surrounded by shrubs and a variety of acacia and jacaranda trees. With its relaxed atmosphere and bar, the White Rhino is a popular meeting place for the local farmers and residents of the township.

***

Later that evening, I learn more about the Poolmans. When we were at the farm, Terry and Henry had recognized each other. Now as Terry and I drink coffee in the hotel lounge after dinner, Terry talks about his school days.

"You know, Gord," he says, "I thought Henry's face was familiar. We were both boarders at the same Nairobi school, but he was in the junior school. Strange how you bump into people you know, although I guess it's to be expected. The white population here is so small compared to the Asian and African communities."

He pauses a moment, and then says, "Did you know that the Poolmans are related to the Hartleys in Rumuruti?"

"You mean Carr Hartley, the white hunter?" As Terry nods, I continue. "No, I didn't realize that. Didn't *Mau Mau* kill Carr Hartley's parents a few months ago?"

"Yes," he replies. He looks down at the table, his fingers playing absent-mindedly with his coffee cup. "Their farm was attacked by a gang while Carr Hartley was away on safari. Only his parents, his wife, and baby son were in the house at the time. His wife was upstairs with the baby when the gang burst in and murdered the old couple. When she heard their screams, Mrs. Hartley took the baby and hid in the attic. Fortunately the gang did not find them." Terry pauses a moment, then adds, "Fancy having to listen to the screams of your parents being killed. Christ, it's sickening."

Terry looks up. "She stayed with her baby in the attic while the gang ransacked the house. After they left, she went downstairs. God, that must have been an awful sight and experience."

Shaking my head, I heave a deep breath. There is an empty feeling in me, a senseless rage at all the killings of both whites and blacks. "What can we do, Terry?" I mutter. "This is not like a war. It's hit-and-run, and you never know when or where the next attack is coming. There is no clearly defined front line like there is in a war. Fortunately, only the Central Province is affected, but that's where most of the white population lives. Thank God it has not spread to the whole country. It would be chaos."

The Old Doldol Farm, Laikipia Plateau

We're off on the road again. *How many farms this week?* I've lost count as our travels over the dirt roads and tracks multiply, and we go from farm to farm, covering a wide area in the foothills and forest areas from Nyeri to Embu. The farms are beginning to look the same to us.

After spending three nights at the White Rhino, we move on to the Silverbeck Hotel in Nanyuki. A quaint upcountry hotel, the Silverbeck's claim to fame is the fact that the equator runs through its bar. Part of the room is in the southern hemisphere while the remainder is in the northern. Apart from this doubtful claim, the hotel is rather drab. Its location is convenient, however, because it is close to the small township's centre of activity. The hotel's dining room, lounge, bar, reception office, and the manager's quarters are all located in the main building, while a line of *bandas* provides sleeping accommodation for the guests.

"Doldol, where the hell is that?" Terry asks as he reads the list of farms. It's nine in the evening, we've eaten the plain, wholesome meal provided by the hotel, and are sitting in the lounge. Late in finishing the last farm in the Embu district, we'd driven hard along the Embu-Nanyuki Road and had just arrived in time for dinner.

"It's a long way off by the sound of it," I say as I spread the large-scale survey map on the coffee table, then compare our list and routing

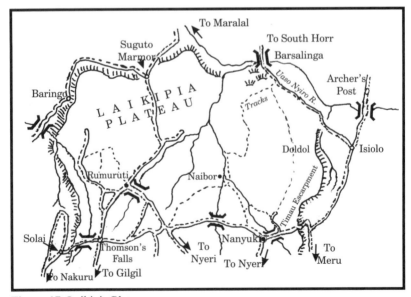

Figure 17. Laikipia Plateau

directions with the map. "From Nanyuki, we follow the Thomson's Falls Road for roughly ten miles, and then take a track heading north across the Laikipia Plateau."

After a short pause, I indicate a spot on the map. "This large area is Doldol, but we'll have to rely on the route instructions from that point." With my finger, I trace the route across the plateau to its far edge. "That's quite a way out. This one is a full day's trip, for sure, Terry, and, by the look of the map, it's across a dried-up wasteland. Why would anyone have a farm out there?"

Terry grunts, "We'll find out tomorrow for sure."

✳✳✳

We were up early, and left the Silverbeck after a quick breakfast. Now, it's mid-morning and we've driven deep into the Laikipia plateau, heading northwest in the direction of Naibor. For miles now, we've been travelling over dusty, drought-ridden plains as we follow the old feeder track to isolated farms.

As he looks at the sparse coarse clumps of grass, stunted thorn trees, and bush, Terry shakes his head. "Yeah, as you said, it's a dried-up wasteland, all right. Not much can grow out here. I wouldn't have thought it could have sustained cattle grazing, especially at this time of year." His eyes squint against the sun.

It's hot in the cab. The only breeze is that generated by the speed of the truck as it rattles and shakes across corrugations and potholes in the track.

It's a moment before I reply, "It's the same to the west on the Laikipia. You should try the Rumuruti-Maralal road sometime; it's just like this. I know a farmer over there, name of Jimmy Keen. He's got the ranch next to Carr Hartley. He told me that, during the hot season, he has to trek his cattle some forty miles up into the hills. But while the rainy season lasts, this is good cattle country."

"I suppose that's why the farmers need so much range land," Terry's face is thoughtful. "It's a case of so many acres per head of cattle, and not the other way around." A turn-off running north appears on the road ahead, and he breaks off to look at the route plan. "That's our turn-off," he exclaims.

Roughly a mile down the farm track, half-hidden in the scrub and bush, the farmhouse suddenly appears when we round a bend. It is a long, rectangular building with a high, sloping thatched roof and thick mud-and-wattle walls. Situated in the midst of acacia trees and surrounded by bougainvillea and canna lilies in full bloom, the house has a picturesque, old-fashioned charm. The scene, however, is deceptive, because, on closer inspection, we can see that the house is badly run down, and the garden neglected. Somewhere behind the house a dog barks, warning its owner of strangers in the vicinity.

Braking, I draw the truck up outside the front door of the house as an elderly woman opens the door to peer out. As we climb out of the truck, she welcomes us with a smile. "Aye, luv," she says, "I've been expecting thee. Come in. Thee must be thirsty. It's a long way from Nanyuki."

The familiar, broad Yorkshire accent makes me smile. It reminds me of my mother, who also came from the north of England. Now as we follow the farmer's wife into the neat, but sparsely furnished living room, I glance at the woman. Her face is deeply lined and her hands are work-soiled, but there's still that air of pride and spirit about her.

"Kimani," she calls, "*Lete chai*—bring the tea."

From the depths of the kitchen, a voice answers, "*Ndiyo, memsahib.*" Moments later an African servant dressed in a white *kanzu* enters the room carrying a tray loaded with cups of tea and hot, buttered scones.

"Aye, lads," she says, as we sit around the table drinking tea and eating scones, "Before he left on safari yesterday, Jack, me 'usband, said you would be coming today."

"Are you here on your own?" I ask.

"Ooh, aye. Jack's often away. He goes off upcountry hunting. We sell most of the meat he shoots, but keep some to make biltong. Of course," she adds, "we've got the chickens and some cattle, but in the hot season he and the boys trek the cattle up into the hills to graze."

When we finish eating, we walk out to the truck to unload the mast sections, cable and beam antenna. Our installation begins in earnest. Inside, the farmhouse has been partitioned into rooms by walls that are eight to ten feet high. There are no ceilings, only the bare, high vaulted roof with its intertwined rough poles and crosspieces. A fireplace and chimney grace one end of the house. We mount and stay the mast and antenna section to this gable end, and lead the coaxial cable into the room beside the chimney.

The house has a peculiar, musty odour. When I smell my hands after I have touched the walls, I realize what the source of the aroma is. The mud walls have been coated inside and out, native-fashion, with a mixture of diluted cow dung, urine, and whitewash.

The cookhouse and servants' quarters are separate from the main building, but connected to it by a covered sidewalk. The small huts built by the farm labourers are a short distance from the house, and screened from it by a thick hedge of bushes and acacia trees. The labourers are squatters who live on the farm with their families. Like the occupants of tied farm cottages in England, the squatters supply labour to the farm when needed in turn for living on the farmer's land.

Because the farm has no electricity to run the radio equipment, we install a small Yardley Wavis generator in the adjacent barn, connecting it to the equipment in the living room using heavy, overhead cable. Then we show her house servant how to start the generator and how to check the oil and fuel levels.

As we test the unit with police headquarters in Nanyuki, the farmer's wife listens intently to the conversation. When I explain that she can put the transceiver on standby and listen to the emergency channel giving out bulletins or talking to other farmers on a separate channel, she smiles with pleasure.

"Yes," she says, "I'll not feel so lonely now when Jack's gone. I've only an old, battery-operated radio, but that only comes on for the news. And," she adds with an air of exasperation, "the batteries seem to go dead just when I want them."

Before we go, I ask her how long she's lived out here. "Oh, it's a long time, luv," she says. "Aye, let me think." She pauses a moment, then continues, "I met Jack in York just after the 1914-18 war—he was a young soldier then—and we came to Kenya in the mid-'twenties. For a while, he worked as a farm manager near Gilgil, and then we got this place. It was going cheap, and we bought it. That was back in 1936. It's nay so bad and 'tis our own, even though it's away off the beaten track."

Thinking back on my mother's early life, I smile. "It sounds familiar," I reply. "My mother was born in Easingwold, about fifteen miles north of York, and she, too, met a soldier and married him in 1919. After they were married, Dad took her south to live on a small farm in Essex. I was brought up on that farm." I shake my head at the memory. "Christ, it must have been a hard life for my parents too, in those days, what with the depression, and no electricity, water or plumbing. The kitchen floor was brick." I pause, closing my eyes, and can see Epping Forest and the farmer's fields behind the house. "My dad used a yoke and two three-gallon cans to carry water from a spring about half a mile away," I say.

"Aye," the farmer's wife breaks in, "and dinna' forget the outhouse. We have a long drop here, but back in the auld country the farm outhouses had bucket toilets. Villages had night-soil men who removed the pails from an opening behind the outhouses, but on farms you had to bury the bloody stuff yourselves."

I shake my head at the thought, feeling my stomach squirm in revulsion. "Yes, after my father died in 1942, I used to help my mother whenever I was home on leave. The stench was terrible. I don't know how she could stand it, week after week."

We talk for a while, and then I climb up into the cab of the truck. The old woman stands on the porch with her dog, a black and white mongrel, by her side. When we reach a curve in the farm road, I glance back in the mirror, but she has gone, and I catch a glimpse of the farm door closing behind her.

Terry and I sit in silence as we drive down the dusty track, followed by a plume of dust. The farm is now hidden by the screening bush. As I change gear, I glance across at him. "Bloody hell, Terry," I say. "What keeps people on a farm like that? They're barely scratching a living from the soil."

"Yeah," Terry replies, his voice despondent and bitter. "Some people say that the farmers are rich and live in mansions out here. Some are, but most of them are having a tough time to make ends meet. Maybe they are wealthy in comparison with their labour force and the Africans who live in the bush or the slums of Kariokor, but not by civilized standards. Still, it's their own little piece of Africa, and they love all that it entails."

Captain Raymond Hook

We've worked right through the weekend. There's a sameness now to the routine as we go from farm to farm installing emergency radio systems. We have installed equipment on farms from Timau and the escarpment in the north, to Mweiga district in the foothills of the Aberdares to the south and southwest. We'd brought extra supplies from Nairobi, and now the truck is almost empty.

This morning, Terry and I were on the outskirts of Nanyuki, where we installed emergency radio equipment into a large and prosperous farm with its own farm manager. The large mansion-style farmhouse provided a sharp contrast to the poverty-stricken Doldol farm. The Bastards—*with the emphasis on 'tard'* (the last syllable)—are influential settlers who have lived in Kenya for several generations. The owners of the homestead were away upcountry when we arrived, so Terry and I talked to their farm manager.

Lunch at the Silverbeck Hotel was a hurried affair, and now we're off on our last farm assignment before returning to Nairobi for another truckload of equipment. As we pull out of the hotel parking lot onto the gravel-surfaced road to Nyeri, Terry glances at the map in his hands. "This one's quite close," he says. "It's old Hook's farm on the outskirts of Nanyuki."

"Aye," I say, "It's just up the road. I'm looking forward to meeting him. The name and his exploits intrigue me. Have you met him before?"

Terry shakes his head, "Like you, I've only heard of him. He must be getting on because he's one of the old settlers. Didn't he introduce cheetah racing?"

I nod, "Yes, back in the 'twenties, or so I understand." I smile at the thought of meeting this old settler, and wonder what he looks like. *He's older than Hunter, the game warden in Makindu. He's probably about Carver's age.* I dismiss the thought from my mind and say, "Well we'll soon know. We're nearly there. This is not a big town."

Terry laughs, "Yeah, as the old Afrikaners say, it's a bit of a *dorp* (village)."

After the installation is completed and the radio tested with the Nanyuki police headquarters, we sit in the Captain's lounge, talking to him, and the conversation inevitably turns to the cheetahs.

Captain Raymond Hook is another of Kenya's well-known characters. He's in his late fifties or early sixties, and his features are suntanned. Unlike Carver, he does not cut a romantic figure because he's quiet and unassuming. "Aye," he says in reply to my question about the cheetahs, "it was back in the 'twenties, early 'thirties, when I started racing cheetahs. I even took them to the UK once, but it didn't catch on."

Pausing, he sips the steaming hot tea in his cup, then reaches out, and takes a cake from the old-fashioned cake stand. It is now late in the afternoon—the Captain, an ex-Indian army officer, refers to it as *tiffin* time—and we are observing the old British custom of having tea and cakes.

Satisfied with his choice, he continues, "The trouble is that, though cheetahs are the fastest animal on four legs, they cannot sustain that speed over a distance of more than a hundred yards or so. That's how we caught them. A rider on horseback would chase the cheetah, and then net it after it fell down exhausted." An interesting man, Hook talks to us about the early days in Kenya, of Karamoja Bell, the white hunter, and life before the Second World War.

It's dusk when we finally leave, and head west along the main Nyeri-Nanyuki road into the centre of the small township. Night has fallen by the time we arrive at the hotel, and the lights of the Silverbeck welcome us. It is Tuesday, January 20, and tomorrow night we'll be back in Nairobi.

For Terry and me, this marks the end of our teamwork. Next week, we will split up and each of us will work alone with our own truck and driver. There are still many more farms that urgently need radio communications. We have not yet touched the south side of the Aberdares, nor the southwest, where many settlers farm the land.

✳✳✳

Chapter 4
Of Murder and Mayhem

Fire Bombing, the Night Patrol

It's dark in the dimly lit streets of Kileleshwa outside Daphton Court. There is no moon, only stars in the clear night sky. To the north, the distant glow from downtown Nairobi lights the sky, and silhouettes the roofs of houses and trees lining Riverside Drive. My partner Harry Boardman and I are walking down the road on patrol.

There's been a spate of fire bombing by *Mau Mau* gangs in Nairobi, and several houses have gone up in flames in the residential districts. The Kenya Police Reserve, which I'd joined as a special police officer in October, has been called out to patrol the streets and neighbourhoods during the nighttime hours. While back in Nairobi between safari*s*, I've been placed on the call-out roster.

Terry and I had left Nanyuki this morning, and arrived back in Nairobi around three o'clock. Terry went off to report to his regimental headquarters, and to receive his new orders, while I left the empty truck in the post office yard and phoned Joan to get a ride home.

When she picked me up outside the main post office, Joan told me about the fire bombings. Talking in short animated sentences as she steered the car through Nairobi's rush hour traffic, she said, "The fire bombing started a few days ago, and then the Kileleshwa Police rang the other night. They're making a roster for police reservists, and gave me a number for you to call."

When I called the police station, a male Scots voice answered my query. "One moment please, Mr. Mumford," he said, "and I'll just check the list." I could hear a rustle of papers, and then his voice returned. "Can you possibly make it tonight? We're a man short on the midnight-to-two patrol. You'll be with Harry Boardman. He lives in your area." I phoned the number that the police gave me, and arranged to meet Harry outside the entrance to Daphton Court.

Now as Harry and I walk along, I glance at my companion. Judging by his shadowy shape, he's a tall man and heavily built. Passing beneath a street lamp, I catch a glimpse of a broad leathery face and dark hair with telltale streaks of grey that put him over forty.

"We patrol as far as the bridge over the Nairobi River," he says, then chuckles, "that's if you can call it a river. Then we head downstream along the bank." Harry pauses an instant. "I'd better lead the way because it's a bit dicey. The bush is bloody thick, and there's only a narrow path along the river behind the houses. That's where we're most likely to get trouble. The path is on the escape route for gangs operating out of the Kikuyu Reserve. Usually, they're small groups, just two or three men."

He continues to describe our route. "Farther down river, there's a feeder stream that cuts across the path. We'll head up it to the back of your place in Daphton Court. It's roughly a rectangle. Then, we do the same on the south side of Riverside Drive, but along MacMillan Close to the river again. That's the limits of our patrolling area."

When the bridge looms up in the night, Harry, with his rifle clutched in his right hand, turns into the narrow path along the riverbank. As I follow Harry's bulky form into the black shadows, I feel a tensing in my muscles and a dryness in my throat. We're not hunting animals here, but men, and it's a very different proposition. Alert to any strange sound, I ease a bullet into the breech and check the safety catch as I hold my rifle at waist level.

The path winds up the uneven slopes of the valley. A canopy of branches from the short, stunted trees that grow along the banks blots out the night sky. We pick our way along the narrow path, partly overgrown with undergrowth and bush. Harry shades his flashlight so that its faint light shines on the ground. Brambles and thorns pluck at my clothing as we stumble up and down slopes along the edges of the properties that abut onto the ravine. Every now and then we stop to check the various houses through gaps in the bushes and fences.

"Aye," Harry whispers, "the gangs come to places like this, and then they throw bottles filled with gasoline and a lit rag onto the wooden verandas or thatched roofs, before disappearing back into the bush."

Although this area is not far from my home, it's unfamiliar ground to me. Up to now, I've taken the long valley with its thick bush and acacia trees for granted as I've sped past in a car or truck. Now, as I patrol at night on foot, the bush seems alive. Sounds made by nocturnal animals and insects set our nerves on edge. The thought of terrorists waiting in ambush is ever present.

A sudden rustle and snapping of twigs freezes us in our tracks. As we crouch there in the dark with the shaded flashlight switched off, I sense, more than hear, Harry release the safety catch on his rifle. Vainly, our eyes try to pierce the surrounding black curtain of bush. My heart pounds in my chest as I, too, slip the safety catch of my rifle. I've used the Mannlicher-Schroner on game many times, but never against men. There is a rush of adrenalin in my body as the tension grows. My mouth is dry as I stare into darkness. Expecting to meet a rush of bodies and hear frenzied screams of dope-crazed thugs at any moment, we wait for the first signs of attack, but only the unnerving silence of the bush mocks our straining ears.

"Aye, Gord," Harry mutters, "It's bloody hair-raising in the bush at night. Humph," he snorts, "it was probably just a bloody animal moving around, I guess. The trouble is that you never know. Just two or three nights ago, my partner and I stumbled on a couple of *Mau Mau* just about here." He pauses, and then continues, "Christ, it scared the shit out of me, and them, too, I guess. In the confusion—everyone's yelling and crashing about—you just fire wildly. We couldn't see a target, not clearly."

He nods towards the revolver I carry on a bullet belt around my waist. "You're much better off with the revolver, because rifles are too cumbersome." After a short pause, he adds, "The racket brought out the army security patrols, but the bastards got away."

With the menace of the bush behind us, I feel a sense of relief. The moon has just risen, and Daphton Court, a rectangular apartment block, looks bleak in the moonlight. It's one o'clock in the morning when we circle the building. Joan is probably asleep; the lights are off in our ground floor apartment.

Now Harry and I are on the second leg of the patrol, and we've toured the neighbourhood, walking along the residential roads and dark back alleys. Near MacMillan Close, we find a log partly hidden in the brush near the river and sit there and rest a while before moving on. As we watch for movement along the length of the road, my rifle lies across my knees.

"Mac, our controller, told me you'd just got back off safari, Gord," Harry says, his voice low as he talks.

"Yeah, my partner and I are putting emergency radio equipment into outlying farms in the Aberdares and Mount Kenya forest areas. We left Nanyuki early today, and got in about three o'clock. The controller said you were short a partner, so I volunteered to take his place."

Harry smiles. "I'm glad you turned up. We need two for patrol work. Imagine going through the bush by the river on your own." He shakes his head. "It's bad enough with two, but it's asking for trouble by yourself." After a brief pause, Harry adds, "Did you listen to the six o'clock news? There's been another murder."

"You mean the young farmer and old settler in Ol Kalou?"

"Yes, Richard Bingley. The old settler was Ferguson. He's been farming in Ol Kalou for more than thirty years. Poor bastards. I'd like to catch those bloody murderers." His voice trails off, and he mutters, "They'd die slowly."

"Aye," I say. "I guess most of us would like to do that. It's hard to believe that someone you've come to trust could turn round and kill you. According to the report, the gang followed their cook into the dining room, and hacked the two men to death."

Harry nods, "Yeah, the attack must have come as a complete surprise. The security report said they didn't even have time to use their weapons. The soup was still sitting on the table, undisturbed."

Shifting on the log, Harry stretches his legs out. "It's bloody bad. It's not just Europeans being killed—there have been relatively few of those at the moment—but they're killing the poor old *munts* (natives) who are loyal to the government. It's not only those who live in parts of Nairobi like Kariokor, Pumwani and the Mathari Valley, but others out on the Kikuyu Reserves."

He struggles to his feet, and we resume our patrol. "Aye," Harry says, starting to speak as we walk along the edge of the road. Then, hearing a rustle in the undergrowth, he pauses momentarily, intently watching the bush on the edge of the road. "It's only a bloody cat," he mutters. "At the moment, the *Mau Mau* are riding on the crest of a wave," he continues. "They seem to be gaining more support in the Reserves with all the oath-taking that's going on."

"That's true enough," I reply. "Just the fact that they can start and sustain fire bombing attacks right here in Nairobi shows that."

"Christ, almighty," Harry snorts. "I'd love to even the score." His hands fondle the rifle slung over his shoulder. "Last week, they burned down several houses in the Slaters and Forest Road areas. All the reservists were called out to help fight the flames, and police the area. Fortunately, apart from some burns and smoke inhalation, nobody was killed or seriously injured."

He pauses a moment, and then says, "Those old wooden houses with thatched roofs can go up in flames in seconds. Some white residents were trapped for a while by the security bars and mesh on the windows, and were lucky to escape." Putting his hand to his mouth, he stifles a yawn. "Yes, bars on the windows are a mixed blessing. They're fine to keep burglars out, but they can be fatal if you have to get out in a hurry. We had to smash some doors so we could drag the people out."

We move on in silence. It is nearing two o'clock, and we watch warily for movement and signs of activity, but the patrol ends peacefully.

The Ruck Family Murders, North Kinangop

It's Sunday, January 25, barely two days since I arrived back home. It's Odede's day off, so I am washing the breakfast dishes when Billy arrives. Joan lets him in, and I catch the word, *murder*. Grabbing a towel, I hurry into the hallway, drying my hands as I go.

Billy is saying, "'Twas on this morning's news. Didn't you hear it?"

Joan's face is solemn as she shakes her head, and turns to me. "Billy's just said there was another murder last night," she says. "It was the Ruck family. A *Mau Mau* gang killed the husband and wife, and then hacked their six-year-old son to death."

"Aye," Billy's voice breaks in, "it was up in the North Kinangop. The Forces Radio Broadcast said that there are white settler protest meetings taking place all over Kenya today. The settlers are planning to march on Government House at noon."

"Did they give any details, Billy," I ask as he follows me into the kitchen.

"No. They said that the police and security forces are investigating and questioning the cook and farm labourers. The report also said that the Ruck's syce may have played a major part in the attack, but security has not released any details. The bodies of Roger Ruck and his wife were found outside the house, and they were both badly mutilated. It looked like he had been held down on a log and battered to death. The boy was asleep upstairs, and was killed in his bed. It's a bloody affair."

"Do you think the settlers' meeting at Government House will help," I say, and then add, "other than giving people a chance to let off steam."

Billy nods, "Yes. At least, it will let the government know what the settlers and expatriates think. People are fed up with the Foreign Office in London regulating things, but I can't really see them handing over the control of the army and security forces to the local authorities. It may be that the Settlers' Association will get more say in decisions, but it's hard to tell."

"They're a hard-headed bunch, the settlers," I add, pausing a moment to wash another dish. "Right now, they're in no mood for games; their homes and their lives are at stake. I must admit that I can't help sharing their views. After all, our lives and work are also at risk. It's not the same for some bloody politician in the British Parliament. If *Mau Mau* succeeds, we're out of here, but personally I can't see the *Mau Mau* winning this one, not in the long run."

After all the dishes have been washed and dried, then stacked away in the cupboards, we enter the dining room where Joan has been dusting the crumbs off the table, and putting the tablecloth away. She looks at us suspiciously. "What've you two been mumbling about out there? No, let me guess. You want to go to the meeting!"

She laughs as she looks at us, reading our faces, "Yes, I thought so. But remember, if there's any trouble, I want out of there. Some of those settlers could start a riot, and that's the last thing I want to be involved in. That doesn't mean I disagree with them. Something needs to be done."

The March on Government House

After parking the car, we join the march in State House Road. Although angry, the crowd is an orderly one, and is being escorted by police on motorbikes. There is a constant buzz of conversation as we enter the grounds of Government House.

Large and imposing, the old world facade of Government House stands at the end of a drive edged with canna lilies, overlooking the well-cut lawns and spacious grounds. Acacia trees and flowering shrubs line the perimeters. The protest marchers congregate in front of a dais, hurriedly erected for the occasion. Various government officials sit on the platform. We can recognize Michael Blundell, leader of the European Elected Members in the Legislative Council, as well as representatives from Nairobi districts, including W. B. Havelock of Kiambu.

Speaking over the loudspeaker system, Blundell addresses the assembled crowd, outlining the aims of the meeting and the frustrations of the settlers. His familiar voice rolls over us as he introduces the group of government officials seated on the platform. Behind them, standing inconspicuously in the background, are the African *askari*s who form the Government House guards.

It is not until the thorny question of the time-consuming court procedures is raised that the meeting dissolves into a shouting match between the speakers from the Settlers' Association and the government officials. The control of the emergency has been referred back to the Governor, and a delegation of settlers will meet him to thrash out a system whereby the settlers will also have a voice in decision making.

"It's aboot time ye've changed the law, you bloody Sassenachs," an angry, burly Scotsman says. "You and your English law. It's nay good out here in Africa. You're dealing with natives, man, and they dinna' understand it, so how can you expect them to respect it. Their own tribal practices and customs are efficient and swift. How can you expect them t'understand long, drawn out trials by judge and jury and the complex systems and rules. It's all very fine in England where the courts can proceed leisurely, but," he pauses for effect, and raises his voice, "it's nay good out here. You have to cut the bloody rules to suit the crimes and quickly."

He stands down to applause from the crowd, as worried officials take notes, muttering amongst themselves. Other speakers take the Scotsman's place, pointing out that there have been delays of six months or more in reaching decisions on sentencing, and quoting instances.

One speaker refers to the murder of Chief Waruhiu. "Aye," he says, standing in front of the dais, and addressing the men on the platform. "They've still not sentenced the men that attacked Waruhiu, or the African driver who shot him. The driver confessed to the killing, and the case is still tied up in the courts. Now, the driver is claiming that the confession was dragged out of him under duress, despite the fact there were witnesses to the killing. That's over six months ago. What sort of impression do you think this has on the Kikuyu? It's no wonder that they fear *Mau Mau* more than they respect British justice."

"He's got a good point there," I say, and Billy nods his agreement.

A farmer standing close to us joins in. "Yeah," he says, "I farm up in the Kinangop not far from the Ruck place. I came down this morning for this meeting. Peter Steenkamp, a superintendent in the Kenya Police, and his team are working on the case. He's got quite a reputation for quick results."

"From what I understand," he continues, "they've caught the syce. He was trying to escape the police net, and, from what I hear, he was in charge of the gang. Evidently the syce lured Roger Ruck out of the house about nine o'clock last night by telling him that a gangster had been arrested. Then the gang attacked Roger."

He shifts uneasily on his feet as he speaks. "Hearing his shouts, his wife, Esme, ran outside. The gang caught her, and forced her to watch as they killed her husband. They placed him on a log, and battered him to death. The gang hacked her to death before going into the farmhouse to ransack it. They found Michael, the six-year-old son, hiding in terror in his bed, and slashed him to death with *pangas.*"

The farmer turns away, absently watching the crowd, but barely taking in the arguments any more. He turns back to us, and continues in a low voice. "I didn't know the family very well, but Esme Ruck was a doctor. She ran a clinic for the Africans labourers on her farm, and also treated any other Africans who came to her."

His voice falters with emotion as he says, "I can't understand it. Only three or four days ago, the little boy had fallen off his horse, and that syce carried him several miles to the farmhouse. Now, he turns around and kills the child. How can any human do that?" He shakes his head, saying, "I just don't understand it."

As various rumours circulate, the mood of the crowd around Government House begins to grow violent. Some rednecks in the front ranks of the crowd are threatening to go into State House and fetch the Governor out. They want him to change the law. A thin line of African *askaris* has now formed and stands between the crowd and the Governor's residence. One heavily built farmer shouts, "Get those bloody *Kafirs* out of the way, or we'll smash our way through them."

Blundell is again addressing the settlers, entreating them, trying to quell their anger. "You're hurting your own cause," he says. Gradually he talks them out of the rage caused by the lack of response from government officials. He assures the meeting that he will try to arrange for a delegation from the Settlers' Association to put their protests directly to the Governor. Mollified, but still angry, the crowd finally disperses and leaves peacefully. We leave with the crowd, silently walking back the way we had come, still deep in our own thoughts.

When we reach our car, I unlock the doors. "Yes," I say, finally breaking the silence, "I can't understand why, or how, the syce could bring himself to murder that child. It doesn't make sense."

Muchoka and the Aberdare Farms

The farm radio project has now taken on a new urgency. As planned, Terry and I have split up, and he works from his own vehicle, which he loads at the Kenya Regiment's supply depot. Soon, we'll be heading back to separate locations in the Aberdares and Mount Kenya regions to install farm radios. This time, I'll be working with Muchoka, a Mkamba tribesman; I've known him for several years now. Although blood brothers of the Kikuyu, his tribe is not directly involved with the *Mau Mau* movement. He'll be very useful to me as both a driver and an assistant when we erect the heavy radio masts and antenna systems.

A young man, probably in his mid-twenties, Muchoka has an open, friendly manner. Taller than average, with a closely trimmed beard and short, curly hair, he has an oval face and the broad, flat nose of the Bantu people. His large expressive eyes reflect his moods and easy-going personality. I instinctively like him.

It's nine o'clock before Muchoka and I start to load the Dodge truck with the radio equipment for the farms. As we work, Muchoka asks, "*Tunakwenda mbali, bwana*—are we going far?"

Shaking my head, I reply, "Not far. We'll be based in Naivasha. You've got your safari allowance and can arrange your own accommodation once we get there. Then we will be working on farms in the Aberdares. *Unajua, kazi ya serekali*—you know, government work."

Muchoka nods his head, and together we spread a tarpaulin over the load, and tighten the ropes, lashing it in place. He grunts with satisfaction as he pulls on the ropes testing them, and then adds. "It can't work loose now."

Handing him the keys to the truck, I say, "You can drive first, Muchoka, and I'll take over later. We'll stop at the Bell Inn; that'll be our base for the first week." I pause a moment then add, "Then we'll probably come back to Nairobi for another load."

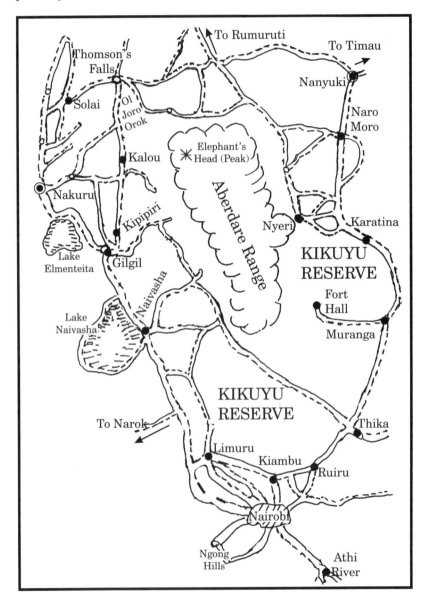

Figure 18. Map of the Aberdares and the Kikuyu Reserves.

Muchoka smiles. *"Ndiyo, bwana,"* he says, climbing into the driver's seat, while I make myself comfortable beside him in the cab.

A Nagging Doubt

Much has happened in the last three months. Muchoka and I have crisscrossed the Central Province, from the Ol Kalou, Laikipia, and the Kinangop in the western Aberdares to Embu and the Mount Kenya forests. We have been installing emergency radios, linking farms and military posts around the Aberdares and Mount Kenya forests with their area police radio communications centres. The weather has changed from the summer heat of January and February to the long rains of late March and April.

We have been lucky, encountering no ambushes or other problems as we travel along the farm and forest tracks in remote areas. Someone up there must be looking after Muchoka and me. It's not that I'm complaining, but it's strange, because so much has been, and is still, happening in the forests and farms these days. There is a nagging doubt in my mind; *something just doesn't add up.*

Daily, there are reports of incidents in the press, and I've read the police bulletins as well. I know the *Mau Mau* have been gaining strength in the forest; it's all over the national newspapers. The army and security forces are fighting terrorists in the forests. There were reports that in a single operation, the gangs can number between five hundred and a thousand men. But somehow Muchoka and I have sailed through it all without a scratch or incident.

For a fleeting second, I ponder the possibility that I'm being used, perhaps as a courier. I look at Muchoka sitting beside me. *No, it couldn't be, not Muchoka. If he had wanted, he could have killed me any time, and taken my rifle and handgun. It would be so easy. No, he's a Wakamba and a good man. I'd bet my life on that.*

Puzzled, but relieved by our good fortune, I shrug my shoulders. *It's the luck of the game.* I think about the latest reports from the police and security forces; they are common knowledge now. The forest terrorists are organized into two armies that operate separately. General China operates in the Mount Kenya region, while General Dedan Kimathi is in the Aberdares. As well as fighting these armies, the Lancashire Fusiliers and security forces have been trying to contain the oath taking and swelling support for *Mau Mau*, which exists in the Kikuyu Reserves.

✳✳✳

Early in February in the midst of a flurry of bad news, the daring act of two women raised the spirits of the white community. Mrs. Dorothy Raynes Simson and Mrs. Kitty Hesselburger displayed exceptional courage and calmness when *Mau Mau* attacked them on their farm in the White Highlands. One evening, they had sat down after dinner to listen to the radio when a gang burst into the room. Their dog, a boxer bitch, went for the gang, and was killed. Within seconds, the two women had opened fire with their handguns, shooting two men. Surprised by the resistance, two other terrorists were injured by gunfire as they fled. A bullet through the bathroom door struck a fifth man, who had hidden there. The women had also shot out a lamp outside the house, a prearranged signal, but they had already routed the gang by the time help arrived.

At the time this incident happened, I was in Nairobi, and I can remember the general elation. Joan's face had lit up as she said triumphantly, "See, we women are not so helpless as you think."

Later that month, a large *Mau Mau* gang had swept out of the forests of Mount Kenya and overran a fortified police post at Timau, killing the defenders. Due to its exposed location, this post was then abandoned. Emboldened by their initial success, *Mau Mau* terrorists increased their pressure on Africans living on the reserves. Loyalist Kikuyu forces and fortified home guard posts came under increasing waves of attacks, and murder and arson were rampant throughout the reserves.

A Gift of Eggs

In late February, Muchoka and I were working in the Ol Doinyo Sapuk area. We had installed the last of our emergency radio equipment in a farm located on the Garissa Road, and were on our way to Nairobi via Machakos. I remember that day very well. The peak of Ol Doinyo Sapuk, rising up two thousand feet above the plains, was partly obscured by the dust following the truck as I drove down the corrugated dirt road towards the Machakos range of hills. Muchoka, who was seated in the passenger seat, suddenly pointed south across the plains to a distant collection of African huts surrounded by a hedge of shrubs and bush.

"*Shamba yangu uko, bwana*—my home is over there." Hesitating a moment, he then asked, "Can we stop there? I would like to see my wife and children."

Pleased to have the opportunity to meet his family, I said, "Why, of course." Then, I added, "Just tell me when to turn off into the bush and we'll surprise them."

Muchoka's eyes brightened with pleasure, and he sat up alert in his seat, watching for the turn-off to his village. "*Uko, bwana, uko* (there)," Muchoka pointed to a dirt track on our right heading south across the plain. I turned off the Machakos Road and onto the potholed bush track leading to Muchoka's *shamba*.

As I drew up close to the huts, a curious group of villagers surrounded the truck. "*Aiyee*, Muchoka," called several local men when they recognized him. Breaking into the Wakamba language, they began plying him with questions as they walked with us to a hut where I was introduced to his wife and children. An attractive, young woman, she was dressed in a yellow, loose fitting, *americani* (cheap cotton) dress. Two young children, a boy and girl, clung to their mother's skirts as she shyly shook my hand.

As I sat on a log in front of the thatched rondavel, we chatted in Swahili, while Muchoka squatted on his heels nearby. Speaking in the Wakamba language, he gave his wife a package that he'd brought with him from the truck. A smile crossed her face as she disappeared inside the hut with it. The children stood close to Muchoka looking with wide-open eyes at the strange white man talking to their father.

When Muchoka's wife emerged from the hut carrying a basket full of fresh eggs, and gave them to me, I was surprised. "They're for your wife," she said in Swahili. Confused, I tried to protest and looked at Muchoka.

"*Ndiyo, bwana,*" he said with a smile. "*Inadesturi yetu*—it is our custom. The eggs are for your wife. Many times, you and I have bought chickens in Karatina market for our wives. They were live chickens that your *mpishi* (cook) would prepare for you. Now this is a little something in return."

I thanked him and his wife for the eggs. These people are poor, and here among them I felt the simple kindness of the old Africa that I'd come to know and like. As we walked back to the truck in a small group together with Muchoka's family, I felt accepted in their society. It was a warm and heartening experience that restored my confidence in the Africa that I knew.

The Lari Massacre and the Naivasha Raid

In March, the news of the Lari massacre burst upon Kenya like a bombshell. The brutality and savagery of the attack on the loyalist Kikuyu guard post appalled whites and Africans alike. The attack took place on March 26, the same night that General Dedan Kimathi led a successful attack against the police station and armoury in Naivasha.

First rumours, then news of the massacre swept through Kenya like wildfire. When I heard the reports, I was staying at Barry's Hotel in Thomson's Falls. Situated at the western end of the Aberdare plateau, the hotel overlooks the waterfall for which the township is named. It was my temporary base at the time, as my area of operations covered the Ol Kalou and Kipipiri farms in and around the forest edge to the southeast. Towering some three thousand feet above the farms to the north of them is the rounded peak of the Elephant's Head in the Aberdares. And it was from the dense forests in this mountain range

Figure 19. Thomson's Falls.

that *Mau Mau* gangs, operating under General Dedan Kimathi, menaced the farms.

"*Ulisikia habari ya Lari*—did you hear the news about Lari?" I asked Muchoka as we drove down the dry dirt road from Thomson Falls past Ol Kalou and up into Kipipiri.

Seated beside me in the cab, he nodded his head, his face downcast as he gazed at his hands, nervously twisting and entwining the fingers.

"*Ndiyo, bwana,*" he said, "The news was all over the hotel. The people where I stayed told me that many Kikuyu have been killed in Lari. They also said that Chief Luka has been killed, along with his wife and *totos* (children). Is it true, bwana?"

"Yes, so I understand, but the police and security forces are still investigating both Lari and the raid on Naivasha Police station." I said. "Both these attacks took place about the same time last night."

As I shifted gear to climb the steep grade, Muchoka looked out of the cab window, his gaze fixed on the Elephant's Head. "*Ndiyo,*" he replied, "that, too, was said at the breakfast tables this morning. The men of the forest are bad men. We heard the *wazungu* say that these forest men had overrun the police station and stolen many rifles and guns." Turning, he looked directly at me, his eyes gleaming with anger. "Those men, they are dividing the Kikuyu people. It is not good, bwana, that Kikuyu are killing Kikuyu; there is great bitterness in the reserves. Now, these men have even more weapons to kill the loyal Kikuyu and the Wakamba, their blood brothers. What is to become of us?"

Sighing wearily, I replied, "Yes, it is bad, Muchoka, but at the moment the *serekali* (government) have not released any details. They said that the army is still tracking the gang that attacked Lari, but they haven't given any more information about the raid on the police station." I paused, then said softly, "We'll get those bastards yet; it's only a matter of time."

Over the next few days, details were gradually released to the newspapers and the Kenya Broadcasting Service. Evidently, there had been a large Kikuyu oath-taking ceremony near the Lari Reserve, which involved some three thousand men and women. Many young men, who had taken the Batuni forest oath that evening, joined the attack on the Kikuyu home guard post, which took place when the men stationed there were out on an anti *Mau Mau* patrol.

The *East African Standard* carried a story and photographs submitted by a reporter with the security forces that showed the terrible carnage. After taking *bhang,* the drug-crazed *Mau Mau* had embarked on a frenzy of killing. More than a

Figure 20. Homeguard post, with moat and drawbridge.

hundred loyal Kikuyu, mostly women and children, had been killed, with Chief Luka among those murdered. According to eyewitness reports, the Chief's wife had been forced to watch as her baby was cut in two and the blood drunk. The corpse was then flung at her, before she, too, was hacked to death.

The attackers also trapped many loyalists inside their rondavels by winding thick cable around the outside walls. Then the attackers threw gasoline onto the thatched roofs and set it alight, and the occupants were burned to death. Persons caught outside the huts were either bludgeoned or hacked to death; and their heads cut off; bodies were mutilated, and pregnant women disembowelled.

As I read these accounts, feelings of revulsion, anger, and disgust swept over me. Although Lari was only twenty-eight miles from Nairobi in the Uplands area (roughly eight miles northwest of Limuru), the news of the attack came too late to save the outpost. Security forces were on the scene at dawn, however, and the combined force consisting of the twenty-third KAR, police, and the Kikuyu home guard, began rounding up hundreds of suspects.

Running fights developed everywhere on the African locations as the security forces, disgusted by the senseless butchery, exacted a heavy toll on those suspected of having been *Mau Mau* or somehow involved in the massacre. The number killed in the round up far exceeded the number of loyalists murdered at Lari.

"Aye, 'tis a fact," said one of the police inspectors in the Kipipiri control centre, when I visited there shortly after the Lari raid. "We didna' reckon on Kimathi carrying out a diversionary attack on the Naivasha police station at the same time that he attacked Lari." He continued, "Yon's not stupid; the attack was successful and drew off security forces from Lari. As the newspapers said, two trucks were used in the attack. His men surprised and overpowered the garrison, then ransacked the police station and the armoury. The terrorists loaded rifles, automatic precision weapons and ammunition into the trucks, then disappeared into the night."

He sighed wearily, "You've got to admit it was a very skilful and determined attack, planned and executed by the Aberdare *Mau Mau* army under General Dedan Kimathi. After this, we can't afford to take them lightly."

Checkpoints and Guard Posts

During the days that followed the raid, tensions were high on the farms that Muchoka and I visited. Army units and security forces were on the alert as we were passed through the checkpoints set up on the main road and on farm tracks near the forest edge. The security forces, seeing a *mzungu* driving the truck loaded with masts and radio equipment and with a Posts and Tels logo on the door, ushered us through the checkpoints ahead of the long lines of waiting buses and native trucks carrying food and market products.

"Come on, mate," a Lancs soldier would call. "Get a move on. Go straight through; we're bloody busy this morning." Grinning, he signalled us on. "'Ave a nice day, guv."

As we installed the antenna on one farm, the farmer there summed up the feelings of all the settlers. "Aye, lad," he had said, "It's about time we got rid of the Foreign Office in London telling us what to do. Since the war, that lot in the UK have gone soft-like."

His Yorkshire accent blends into his speech, lending passion to his words. "They should send us more troops and let Blundell and the settlers take over. We know the country. That bastard Dedan Kimathi is bloody cunning, but we'd get him. As for Kenyatta, he and his henchmen should be hung, not kept in jail in Lokitaung. Humph," he snorts, "and his bloody lawyer, that twit Pritt from the UK, and Kapila, his sidekick, should both be kicked out of the country."

✳✳✳

The rains are late this year, and it's the end of March before the skies really open up, turning the roads into a morass of mud, stalled vehicles, and frustrated drivers. The bulk of the farms have been equipped with emergency radio systems, while those in and near the forest areas have installed barbed wire defences around the farmhouses.

Figure 21. Typical homeguard post built to safeguard the loyalist Kikuyu.

It was a few weeks after Muchoka joined me on the farm radio project that curiosity got the better of me. The Kikuyu guard posts in the Fort Hall area and elsewhere had been heavily fortified, and, seeing the watchtowers and surrounding barbed wire entanglements, I stopped to photograph the post and the surrounding moat. The guard post had been constructed like a fortress, with sandbagged firing points arranged strategically around it. To me, it looked like a medieval fort that had been grotesquely draped with razor-sharp barbed wire. Spears and *pangas* would probably be useless against those defences: only guns and grenades could prevail.

"Look, Muchoka," I said as he sauntered up from the truck. "They've put hundreds of bamboo spikes in the bottom of the moat. I'd hate to fall in there."

Muchoka nods. "*Kama unaanguka chini*—if you fall down there, you will die." He grins, and says, "*Ona milango*—do you see the door?"

When I look beyond the spikes to the inner barbed wire fence and watchtowers, I can see the drawbridge. Attached to thick posts with strong sisal ropes, the crude, hinged wooden gate can be lowered or raised across the moat at will.

As we walked back to the truck, Muchoka looks back at the guard post. "*Mahali uko hodari sana*—that place is very strong, impossible to defeat," he said. Shaking his head, he adds, "It is very good."

Yes, I think, *unless there is treachery within.*

The Lone Patrol

Since the Lari massacre, there's been a dramatic increase in the number of loyal Africans murdered by terrorists in the reserves and also in Nairobi. The home guard patrols in the European residential areas in Nairobi now take place both day and night, with special protection being given to women who live alone.

It was on a Sunday night, a few weeks after I had started on the home guard patrols that my partner, Harry, had to go out of town. It was the midnight-to-two patrol again, and I was to have a new partner that night. I'd arranged to meet him in front of Daphton Court. As I kissed Joan good-night, I said, "I'll be back a little after two." Joan was in bed when I'd slipped out of the apartment, closing the door softly behind me, and locking it.

It was gone midnight as I waited outside the apartments on Riverside Drive. The luminous dial of my watch gleamed faintly in the light from the street lights, and in the dim light I could make out the time with difficulty. At twenty past, he had still not turned up. I felt the frustration building within me as I paced up and down. I didn't know where he lived; all I knew was his first name, Frank, and his telephone number. By then, however, I didn't want to go inside and phone him. It would wake Joan, and she had to get to work in the morning. At least I could doze in the truck en route to Naro Moru.

"To hell with him," I muttered under my breath; "I'll patrol on my own." It was eerie patrolling at night, even with a partner. On my own it was worse! Trying to be inconspicuous, I kept to the shadows under the acacia trees that lined the roadway. Then as I peered into the driveways, it was only to find that the houses were partly obscured by thick thorn hedges, and set well back from the road with spacious lawns and long drives. They were difficult to see, and as usual, only the security lights were lit. I began to regret my decision, but my stubborn pride kept me patrolling the lonely, residential streets.

Approaching the Nairobi River, I heard the soft trickle of the water and then the dark pillars of the bridge took shape. At the entrance to the narrow, overgrown path that Harry and I used to check behind the houses, I hesitated. Then, stepping onto the path and into the shadows, I felt the undergrowth closing around me, and could hear my heart pound. For a moment, I shone the small flashlight I carried onto the footpath, and then I moved cautiously along the bank to check some of the houses through gaps in the fences.

Standing there in the dark, I could see the houses silhouetted against the skyline. The silence in the bush was broken only by the high-pitched hiss of crickets and the occasional squeal from some small animal scurrying away. As I watched, I shivered, although the night was warm.

The rains are overdue; they'll be on us in late March or early April, I thought to myself. *That'll cool us down.* For a moment or two I considered going further down the trail, but common sense prevailed. It was either that, or the primitive superstitious fear of man that induced me to head back for the bridge.

There was an uncanny feeling at the back of my neck, and I was glad when I emerged from the bush path and saw the bridge again. As I leaned against the parapet, my breath came fast, and gradually I felt my muscles relax. I had my rifle over my shoulder, but instinctively my right hand dropped to touch the butt of my revolver in the holster at my waist. Reassured, my eyes searched the dark shadows of the bush. Nothing moved and gradually my nerves calmed down.

Hearing the sound of a car coming along Salisbury Road at speed, I watched the T-junction beyond the bridge where Riverside Drive meets the main road running from Nairobi to Westlands. The tires screeched on the tarred surface as the car, barely checking its speed, turned into Riverside Drive. Dazzled by the headlights, I was too surprised to raise my rifle and halt the vehicle, but the car pulled up beside me.

"I might have known it, a *mzungu.*" grated a voice, and I found myself gazing into the barrel of a forty-five-calibre police revolver.

"You a special police officer?" said another voice. "We're the Nairobi Central police."

"Yes," I replied, "I'm attached to the Kileleshwa station."

"We received a report of a *Mau Mau* terrorist in the neighbourhood." His laugh is cynical. "You're lucky they didn't take a shot at you. Where's your partner," he said, his voice softening in tone.

"He didn't turn up for our shift, so I thought I'd go it alone. It seemed the right thing to do," I said.

They'd turned on the overhead light in the police car so I could see who they were. The police officer shook his head. "I'm afraid it wasn't. If you'd come across any terrorists, they'd have taken you out easily, before you even knew they were there. You've no one to guard your back. That's why we insist that two men patrol together. You'd better call it a night, and get home while you're in one piece."

They sat in the squad car, watching as I walked back up Riverside Drive. Hearing the car reverse, I looked back as they took off in a U-turn back to their headquarters. *Joan'll be surprised to see me,* I thought as I neared the gates of Daphton Court.

Recalling my conversation with the police, I smiled. 'Our statistics show there has been a marked drop in crime and arson in the residential districts since the local patrols have been set up,' they had said. *It had been encouraging to hear that the patrols were having an effect.*

When she heard the front door being unlocked, Joan called nervously,

Hurriedly, I reassured her. "Yes, it's all right. It's only me," I said as I entered the hall. "My partner didn't turn up, so I started the patrol alone. Trouble was, someone reported me as a terrorist." As I undressed, I related the whole story.

"Gordon," she had said sleepily. "You're bloody crazy."

I had to agree with her. It had been a stupid thing to do. I should have come home. "Ah, well," I said, "you live and learn"

"Yeah, if you're alive!" she replied. We cuddled up in bed and fell asleep. It had been quite a night.

Mathari, the Valley of Death

It's early April, and Muchoka and I have been busy all day on the farms. About four, we had returned to Thomson's Falls from a farm in Ol Kalou. As I sat in the lounge of Barry's Hotel after dinner, the local newspaper's headline—*Valley of Death*—caught my eye. Beneath the headline was a photograph showing a valley where bodies were being exhumed from nearby shallow graves.

Interested, I read on. "Nairobi," it said, "was the scene of some gruesome discoveries. Seventeen bodies of loyal Africans were discovered buried in and near illegal native villages in Mathari Valley and Maparani." The article went on to say that a *Mau Mau* 'court' had operated in the vicinity. "Death sentences, usually by garrotting, were carried out on the spot. Some of the bodies were found a few feet from the doors of the huts. Other bodies have been found in Mathari Valley, mutilated, and burned beyond recognition. A large-scale police and army operation is being carried out in the area, and the villages are being bulldozed to the ground."

The next day in the truck, when I mentioned this article to Muchoka, he had nodded. "Ah, *ndiyo, bwana*," he had replied. "It happens all the time in the reserves. People are afraid now because *Mau Mau* is very strong. Brother no longer trusts brother; and there is no justice any more." Deep in thought, he lapsed into silence, his face blank, and then murmured, "I, too, am frightened."

✳✳✳

It was a few days later at midday on Friday, April 10, that, having completed the last farm, we left the Kinangop for Nairobi. Dark heavy rain clouds hovered over the Elephant's Head, partly masking the peak and the forests of the Aberdares. Empty, the truck was heading down from the forest belt onto the lower slopes when, suddenly, the rain and wind caught us broadside. Startled, I jerked the steering wheel round to the left, countering the truck's slide.

Slipping and sliding on the surface of the dirt road, despite chains on the wheels, the Dodge ploughed on over forested ridges and down valleys. Beside me in the cab Muchoka sat silently, one hand gripping the armrest, his body jerking with the truck's movement. Fleetingly, I thought that he was unusually quiet, but then my attention was fully occupied fighting the steering wheel, and trying to counter the truck's tendency to slide off the crown of the mud-slicked road.

When we finally reached the all-weather road that winds its way down from Kipipiri to Gilgil, the tension drained from my body. Grinning at Muchoka, I settled back in the driving seat. "Ah," I said with a feeling of relief, "that's better, Muchoka. God, will I be glad to get home. This bloody rain depresses me."

Muchoka laughed in reply, "*Ndiyo, bwana,* but we need the rain for the *shamba*; my wife will be pleased. Now the *mealies* will grow tall, and the *ngombe* (cattle) will have plenty of grass to eat. When the land has new grass, *watoto yangu* (my children) can herd the cattle closer to home."

I smiled, remembering when I had met his wife and children on the Mkamba Reserve, and said, "Yes, farmers are all the same, always looking for rain, and then looking for sun when the rains last too long."

We talked on as the truck rumbled across the floor of the Rift Valley, then crossed the escarpment into the Kikuyu Reserve and on to Nairobi. Like me, Muchoka was anxious to get home for the weekend. We would load the truck the next day ready to be off early on Monday.

Muchoka, of All People

But, when we entered the post office yard and parked the truck, events took a turn that left me stunned and shocked. Figures dressed in dark, navy blue police pullovers suddenly swarmed round the truck. Muchoka cried out as the cab door was jerked open, and he struggled as the police pulled him out. Mesmerized, I sat transfixed, watching his head weaving in the midst of a ring of *askaris*.

There was a white man, an inspector of police, interrogating him, and, as I got out of the cab, the inspector's fist lashed out, knocking Muchoka to the ground, where he sat, his face bleeding.

Pushing my way through the *askaris* to the police inspector, I demanded angrily, "Why, why did you do that to him? He's my driver, a good man. I've known him for years."

His face red with anger, the inspector turned to me. "A good man, you say! He's nothing but a bloody murderer, a *Mau Mau* terrorist." His Scottish accent became broad, and his voice grew loud in his anger. "We've enough evidence to hang the bastard. He was a guard and executioner in the *Mau Mau* courts set up in the Mathari Valley. Have you not seen what they do to their victims?"

Shocked, I shook my head, unable to reply. I'd seen photographs of victims, burned, and mutilated beyond belief.

"Aye, laddie," the inspector's voice quivered in anger, "So I thought." Calming himself, he nodded towards Muchoka's bent form, which was being thrust into an enclosed police van, urged on by rifle butts. "That's one less," he paused, and then looked back at me. "He gave me cheek, the cocky bastard; that's why I knocked him down. He's well known in the Mathari Valley. They mutilate and garrotte their victims, mainly Kikuyu loyalists and anyone else opposed to *Mau Mau*, including police *askaris*, and sometimes they even burn them to death."

Wearily, I said, "Yes, I've read about Mathari Valley and Lari. I thought I knew Muchoka, and certainly I trusted him. I've even been to his village where I met his wife and kids."

The inspector's voice softened, and became more human. "You were lucky that you weren't killed," he said. "You were spared because you were useful to them. They used you as a courier; it's as simple as that."

✳✳✳

The inspector, the *askaris*, and Muchoka are gone, leaving me sitting on the cab step, momentarily alone with my thoughts. Shaking my head, I mutter, "Muchoka, why you? I trusted you." I feel tired, betrayed. *Who can I believe? The inspector represents the law of the land, and I have to take his word for it. The courts will decide. If they can prove their case, Muchoka will hang.*

My mind grasps at straws. There must be some mistake, false witnesses, enemies. The hopelessness of the situation is compounded in my own mind by our safe passage through hostile country over the last three or four months. *Was it just luck, or was he really using me as a courier?* My mind is confused. *Why, why Muchoka?*

In a daze I get up and pass through the little crowd of African employees who had stood silently by, watching the unfolding drama of Muchoka's arrest. There is a sick feeling in my stomach and my throat hurts. Mounting the stairs to the general office in the main post office building, I go into the office. There is still work to be done, and next week's load to be prepared and loaded onto the truck. The program is nearly over, and I must find another driver. *Yes, a lot has happened.*

✳✳✳

Chapter 5
Nairobi, the Big City

A Time for Reflection

This is my last safari before I go on overseas leave. It is May 8, and we've completed the last farm on our list and, with it, the emergency farm radio program. As I glance back at the tall mast and antenna clamped to the gable end of the farmhouse, a sense of accomplishment spreads through my body. Climbing into the cab of the truck, I give a final wave to the farmer. Then, with Kamundu seated beside me in the passenger seat, I drive down the farm track to the rough stone road from Kipipiri into Gilgil. We are on our way home.

After Muchoka's arrest, I selected Kamundu as my driver: he'd been with me in the NFD and on the VHF survey. We've now worked together on the farm radio project for roughly four weeks. Each weekend, we return to Nairobi for more radio equipment for farms located on the western slopes of the Aberdares from Laikipia to the North Kinangop.

The rains are petering off, and slowly the land is drying; the Kipipiri roads are no longer a mud bath. All the farms have been equipped with emergency radio equipment, and they are now linked to the local police communication centre, which is their area control. With the farms in radio contact, they are no longer isolated; and can exchange information regularly with their neighbours and with the police concerning terrorist movements. The farm radio scheme has proved to be a successful morale builder, in addition to providing the police with valuable information.

As we join the main Nairobi-Nakuru road, I think about Muchoka, because this is the road that we'd taken on our last journey together. I wonder where he is now, and whether he is still alive. Thinking about Muchoka reminds me of the circumstances surrounding his arrest. *The police inspector had referred to him as a Mau Mau guard and an executioner. How could I have been so wrong about Muchoka?* With an effort, I clear my mind of these thoughts as we drive over the Rift Valley plains and up the escarpment to the Kikuyu Reserve.

It is early evening when we crest the foothills, and can now see in the distance the familiar sparkle of lights on the edge of the Kapiti plains. Nodding towards the far-off lights, Kamundu says, "*Karibu sasa, bwana*—Nairobi is close now." Then he adds, "I hear that you will be going on leave, is it not so?"

"*Ndiyo*, Kamundu," I smile as I reply. "We are leaving by ship from Mombasa in two weeks' time."

Kamundu nods solemnly. "It is good that we have finished the farms. Now you will be able to stay in Nairobi until you and your *memsahib* go down to Mombasa to catch the ship."

"Yes, there are many things to do," I say absent-mindedly as I concentrate on the road ahead. The headlight beams cut through the darkness, picking out the curved, rounded edges of the shoulders. "We'll be away for a few months. Our apartment goes back into the housing pool, and we have to put all our belongings into the post office stores. If the government need me back quickly, however, they could cut my leave."

✳✳✳

Joan is expecting me. The roar of the truck entering the driveway brings her to our door.

"*Jambo, memsahib*," Kamundu calls as he steps down from the cab. He climbs into the back of the truck to look for my personal belongings, which are hidden under the tarpaulin. He and Joan know each other well, and she talks to him briefly as he hands my things down to me. "Áh, *memsahib*," he says, "you are soon going on leave to England on a big ship. The land of Kingi George is far away."

She laughs, and then says with a smile. "Yes, Kamundu, we leave on the twenty-first on the *Rhodesia Castle*. The ship goes through the Suez Canal and the Mediterranean, and will take three weeks to reach England."

"You will see your *mama* and *baba* there?" he asks.

"My father died many years ago, but I will see my mother and family. I have two brothers and three sisters."

"*Aiyee*, your mama has big family like Kikuyu people! That is good."

Joan murmurs a noncommittal reply. She had decided long ago that she does not want children. Perhaps it's because her mother had to raise six kids on her own. That must have been no easy task during the depression years in the early 'thirties.

Standing together in the drive, Joan and I watch Kamundu climb back into the cab and start the engine. The truck moves through the gateway of Daphton Court, a hand waves from the cab window, and he's gone. As we walk side by side into our apartment, Joan turns to me. "I like Kamundu," she says. "He's a good man. He's travelled all over the country with you for many years now, and I feel you're safe with him." She pauses, and murmurs, "But then, I felt the same way about Muchoka. I'll be glad to get back to England, at least for a while. It will give us both a break."

As the front door closes, Joan turns to me in the privacy of the hallway. "I've missed you, Gordon," she says, as we instinctively come together. She is in my arms and our lips meet. A warmth enters my heart as we kiss and cling to each other. *It's strange*, I think to myself as I follow her into the dining room, *how society rules and moulds us into conformity. We never kiss in public. In East Africa, to show affection, especially in front of Africans, is taboo. It is demeaning in the eyes of Europeans, yet it is an instinctive and natural act. I wonder what Kamundu thinks? Do the Africans kiss their wives, too?* White people take hugging and kissing for granted, but I cannot recall seeing any similar outward signs of affection between black men and their women.

✳✳✳

A week has passed since Kamundu and I returned from Kipipiri and the Kinangop, a week filled with the bustle of packing and crating our personal belongings. Except for the refrigerator, the "hard" furnishings—beds, tables, chairs, sideboards, tallboys, cooking stove—belong to the government. All the things that go to make a home—kitchenware, bed linens, curtains, cushions, pictures, and a vast assortment of African curios—are ours, and must be packed, either to go into storage or to be taken with us to England.

Like a magpie, I hoard things, treasuring them for the memories that they hold. I have everything, from the Japanese officer's sword I got in Bangkok at the end of World War Two, to a camel bell, carved from a large seed husk, bought in Wajir two years ago. Joan helps me to wrap my cherished souvenirs in soft tissue paper and pack them into a wooden box. "It's a good thing you didn't keep those smelly old antelope horns that you used to decorate the safari vehicles," she says. "We'd never have room for them all."

Yes, I think, *I wonder why I didn't. The horns of that waterbuck that I shot in the Olambwe Valley would have looked great mounted on a plaque.* I shrug my shoulders. *There'll be other safaris; there's still plenty of time for that.*

While we pack, our house servant Odede is busy cleaning the walls and polishing the wooden parquet floors. "*Nitangoja kwa wewe, bwana*—I will wait for you," he says.

"Ah, *mzuri*, Odede," I reply, "I would like that, *lakini iko tabu*—but there is a problem. We will be away for six months, and it will be too long for you to wait."

Odede nods his head, his face downcast. *"Ndiyo, bwana, nafahamu—* I understand."

We've employed Odede since September last year when we first got this government quarters. Joan and I both like him; he's a good cook, and has proved trustworthy and honest, qualities that are sometimes hard to find. His face brightens when I say, "If you like, I'll put an advert in the newspaper and try to find another position for you." Odede is pleased and accepts my offer.

Homewood Hotel

It is late afternoon on Saturday, May 16, and, with Billy's help, we've moved into Homewood Hotel where we'll stay for a few days. Billy is still based in the Gilgil workshops of the Kenya police transport section, but has taken some leave to help us move. This was our last day in the apartment, and this morning, a department truck and labourers collected our crates and possessions, including the refrigerator, and took them to the storage depot.

Billy is seated on a small chair, reading the newspaper. "Aye, they're planning the *Coronation Safari*, but you'll miss it; 'tis in June." Billy's soft Irish accent is pronounced in his excitement as he puts down the paper.

I've been unpacking some clothes from my overnight case, and am putting a couple of shirts in the dresser drawer. Pausing, I look up, amused by this information. "You mean they're actually getting down to finalizing the race. They've been talking about holding a motor rally for months now. First it was going to be called the *Three Capitals Rally*, and now it's the *Coronation Safari*." I shrug my shoulders. "Well I guess it's logical, after all this is Queen Elizabeth's Coronation year. When is the rally being run?"

"May 30 to June 1," Billy says. "They're leaving out Dar. They start and finish in Nairobi, turning around at Morogoro in Tanganyika, and heading back through Nairobi and up to Kampala. It's roughly a two-thousand-mile route with three days to do it. They'll have to travel some over those roads."

Closing the dresser drawer, I get to my feet, and move to the sofa where I sit beside Joan. "What are they going to do about the Langa-Langa track at Gilgil then?" I ask. "The Automobile Association was developing a three-mile motor racing track there." I grin as I think about the old course. "It used to be just a dirt track laid out on a rancher's land," I say. "Do you remember going up there on a weekend, Joan, and all those farmers and motor crazies tearing around the track. They had a beefed-up engine mounted on an old truck chassis that they drove hell-for-leather around the circuit. It's a wonder they survived, but they seemed to."

"Yes," she says, "but remember when Rivers-Royston was the Clerk of the Course? He captured the imagination of everyone in Kenya," she chuckled, adding, "and some of their money, too."

"You couldn't but admire the nerve and confidence of the man," I add. "My God, what a character! Did you ever see him, Billy?"

Billy laughs, "No, it was a bit before my time. He'd gone before I arrived here, but I've heard of him. He took Kenya high society for a bundle, didn't he?"

"Yeah, that's him," I say. "I remember him being driven around the Langa-Langa track to the cheers of the crowd. As he stood in the moving car, waving, his flaming red beard and hair were swept back by the wind. The crowd loved him. I can see him now, steadying himself with his left hand on the windshield of a big red American convertible. He was immaculate. He wore light grey flannel trousers and a navy blue blazer, with a yellow paisley cravat tucked into the vee of his open-necked white shirt."

"Rivers-Royston moved in high circles, all right," Joan says. "He came up from Jo'burg, and was very friendly with Stratton of *Kaplan & Stratton*, the law firm I used to work for. Stratton was one of the leading lawyers, but Royston took him in with his schemes and investments. His victims even included the governor, Sir Philip Mitchell. First Royston would borrow small amounts of money, and then quickly repay them at a very generous interest rate. Over the months, he gained the confidence of his backers. Finally, he borrowed thousands of pounds sterling, only to disappear into the blue one night with his wife and all the money. It was in all the newspapers at the time, and caused quite a sensation."

"Yes," I add, "The last we heard of Rivers-Royston was some months later. The newspapers reported that he had been arrested in Paris for smuggling diamonds. Nairobi is pretty much a small town, despite being proclaimed a city in 1950. The white population is not large; there are only fifty thousand or so whites in the whole country and, like any small community, everybody seems to know everyone else's business."

A Night on the Town

"Stay here for dinner with us, Billy," Joan says. "I can easily arrange it. Mrs. O'Connel treats us all like one large family, and we've known her for years."

Billy laughs as he gets up and walks towards the door of the rondavel. "I've promised Paddy and Mary that I'd be back for dinner. Besides I've got to change into evening clothes. Remember, we're going out on the town tonight." He calls back to us as he makes his way to the car park, "I'll be back about eight-thirty."

Automatically, I glance at my watch; it's just gone six. "We've plenty of time," I say. "There's a good two hours."

Joan nods, pausing as she hears Billy's car roar into life. As we watch, the red rear lights of his car move through the hotel's archway onto Valley Road. "He's gone," says Joan as I put my arm around her, and we go back inside our rondavel.

"Come on, woman," I say, laughing. "Let's have dinner now, and then get ready."

✳✳✳

Dinner is over, and I've had my bath. From experience, I know that Joan likes to lie soaking in the warm, soapy water, so I beat her to it. Now, as I sort out my evening clothes, I can hear the reassuring splash of water. *She's still moving, so she's not gone to sleep.*

It's a funny world, I think to myself as I slip on my white dress shirt, and get out my tuxedo jacket and black trousers. *We dress up for everything out here in the colonies, even if it's just to go to the movies. We go all dressed in our tuxedos, bow ties, and evening suits, like so many penguins on parade. Why do we do it? I don't really know, any more than I know why the D.O.'s and D.C.'s dress for dinner in the bush. Is it to impress the natives? Or maybe it's to keep their sanity and keep in touch with things, or perhaps it is tradition.*

I smile to myself. *Our survey safaris are very different from the ones taken by Foreign Office types. We wear khaki shirts with long trousers, if it's a mosquito-ridden place, or khaki shorts with knee-high stockings and safari boots or ex-army boots. Back in Nairobi, however, I readily observe the dress codes. It's simply a carry-over from my Merchant Navy days and the ship's wardroom where we always dressed for dinner. It's just a matter of changing one uniform for another.*

Joan's out of the bathroom now, and is changing into a strapless evening gown. Her white and gold earrings match the swirling gold patterns on the bodice of the white gown. As I do up the zipper at the back of the dress, I smile. "You look great, Joan," I whisper, my lips close to her ear.

She laughs and pivots around, making the full skirt swirl out and revealing her matching shoes. "It should look great," she says, "considering what it cost. But, of course, it's imported from Europe." Joan has a great dress sense. She is petite, five foot two inches, with a trim figure, and her shining black hair contrasts nicely with her white-and-gold outfit. I feel a sense of pride as I watch her.

A knock on the door interrupts my thoughts, and I hurry to open it; I smile when I see that it is Billy. Hurrying into the room, he kisses Joan on the cheek. "'Tis a fine lot that we are tonight," he says, and turns to me. "Ah, Gord, it looks like we're ready to go."

Ben Hur, a Cecil B. DeMille spectacular starring Charlton Heston, is the movie showing at the Empire Cinema in Harding Street. During the intermission, I look around at the predominantly white audience. There is a smattering of Asians, some wearing their distinctive Sikh turbans, but there are no Africans present, but that's true everywhere in Africa. Somehow, I don't think that my mother would approve, particularly with her communistic views.

I can't help contrasting the life that we lead in East Africa to that existing on the African reserves. There are two distinct societies here, three if you include the Asian segment of the population. The Asian community is made up mainly of artisans, and they act as a buffer that separates white society, comprised of settlers and government officials, from the Africans. There are roughly eight million Africans under British Administration, spread out in different tribal units over the whole of East Africa. Kenya is a colony with settlers, but Uganda and Tanganyika are both protectorates.

The difference between the societies is as clear-cut as the class system in Britain or the caste system in India. The old battle lines are drawn between rich and poor—the squalor of Kariokor and the splendour of downtown Nairobi—each fighting to maintain their standards. *Yes*, I think, *what would Mother say, as if I don't know.*

Mother hates the ruling class. Her family was once well-to-do. They were millers in Yorkshire until the mills failed in the mid-1800s and the family fortune disappeared. Since marrying my father, she's been reduced to living in an old farmhouse without electricity, tap water, or plumbing, just candles, well water, and an outhouse. It's no wonder that she's bitter.

At times, I'm bitter, too, but I've fought against it, against the feeling of inferiority. Now, ironically, I am upper class in comparison to the African masses. But even here, the old class distinctions still exist among the whites themselves.

I can understand the anger in the Reserves, but Mau Mau is not the right way. I shrug my shoulders. *Sometimes, however, force seems the only way out. But to murder your own people? No, I can't understand the hatred that drives Mau Mau, and I probably never will. It is something bound up in their binding oaths and superstitions that is beyond my comprehension.*

As we join the people disgorging in a steady stream from the movie theatre into Harding Street, Nairobi's nightlife beckons. It's eleven-thirty, but the Equator Club, a regular haunt of ours, is open to all hours of the night. On our way, we pass the Jamal Mosque behind the

MacMillan Library. The mosque's imposing archway and its ornate parapets and cupolas, are festooned with strings of coloured lights. Against the green background of the arch, gold lettering proclaims in English: *There is no God but Allah, Mohamed is his Prophet.* We pause momentarily, taking in the display. The mosque glitters like a Christmas tree in the night.

"Aye," says Billy, "even the mosques are celebrating the coronation of Queen Elizabeth II, and she's not to be crowned for two weeks."

"Yes," says Joan. "By that time, we should be in the Red Sea."

After one last look, we wander on, pulled along by the crowds, until we reach the Equator Club and climb the stairs to the ballroom.

The Equator Club

Two men with a woman, is that so exceptional? I ask myself as I watch Joan and Billy together on the circular dance floor. Billy has become so much a part of our existence, that it's hard to imagine life without him. The two of us take turns dancing with Joan. She's a good dancer, light on her feet. As I watch, the two of them blend into the dance crowd, moving out of my line of vision in the subdued lighting.

The band is silhouetted against a backdrop of changing lighting effects. They're playing the blues now, and the background is tinted blue. There is a spotlight shining on a rotating ball suspended from the ceiling; its mirrored facets reflect rotating beams of light around the room. A young, blonde woman, wearing a light blue, snugly fitting dress, is singing, and the haunting melody fills me with yearning. I want to dance with a woman in my arms, and submerse myself in the hypnotic spell of the music. Restlessly, I watch, my fingers softly drumming on the table, while on the dance floor, Billy and Joan float by, appearing and disappearing in the crowd.

My thoughts wander to another time, another place, and another melody, *Lilli Marlene.* Now, as I sip my beer, I remember the small nightclub in Tripoli in 1943. I had just turned eighteen, and was on my third ship, a seasoned seaman, or so I thought. The melody and the singer, a young Italian woman, had held me spellbound in its grip, bringing out all the intense longing of my youth and the grief of war.

Now, similar feelings and sentiments return. Maybe it's the association of the young woman on the stage that triggers the memory, or, more than likely, it's the beer that's to blame. I sigh wearily, my mind absorbed in the music.

When I hear my name, I jerk awake, my thoughts momentarily confused. "Gord, are you asleep?" Billy says.

As Joan and Billy sit down at our table, I stretch and laugh. "No, I was just deep in memories." My fingers fold around the glass, absently turning it, as I gather my thoughts. "It must be the beer," I say, then add, "and the music. You know the blues always fascinate me, and bring out my sentimental side. It takes me back to the past."

Smiling at Joan, I say, "Remember the Royal Forest Hotel during the war?"

"How can I forget it," she says. "You'd changed from a young kid to a grown man in uniform."

We talk on into the small hours of the morning, Billy, Joan, and I, intermittently dancing to the hypnotic rhythm of the band.

∗∗∗

It's Monday now, and Billy left after dinner last night to rejoin his unit in Gilgil. We'll be off to Mombasa Wednesday on the overnight train. The excitement of saying goodbye to our friends and buying last-minute gifts from the curio dealers in Bazaar Street brings with it the trauma of parting. Yet, at the same time, we are eager to leave, savouring the excitement of travel and the coming reunion with our families and longtime friends.

Despite the emergency, Nairobi is in a festive mood because of the coronation. Delamere Avenue and the adjacent streets are alive with decorations and lights. A long line of golden crowns hovers above Delamere Avenue, and stretches from Delamere's statue opposite the New Stanley Hotel, to the triumphal archway that spans the avenue, not far from the railroad crossing next to the post office. Joan and I tour the city like tourists, photographing the colourful displays to show our family and friends in England.

We have ordered a new car through the Nairobi agent—a six-cylinder Vauxhall Velox—and will take delivery of it in England. We will use the car to travel in Europe, and then have it shipped here at no extra cost to us. Delighted with the arrangement, we signed the contract yesterday. We will keep the Austin as a second car.

Figure 22. Coronation decorations.

On the morning of our departure, I drive the Austin to the post office *go-down* (store) in the industrial area, followed by Eric in a Land Rover. After completing the formalities with the clerk, Eric and I disconnect the battery, and leave the car under a lean-to.

"Do you think we should put it up on blocks?" Eric asks.

After a moment's thought, I agree. "Yes, it'd probably be better. That will keep the weight off the tires. We can take the wheels off and store them in the back."

Our task finished, we stand back to admire our handiwork. The car sits on blocks, with its wheel studs protruding from the four, dirty, black hubs where the wheels had been.

"There," says Eric, "she'll be right as rain till you get back." He pauses and adds, "I won't be a minute, I just have to check with Jack Munro about an S-five order form that I put in a while ago for some equipment."

While he's gone, I cover the car with a tarpaulin and tighten the ropes, leaving the Austin trussed up like a turkey dinner. Hearing Eric call, I take one last look at the car, and then hurry over to the Land Rover.

Eric grins. "You're like an old hen about that car," he says. "Don't worry; it'll be safe. The stores are guarded day and night by security men."

The Boat Train

On Wednesday afternoon, John and Connie Gummer collect us at the hotel in their car. John and I manhandle the four large suitcases into the car, but it's a tight fit. "You'd better sit in the back with the overnight bags," John says, "while Joan and Connie can sit in the front with me."

We've known the Gummers for about four years now. Shortly after I arrived in March 1949, I met John in the Thika Road House, a transit point for new government personnel. An ex-hurricane fighter pilot, John is a thickset, burly man in his mid-thirties. He and Rex Wale had come down together from Palestine where they'd worked on police contracts, while I'd flown in from the UK. For a time, Joan and Connie had worked together at the Nairobi law firm of *Kaplan and Stratton*.

It's a short drive from the hotel to the railway station on Government Road, close to the Whitehouse Road intersection. A railway porter, one of many vying for our favour, loads our luggage onto his pushcart. Carrying our overnight bags, our little group follows him to the railway office.

"Aye," says the grey-haired baggage clerk, "the luggage compartment is attached to the boat train section. Let me have your tickets, and I'll process them." He returns within minutes. "That's settled," he smiles. "Your carriage will be shunted off in the Mombasa marshalling yard, and goes directly to Kilindini harbour. The luggage will be put on board the ship, where the shipping agent will check it in with you."

The railway station is bustling with activity. The crowd is mostly Europeans, although there are some Asians. Kenya's white population treats arrivals and departures as social events. Rex Wale and his wife Nora, along with many other friends, are already on the platform waiting to say goodbye.

Free of our heavy luggage, we push through the crowd, looking for our boarding number and code on the reserved passenger carriages in the boat train section. We've reserved a coupe, a self-contained compartment for two persons. John has forged ahead of me in the press of people. "You're in here, Gordon," he calls.

Joan has lagged behind me, talking to Connie and Nora. As I board the train to check our compartment, she hurries over. It's almost six o'clock, and dusk is falling. The old steam engine gives a warning blast on its whistle, and steam gushes beneath the carriages. I step outside the train to rejoin Joan and our group of friends. There's just a few minutes left, just enough time to say goodbye.

As the stationmaster blows his whistle and calls, "All aboard," Joan and I step aboard the train. Hurrying to our compartment, I open one of the windows and we wave to our friends. Their voices are indistinguishable above the hiss of steam as slowly the wheels begin to turn. As the train gathers speed, it moves out of the station, but I stay by the window, waving, until I lose sight of our friends in the billowing smoke. Shutting the window, I sit down beside Joan. "Well, we made it," I say. "We're on our way."

As I put my arm around her, her eyes are red. "I want so much to go," she says, "but I still don't like leaving all our friends. Strange, isn't it, how you can want a thing so badly, but when it comes, it's hard to let go."

"Yes," I nod my head. "It's so often the way. You get used to having your friends around, and then suddenly they're gone. It's like starting over again." As I kiss away her tears, I say, "We'll be back in a few months," I laugh. "It may even be sooner, if they cut short my leave. But we'll be in England in three weeks."

The brief African twilight has already turned to night as we settle down in the comfort of our compartment, with her head on my shoulder. The industrial area disappears rapidly as the train increases speed. By the time we pass through the small settlement of Athi River, it is dark, but I don't need the station lights to tell me where we are. I wrinkle my nose as the distinctive odour of the cattle abattoir finds its way into the carriage. "Phew," I say to Joan who is also covering her nose with a handkerchief. "The wind must be in the wrong direction. I'd hate to live in Athi River with that bloody smell."

Joan laughs as the smell lessens and disappears. "It's about the only industry here, that and the cement factory. Although the farmers near Machakos also use the railroad to get their cattle to market."

Outside the night is black, and the countryside seems peaceful. Looking across the Kapiti plains, we can see the distant lights of the *Mau Mau* detention centre, a reminder that there is a savage mini-war raging in the country. The steady rhythm of the train wheels on the track merges into the background noise as we talk.

When we hear the distant sound of a gong being struck in the corridor, I look at Joan, "That's the steward taking bookings for the dinner sittings." A knock on the compartment door confirms my suspicions. We choose the first sitting, and the steward scribbles our compartment number in his book, and then says, "Dinner will be served at seven o'clock."

✳✳✳

The gleaming polished woodwork and the gold damask curtains that block out the darkness give the restaurant car a quality and air of a more leisurely age. The subdued light from small, ornamental brass wall-lamps spreads over the starched white damask cloth, place mats, cutlery, and silver-plated condiments.

Joan studies the menu as the table steward stands nearby. "It's a full, four course, set meal," she says, then adds, as she reads from the menu, "with an alternative for the main course. There's either grilled lamb cutlets with roast potatoes or steak and kidney pie with mashed potatoes. I think I'll have the grilled cutlets. What about you?"

"Well, just to be different, I'll have the steak and kidney," I say with a laugh, then add, "Would you like something to drink to celebrate?"

"Why not," she says, reaching for the wine list.

We've finished the soup and fish courses—cream of tomato soup and *talapia,* a fresh lake water fish from Lake Victoria—and, having demolished the main course, we now sit back, satisfied, with the half-empty bottle of wine between us. "Yes," I say to Joan, as I clean the remnants from my plate, "I must have been hungry; I enjoyed that."

"There's still dessert and coffee to come." She looks at the menu and says, "Crème Brulée or Crêpes Suzette?"

"What is a Crêpes Suzette?"

"They pour heated rum over a thin, rolled pancake, then set it alight." There's a twinkle in her eyes, and she laughs as she adds, "You'd like that."

It's almost eight o'clock and the dining room stewards are beginning to clear the tables for the second sitting. The wine bottle is empty when we leave the table and make our way back, a little unsteadily but happy, through the interconnecting corridors to our compartment.

While we were at dinner, the room attendant has pulled out the two facing bench seats and arranged them as beds. Pillows, sheets, and blankets have been provided. He's also closed the Venetian blinds and pulled down the roll curtains. There's a washbasin between the two windows, with a large mirror above it, and racks on either side that hold fresh towels and matching washcloths.

As we enter the compartment, Joan smiles. "Good," she says, "the beds have been made up." She pulls down her carryall bag from the overhead rack, and, sitting on one of the beds, rummages in the bag for her nightie. We talk while we unpack our nightwear and toilet necessities, and then Joan washes her face and arms in the washbasin. "Aye, Joan, the only thing missing in the compartment is a *choo* (toilet)," I say, using the local word (which rhymes with "joe"). Laughing, I add, "But that's no problem; there's one at either end of the corridor."

＊＊＊

Tired out from the excitement of the day and the frantic, last minute preparations, we both feel mentally drained. We have brought books to help pass the evening hours, but, lulled by the rhythm of the train, sleep is not long in coming.

Sometime in the early hours of the morning, a violent shaking and the clash of carriage bumpers wakes me. Curious, I pull aside the curtains, and peer through the Venetian blind. Outside, the station where the train has stopped is ablaze with light. As I watch the activity in the marshalling yard, the carriage shudders and jerks. My sleep-fogged brain realizes where we are. "It's Voi," I say. "They're uncoupling the Moshi-Arusha sections of the train."

"Get back into bed," Joan says sleepily. "We need our sleep. The train will be in Mombasa in a few hours." Turning over, she goes back to sleep, but I continue to watch a little longer.

The Mombasa train has cleared the small settlement of Voi, and the compartment is once more pitch dark. Occasionally, a small light pierces the night like a pinpoint, and I wonder whether it is from a campfire or a lantern. The Tara desert—the area we are now entering—is an inhospitable and waterless expanse that was a barrier to the early explorers. The coming of the railroad at the turn of the century has changed all that.

Yes, I think, *the lights are probably from remote African villages on the slopes of the Teita Mountains.* This is Wateita country. It'll be mostly flat, dried-up plains from here until we reach the fertile coastal strip.

As I recall the time that I was on Mbwinzau, a thousand feet above the road and rail tracks, I grin. I'd kept the fire burning there all night to ward off leopard and other animals. Perhaps another traveller may have seen my campfire, and wondered what was there.

Closing the blind, I get back into bed. Soon I, too, fall asleep to the rhythmic noise of the wheels as the steam train chugs across the uninhabited, deserted bush. When I wake again, it is dawn. I pull back the curtain as we flash by another station, but I catch sight of the signboard, *MacKinnon Road*. During World War II, there was a British army camp here, but now it is just another small settlement, forgotten in the bush.

It is seven o'clock when the train passes Mariakani, roughly twenty-five miles or so west of Mombasa. Joan is up, and we are both dressed, ready for breakfast. Hearing the breakfast gong, we hurry to the restaurant car, to be in time for the first sitting. Breakfast—fruit and cereal, bacon and eggs, followed by coffee—is a hurried affair.

Mombasa and the *Rhodesia Castle*

When the train begins the long winding descent from the hills above Mombasa, we are back in our compartment. The countryside slides past the windows, and the Indian Ocean is now a distant blue haze on the horizon. As the train bisects roads and passes close to small villages, palm tree plantations and native villages swim past in a colourful diorama. Women with loads of produce on their heads stop to watch the iron monster that puffs steam as it passes them. They smile and wave to the passengers, and then adjust their loads, and continue walking to the local markets.

As we watch from the carriage windows, the train approaches the Makupa causeway linking the island of Mombasa to the mainland, and the harbour comes into view. The train sweeps around bends, and the track spirals back on itself. From the high ground, the harbour and creeks of the island spread out before us like a map.

"Look over there," I say, "It's the *Rhodesia Castle* alongside the Kilindini dock." Grinning, I add, "It won't be long now."

The ship's distinctive red funnel, encircled with a black band, the white upper structure of its bridge, and the passenger decks are all clearly visible above the dockside warehouses. In the distance, the Likoni car ferry, looking like a small bug, creeps across the narrow mouth of the inner harbour. There it disgorges cars and passengers onto the far ramp leading to the Tanga coastal road and the seaside resorts that line the southern coast. The train thunders across the causeway, and our view of the harbour disappears. We now see Port Tudor to our left, while on our right, separated by a swampy creek, is the Kipevu Causeway.

Joining Port Reitz to the Mombasa dock areas, the causeway also carries both road and rail traffic.

Entering the marshalling yards, the train slows to a crawl. As we watch, small groups of African railway workers wander along the line, and we can also see crammed third class coaches, with people hanging out of doors and windows. Chattering and gesticulating, they watch with undisguised interest as the railway workers unhitch the boat train section from the main train. The third class carriages move slowly past us into the main terminus, leaving the boat train sitting in the siding.

Figure 23. Gordon on ship in Mombasa.

A sudden jerk startles us. There is a bustle of activity as our carriages are coupled to a small engine. Then, with escaping steam hissing, we are slowly moved into the sheds and warehouses lining the docks, and come to a stop next to the customs and immigration shed. On the other side of the long converted warehouse, lies the ship. We have arrived. I glance at my watch. It is 9:15 a.m., May 21, 1953.

With the immigration and customs formalities completed, Joan and I supervise our luggage as it is brought into our cabin. That finished, we wander out on deck. The ship, a large vessel of roughly twenty-six thousand tons, has cleared the harbour and reef, bound for Aden, the Red Sea, and the Suez Canal. Heading north into the Indian Ocean, the ship passes the palm-fringed beaches of Nyali on the port side, and follows a course for the Gulf of Aden.

The lunch gong sounds, as I look back to the disappearing coastline. I feel a twinge of regret at leaving, even though it is only briefly, because Africa is now our home. *But we're coming back,* I think, smiling to myself.

✳✳✳

Chapter 6
Recalled from Leave

The Parting

Mrs. Green's worn face registers concern, and her voice is low and worried as she hands me the envelope marked *urgent*. "It came earlier today when you and Joan were away visiting your mother," she says.

Standing in the hallway of my mother-in-law's neat, suburban house in Chingford, I take the envelope, and hurriedly tear it open. Dated August 2, 1953, the cable is from the Crown Agents. My eyes scan the terse message:

> Leave cancelled due emergency. Report to Crown
> Agents Office in Millbank, London, for documentation
> and processing of air passages to Kenya.

My feelings are mixed when I hand the telegram to Joan. *The position must be deteriorating in Kenya. I want to get back, but it is hard to break the news.* "I'm sorry, Mrs. G," I say, "but it's what we expected. I've got to report to the Crown Agents. The department needs me back urgently, so I'm afraid we'll have to return to Kenya."

Joan puts her arms around her mother's frail body and hugs her. "Yes," she says, her voice soft and compassionate, "We thought this might happen, Mum."

"We'll be all right, Mrs. G," I say. "Joan's in Nairobi. It's a big city, and she's safe there. Granted, I have to go into the bush because my work takes me there, but it's not so bad as the newspapers make out."

Mrs. Green holds Joan tight, sighs, and then rubs away her tears. "I worry about you both," she says. "When we read about the Lari massacre and fighting in the forests, and those awful murders of Africans and white settlers, it seems that the whole country is in chaos."

"Yes, that's true. Unfortunately the newspapers often don't put the news in perspective. They make it sound like the whole country is in revolt." Pausing, I look at Mrs. Green; her eyes are downcast as she listens. "It's only the Kikuyu tribal areas and reserves around Mount Kenya and the Aberdares, including Nairobi and the White Highlands, that are involved. There may be a few dissident tribesmen of other tribes living in the area, Mrs. G, but on the whole *Mau Mau* has only affected one tribe, the Kikuyu." I smile as I add, "There's a whole division of British army troops operating in Kenya, and they're looking after us."

Her eyes are red when she looks up at me and nods. "Yes, I understand, Gordon," she says. "I know you have to go." Giving her daughter a last affectionate hug, she murmurs, "Look after my girl. I can't help worrying, but that's life, I guess." She pauses then continues, "When do they want you back?"

"Within the week, give or take a day or two," I say. "Tomorrow's Monday, so I'll take the train to Liverpool Street in the morning and see the Crown Agents."

I've always liked Joan's mother. Small and sparrow-like, with a loveable personality, Mrs. Green made me feel at home since I first met her back in 1945. She hasn't altered in that time. Her tired ageing face reflects the care and feelings that endear her to me. She has six children, quite a large family, but it's a loving and supportive one. I suppose they had to be, because Mrs. Green was on her own when she raised them.

I never met Joan's father. Drink, gambling, and women had evidently been his ruin. He lost his coal delivery business, his wife, and his family. Mrs. Green had divorced him long before the Second World War. What happened to him in the end, I don't know, because that lies buried deep in Mrs. Green's past.

The Flight Back, Tripoli

It is August 9, 1953, roughly three months since we left Kenya. With the emotional stress of parting over and with our seat belts fastened, we settle back in our seats as the aircraft takes off from London airport. Joan is quiet, her face pensive as she looks out the window. The tiny houses with their small backyards and the intersecting streets of London's sprawling suburbs fall away below us. Her hands grip the adjustable arms of the seat, and then relax as the aircraft levels out. She shakes her head. "I couldn't see them on the waving base, just a mass of people in the distance. It'll be another four years before I see Mum again."

My hand finds hers as I reply, "At least we've been able to see them, and renew our family ties."

We talk on a while, reminiscing about our holiday. Then Joan picks up her book and lapses into silence. I lean back in my seat, alone with my thoughts, remembering my first flight to Kenya back in March 1949, when I was on my own. Then, the noisy, converted York bomber had lumbered across leaden, overcast skies, and the loud, constant throb of its engines drilled into my skull, giving me blinding headaches. Today, the sound of the engines is muted, Joan is flying with me, and the sun is shining in a clear, blue sky.

There are still no navigational aids available on the African continent, so night flying is banned. The journey will take three days with two overnight stops. It is early evening when we make our first stop, touching down at Castel Benito in Tripoli, on the North African Coast. As we travel along in the bus to the local transit hotel near the harbour, the seafront promenade looks familiar to me.

"You know, Joan," I say as we go up to our room on the second floor, "this is the hotel where I stayed in 1949. I was also based here during the war back in 1943 and 1944. In those days, the hotel was used as an Officers' Club. We visited it often because it was within walking distance of the docks."

Our room has a veranda, and we stand there in the warm evening, looking out over the Mediterranean. The sun has gone down, but the moonlight reflects off the water. Beyond the breakwater to the east are the lights on the docks, while to the west is the sweep of the beach and bay. The pounding of waves on the shoreline and the distant lights bring back memories of wartime, and I think about the *Empire Harmony*, the heavy lift ship that I served on, and the Sicilian landings.

It was from this port that we moved up to Naples in early 'forty-four, soon after that port had fallen to allied forces. We operated under the US Fifth Army, and were based in Naples. It seems like only yesterday, but it is nearly ten years ago.

As we go back through the French doors, I smile as I remember the amusement caused by the bathroom arrangements when my flight landed here in 1949. Turning to Joan, I say with a grin, "Be careful to lock the adjoining door when you're in the bathroom."

Joan looks up at me quizzically. "Is the bathroom shared with another room?"

"Yes," I say, opening the bathroom door to point out the other door. "There's a bolt on the inside, and the doors can be locked from either side. It's common practice throughout the hotel; and it caused some hilarious incidents amongst the passengers when I was last here. You mustn't forget to unlock the adjoining door when you're finished in the bathroom, and then lock our door on this side."

※※※

We're airborne, and Tripoli, with its churches and mosques, is rapidly disappearing behind us. An early morning heat haze is beginning to form over the coast and sea, while ten thousand feet below us the semi-desert coastal strip is edged by a thin line of white breakers. The receding blue of the Mediterranean coastline contrasts with the yellowish tinge of the sand dunes and occasional scrub and palm tree plantations, and then it too disappears as we head south east across Tripolitania for Libya and the Sudan.

The air hostess has come and gone. With breakfast over, Joan's settled down with her book. Leaning forward in my seat, I watch the never ending sea of sand and sand dunes stretching monotonously from horizon to horizon as the aircraft flies on its set course, diagonally crossing the vast Saharan desert belt. Tiring of watching, I doze in my seat, keeping my seat belt fastened loosely because I remember that back in 'forty-nine, heat thermals off the desert had bounced the aircraft unmercifully.

My hand instinctively feels for the comforting presence of the packet of airsickness pills in my pocket. I took one before we left, but you never know, I might need another. Thinking about the Dramamine pills, I smile to myself. *If we'd only had them in the war, they would have saved me countless days of misery.* I glance across at Joan who's engrossed in her book; she doesn't suffer from motion sickness. I smile ruefully as I remember crossing the English Channel when we were returning from our honeymoon in Jersey. *There was a gale blowing, and I was violently sick. As I was in naval uniform, I never did hear the end of it.*

The Nile, Wadi Halfa and Khartoum

The sun is behind us, and it is late afternoon when we first see the Nile like a snake winding across the desert below, its border of green vegetation contrasting with the dirty pale yellow of the sand. The voice of the pilot comes over the intercom. "We will be landing at Wadi Halfa in ten minutes," he says. "Fasten your seatbelts for landing, please."

Joan grimaces. "It's the takeoff and landings I don't like," she says, holding the arms of the seat tightly as the aircraft touches down smoothly on the asphalt surface of the runway. The light is beginning to fail, as, along with our fellow passengers, we walk in a straggling line across the apron in front of the control tower and into the passenger reception area. Loaded with passengers, the airline coach pulls away from the terminal, transporting us to the one-and-only hotel in this small border town.

The brief African twilight has turned to night; and in the headlights, shadowy forms scurry across the dirt road and disappear into mud-and-wattle tin-roofed shacks that line the airport road. On the outskirts of the town, the coach draws up in the driveway of a hotel on the banks of the Nile, framed by the shadowy backdrop of palm trees lining the riverbank. A glint of moonlight sparkles on the surface of the slow moving river.

Dinner is over, and it is peaceful as we sit on the veranda with other transit passengers, sipping our coffee, and watching the reflected moonlight shimmer on the waters of the Nile. The croaking of bullfrogs in the nearby papyrus swamp mixes with the high pitched, undulating sound made by crickets and the whine of mosquitoes which breed in the swamps and irrigation ditches. The night sounds are soothing and familiar to our ears. Wearing trousers and long-sleeved jackets, we sit undisturbed by the mosquitoes; our clothing thwarts their efforts, and, apart from the most persistent, they are easily ignored.

Distant specks of light glitter on the opposite bank of the river. Joan nods towards them, and echoes my thoughts. "It looks like a small village over there," she says, slapping a mosquito on the back of her hand. "Got the bloody thing," she mutters, as she inspects the mangled remains, then continues, "I didn't realize the Nile was so wide this far from the coast."

✳✳✳

The early morning light finds us on our way in the airport coach again. Airborne, the aircraft follows the general line of the river, which wanders in curves through the folds of the parched land, sometimes doubling back on itself in an arc before continuing to Khartoum, roughly five hundred miles to the south. Famed for General Gordon's last stand against the Mahdi and the subsequent recapture of the city by Lord Wolsey's forces in 1885, Khartoum emerges out of the dust and sand of the desert below us. It is here that the Blue and White Niles join, one river flowing from Tississat Falls in Ethiopia and the other from Lake Victoria.

As the aircraft sweeps in from the north over the town, the confluence of the two rivers is clearly visible. Losing height rapidly, the plane comes in low, and I catch a glimpse of a long steel bridge with many spans connecting the west and east riverbanks. Then, the bridge disappears from view, hidden by the blur of shanty housing estates as the aircraft throttles back and touches down in the dusty airport on the outskirts of town.

The heat hits us like a warm blanket and, disembarking, we walk in small straggling groups across the tarmac to the passenger terminal. A large ceiling fan stirs the warm air in the sparsely furnished transit lounge where we sit on leather-covered chairs around a table. "Well," Joan says, as she sips the cold soft drink supplied by the airline, "this is better than sitting in the aircraft with the air conditioning turned off."

Figure 24. Khartoum, showing the bridge over the River Nile, with the confluence of the Blue and White Niles in the background.

Kenya Bound

An hour later the aircraft climbs into the cloudless sky, leaving Khartoum behind in the heat haze. Avoiding the highlands of Ethiopia, we head southwest over the arid desert and semi-deserts of the Southern Sudan, crisscrossing the White Nile, which winds like a silver thread across the sandy desert below. The weather is clear now, and there is only the occasional heat thermal to bounce the aircraft around.

In March 1949, however, weather conditions had been quite different. That year, the rains in Ethiopia were late, and, when we neared the Ethiopian border en route to Entebbe, the pilot had warned us of turbulence ahead. Through the window, I had caught an oblique view of a massive cloudbank, rising thousands of feet in the sky.

The aircraft had veered to one side, climbing steeply in an attempt to work its way clear. Unable to climb above or otherwise avoid the towering thunderhead, the plane had hit the cloud and we had passed into a world of white. An air pocket—a ferocious downwind common to these cloud formations—had caught the sturdy old ex-bomber, and we had dropped vertically several hundred feet. It felt as if we were falling down an elevator shaft. For one fearful moment, I had thought that the wings would rip off when we hit the bottom of the air pocket. Thankfully, the old aircraft simply shook herself violently like a dog, and carried on through the thunderhead. That was a moment that I will not easily forget.

∗∗∗

Northern Uganda spreads out like a map below us as we cross the Sudan border. The pilot's voice comes over the intercom, giving our position. "You can see Lake Albert on the right-hand side of the aircraft," he says. "The settlement you see to the west is Nimule, on the Sudan-Uganda border. Our estimated time of arrival at Entebbe will be fifteen hundred hours, or three o'clock in the afternoon."

Joan is wide awake now. "Nimule," she says as she glances down at the ground six thousand feet below. "Do you remember the paddle wheeler?" She pauses, and then adds, "That must be Pakwach over there, where Lake Albert flows into the Nile."

"Yes," I answer, "and that faint white spray must come from Murchison Falls."

We talk animatedly because we're seeing familiar landmarks from our 1951 trip to the upper Nile headwaters. Looking down on the Nile and Uganda gives me a different perspective of the area where I have worked and travelled so extensively in the last four years.

Our flight is on time, and Lake Victoria lies just ahead, its glistening waters extending unbroken to the distant, southern horizon. The aircraft loses altitude as the pilot prepares to land at Entebbe's international airport, located roughly fifteen or twenty miles from Kampala. My stomach muscles tighten, and unconsciously, like Joan, I grip the armrest. A fleeting vision of islands flashes by on the right-hand side of the plane, followed by a glimpse of the airfield's boundary fence just below us. The wheels seem to hover a long time over the runway before they touch down.

✳✳✳

Impatient to be off on the last leg of our flight, we find that the delay at Entebbe is interminable, but it's only an hour later that the aircraft heads out across Lake Victoria and over the hills and mountains of western Kenya. The Great Rift Valley, a huge gash in the mountainous terrain below, passes quickly and the snowcapped mountaintops of Mount Kenya and Kilimanjaro appear on the horizon. Joan sees them first. "Look, Gordon," she says excitedly, "it's Kilimanjaro; we're nearly there. I wonder if Billy will meet us? I cabled him with our flight number and arrival time."

I smile as I place my hand over hers. I can feel her trembling, and tighten my grip. "He'll be there," I say; "don't worry."

An answering smile crosses her face and she nods. For an instant, I feel a pang of jealousy, but I dismiss it as an unworthy thought. Billy is my friend, too. The three of us have been close friends since I met him back in 1952. I smile as I remember how Joan's letter telling me about Billy arrived via a cleft stick runner (an African courier). Then silently laugh to myself when I recall how Doug Price reacted when I arrived

Figure 25. View of Mount Kenya, taken from aircraft.

home early, with my rifle slung over my shoulder. *Did he really think that I was going to shoot Billy?*

With Mount Kenya on the left, the aircraft sweeps in a large circle over the Ngong Hills, and begins its descent into Eastleigh Airport on the outskirts of Nairobi. As the aircraft taxies towards the terminal, I can see the control tower where I first worked back in March 1949. So much has happened in the last four years. I am glad to be back.

Now, as we exit the aircraft, I glance at Joan by my side. I can see that she is happy, too. There's a spring in her step, and she's smiling as we enter the airport.

Eastleigh Airport, Nairobi

When we step out of the customs and immigration exit, there's a crowd of people lining the sides of the roped-off pathway, all pushing forward, eagerly striving to get a first glimpse of returning friends and relatives. A welcoming Irish brogue attracts our attention, as Billy calls, "Gordon, Joan, over here." Recognizing the familiar, brushed-back red hair and wide grin in the sea of faces, Joan smiles.

Laden down with luggage, I nudge her with my elbow. "There he is," I say.

Billy greets us at the end of the roped-off area, and I gladly relinquish some of my load. Accompanied by Billy's nonstop banter, we move out into the waning daylight. It's nearing the end of the cold season in Kenya,

Figure 26. Control tower, Eastleigh

and there's a nip in the air. The sun's gone down now, and the evening temperature has dropped to about fifty degrees Fahrenheit. I'm glad of the sweater that I'd put on in the aircraft.

After piling the luggage on the back seat, we get into Billy's car. There is a wide bench seat that takes three comfortably. Now, with Joan between us, Billy drives out of the airport gates and into Racecourse Road. It is not until we have gone a few hundred yards that I question him about the emergency.

"Aye," he says, "Did you hear about the fighting in the Aberdares and Mount Kenya forests?"

"I've read some newspaper reports, but after three weeks at sea on the *Rhodesia Castle* and six weeks touring the continent, we've been out of contact with English newspapers and radio." I laugh as I add, "To be quite honest, Billy, I guess we wanted to get away from it all for a while. I did hear that General Erskine has taken over military command and that Major-General Hinde is in charge of army operations. Also, I read several newspaper reports on the forest operations, but it was all very sketchy."

Billy nods, "Yeah, that I can understand." He is silent a moment, concentrating on the road ahead, then says, "Erskine and Hinde seem to know what they're doing. They headed the operations against the Communists in Malaya, and both are experienced in guerrilla warfare. Right now the Buffs and the Devons are in the thick of the fighting in the forests against General China's gangs."

He shakes his head. "The *East African Standard* says that gangs of over a thousand men have been fighting in the Mount Kenya forest under China's command. The armed forces have a tough job on their hands what with China's gangs and Dedan Kimathi's army in the Aberdares." Billy's voice tails off, and he adds, "You know yourself that Kimathi is not stupid. He proved that in the raid on the Naivasha Police Station and the Lari massacre operation."

Billy pauses for a moment as he shifts gears, then he continues, "About a month back, three Kenya army men were killed in the forests. I'm told that *Mau Mau* overran their Bren gun position and wiped out the crew. But the big news is Othaya in the Fort Hall area. The police, along with the Kenya Regiment and the Kikuyu Home Guard, together beat off a massed frontal attack on the Othaya Police Post in the Kikuyu Reserve. The terrorists used automatic weapons and grenades, but their losses were heavy. There were about sixty to eighty dead and wounded." Billy laughs sardonically, "I doubt whether they'll try any more direct assaults on army units."

Night has fallen by the time we reach the centre of town. "I assume you've booked into Homewood, Joan," Billy says, glancing at her.

She nods, "Yes, I cabled Mrs. O'Connel as soon as we knew our arrival date. She's expecting us."

The car rumbles across the railroad tracks bisecting the south end of Delamere Avenue, and turning up Valley Road, carries on past the cathedral to the small residential hotel near the top. A sense of homecoming spreads through me, when we drive in through the ivy-clad archway into the parking area of the hotel. The owner, Mrs. O'Connel, greets us warmly as we park the car, and unload our luggage.

We've got the rondavel again. Compared to the rooms in the newer, L-shaped addition, it's rustic, but, knowing we like it, she has managed to keep it for us. Billy stays for dinner, and it is late in the evening when he leaves. He's staying with Paddy and Mary tonight, and will go back to Gilgil tomorrow.

The Apartment, Marlborough Road

Two weeks have gone by, a very hectic two weeks. We've been allocated government housing in Spring Valley. Having served one four-year tour, I now have some seniority, and my name is higher on the housing list. "You're lucky," says the

Figure 27. Joan on stairs leading to our apartment on Marlborough Road

Figure 28. EAP&T block of flats.

housing officer. "There's an apartment available in Marlborough Road."

We drive out to the valley with him to look at it. The two-storey building, with individual garages beneath, overlooks a small stream bordered with acacia and jacaranda trees. Like many residential buildings in Nairobi, it was built by Asian *fundis* (craftsmen) and African labourers with locally quarried granite blocks. We're being offered the end apartment, which has a wide veranda atop the garage. There are two bedrooms, a dining/sitting room and a kitchen along with the usual amenities, including separate servants' quarters located behind the building.

"It's just been redecorated, and it's ready for occupancy," says the housing officer. "Do you want it?"

"Well," I say, "we were nearly four years on the housing list last time. We finally got the apartment in Daphton Court just a few months before we went on leave." I pause momentarily, and then say, "Yes, we'll take it. We don't want to wait another four years."

The housing officer grins and nods. "That I can understand," he says. "I suppose you know that you can transfer to other quarters when something comes vacant? That is, if you don't find this apartment to be suitable."

A few days later we move in; the empty rooms are furnished, and made habitable. The department's hard furnishings have arrived, plus our own personal things—the curtains, sheets and blankets and all the *taka taka* (odds and ends)—are retrieved from the post office *go-down* in the industrial area. Joan is happily rearranging furniture and curtains, putting down small rugs on the parquet floors, and adding all those personal touches that go to make a house feel like home. She loves the apartment, and soon cane chairs and tables, purchased from itinerant roadside traders, are painted red and decorate the veranda.

Mac's Office Again

"Ah, yes, Mumford," says Mac, adjusting his glasses as he reads the fine print on the map in front of him. We're in his office in the corrugated iron and wood shack that he seems to prefer to the main office building. Straightening up from the map table, he leans against it and looks at me. "Now that you've settled in your house, we've a job for you." He pauses, removing his reading glasses. "It's on Mbwinzau. The survey is almost finished now, and we're entering the construction stage all along the routes from Uganda to the coast. I want you to cut a Land Rover track up the ridge. We'll have the building section make a permanent road for trucks at a later date."

Thoughtfully, he strokes his short Van Dyke beard, and then continues. "The Kampala and Nakuru offices are responsible for constructing the roads and buildings on the western route from Nakuru to Kampala. Scales, Williams, and Perrins have been helping out up there. We still need to finish the Shimba Hills survey on the coast and Zanzibar, but we're stretched thin. We need all the men we can get to finish off the routes, construct the buildings and get the equipment installed, hence your early recall from leave."

Mac's face crinkles, the crow's feet deepening, as he grins. "I'm sorry about that, but it couldn't be avoided. What with all the extra emergency work we've had to contend with, we're behind schedule with the VHF route."

He selects a large-scale map of the Mbwinzau area, and, as we lean over the table, he follows the pencilled trail around the back of the mountain with his finger. "I had a quick look at our repeater site, and the north side of the mountain seems the most likely route. The slope is easier on that side, so the gradients will be less." We talk on, discussing the route and other details.

"Yes," Mac says with a sigh. "I've talked to the District Officer there as well as the local chief, Jeremiah Miu. We'll take a truck down with the camping and road building equipment." Mac looks at the calendar on the wall. "Let's see," he says. "It's Wednesday now. You'll leave Monday morning, August 31. That will give you time to get the truck loaded and organized." He grins as he adds, "And you'll have the weekend in Nairobi."

As we prepare to leave the office, he says, "I'll come along in my station wagon, and stay at Pearson's Rest House for a couple of days. That'll give us a day or two to go over the track before work begins. You'll probably need a hundred labourers. The chief can help you with labour and you can arrange a meeting with him through the District Office. I also need to see the D.O. concerning some last minute details."

✳✳✳

Chapter 7
Mbwinzau, September 1953

Off to Makindu

The small Austin A40 edges out into the Monday morning traffic on Saddler Street from the post office yard where Joan has dropped me on her way to work, and disappears into Delamere Avenue. With a last look at the traffic, I turn and walk into the yard.

Idi, his red fez set at a jaunty angle, stands near the three-ton Dodge truck. Seeing me, he comes over, and asks, *"Tunakwenda sasa*—do we go now?"

I nod, *"Ndiyo*—yes, follow Katumo and me; we're in the Land Rover. Karanja the *neopara* and two labourers will go with you in the truck. Bwana Gregory is going in his own car with Unwa."

The truck is loaded to capacity with road building implements. A heavy green tarpaulin covers the load of tents, camping equipment, water filters, axes, *jembes*, ropes and tools plus a hundred and one necessary items. There are also all our personal belongings as well as food supplies. Perhaps one of the most essential items is our medical kit, which includes a Fitzsimmons snakebite kit and a complete first aid box, plus extra supplies in case of injury.

Idi and Karanja climb into the cab of the truck, while in the back the two workers make themselves comfortable, partly covering themselves with the tarpaulin. As I wait for Idi's signal, I say to Katumo, "Those two are going to get covered in dust."

"Vumbi ni mbaya—dust is not bad," he says. "Our people are used to it."

Katumo is a Mkamba tribesman. Like most of the regular drivers, I've known him for several years, and requested that he come with me this time. Mbwinzau is in Wakamba country, and it will be helpful to have Katumo as an interpreter as well as a driver.

Seeing Idi's hand signal, I start my engine. With the Land Rover in the lead, our vehicles move out of the yard into the busy streets.

***

Leaving Athi River and Nairobi far behind, we cross the Kapiti game plains. Our vehicles are now well spaced out to avoid the dust clouds

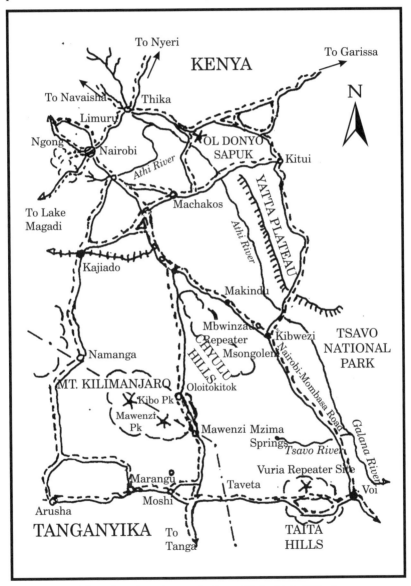

Figure 29. Map showing the route from Nairobi to Mbwinzau.

churned up by our wheels. As I glance in the rear view mirror, I catch a glimpse of the truck. Idi has fallen behind, but I can see his dust, and occasionally the vehicle, as I drive past the rising land near Lukenya, the high cliffs that mark the southerly end of the Machakos range of hills.

Our small convoy climbs the Mua Hills, and then drops down into Sultan Hamud, and onto the game plains, passing through the small settlement about noon. As I concentrate on the dirt road ahead, trying to avoid potholes, the familiar landscape unfolds. Emali passes in the dust, and now, when I look to my right, I can just see Kilimanjaro's white snowcap shimmering in the heat haze across the Nyiri desert. The dried-up, coarse yellow clumps of grass and stunted thorn trees seem to thrive in the adverse conditions of these barren, flat grasslands.

***

The plains are thick with game. There are small and large herds of Tommies (Thomson gazelle), wildebeest, and zebra, mixed with giraffe and ostrich. I slow to avoid some animals that are grazing near the side of the road as we skirt the Chyulu Hills on our right. The dirt road built over the swampy bog of Kiboko Drift has passed and we are nearing our destination, Makindu. A Hindu temple suddenly appears, then as quickly disappears in a cloud of dust. Topping a rise in the land, I can see the small settlement of Makindu just ahead. The administrative *boma* and native village are built around a railroad whistle-stop.

At the far side of the settlement on the right-hand side of the road is Pearson's Rest House, almost hidden in the bush. As we drop our speed, the gap closes between our vehicles, and, when I turn into the drive, Idi follows me closely in the truck. It is mid-afternoon. We park the vehicles near the *bandas* clustered around the main building.

Pearson's Rest House

Pearson, an older man in his late fifties or early sixties, is behind the bar that does double duty as a reception desk. When I enter, he recognizes me, and a smile flickers across his worn features. "Ah," he says, removing his reading glasses and reaching for the registration book. "You've been here before. You're with Gregory's mob, aren't you? Are you still working on Mbwinzau?"

"That's right," I say. "You'll probably see a lot more of us in the near future." As he pushes the book across to me, I continue, "This time I'm cutting a Land Rover track through the bush and up the ridge to the site. Later the transport section is going to make the track into a road capable of taking trucks and heavy vehicles. Then the Posts and Tels building section will construct a repeater station at the top."

The old man chuckles. "Sounds good for business," he says, looking around the bar and lounge. "Christ knows I could do with it. Nobody much stays here these days, only you boys on safari. The upcountry folks mostly stop at Mac's Inn in Tsavo, and then go on to the coast. Sometimes the locals from the DWA plantations come into the bar for a chat. And occasionally John Hunter, the game warden from Makindu, comes along when he gets lonely."

As I sign the register, I notice the name, M. Gregory, in the book. "I see that Mac's got here," I say. "Did he leave any messages for me?"

"Oh, aye. I almost forgot. That's the worst of old age, lad. Mac's gone to see the D.O. in Makindu, and will be back later this afternoon."

***

Katumo has gone off, probably to stay with friends close by, and no doubt saving his safari allowance. All our drivers get an allowance to offset the cost of food and lodging on safari. When we're not under canvas, they either get cheap accommodation in the servants' quarters at the hotels, or stay with friends and relatives in the vicinity.

The facilities at Pearson's are very basic. I've booked into the room next to Mac's in one of the *bandas* near the main building. The bathroom is a separate building with a large water tank on the roof. The water is pumped up into the tank from the borehole. It's nearly five o'clock and I'm bathed and refreshed, when I hear Mac's ancient Ford station wagon draw up.

Wandering outside, I greet Mac; then the two of us walk back to the lounge. Over coffee we talk about his meeting with the District Officer. "Aye." he says, "We'll leave early tomorrow morning for Mbwinzau to check the route up the back of the range." Outlining his plans, he continues, "It starts off on higher ground where the slope up to the ridge is not so steep as it is on the south side." Mac pauses, his face is thoughtful. "We'll go in the Land Rover, and take your driver. He's a Mkamba, isn't he?"

"Yes, from Machakos," I say. "Katumo will be useful as an interpreter. He's been here with us before, and knows the local people."

Figure 30. Mr. Pearson looks on as labourers skin a gazelle shot near Makindu.

"That's good," Mac says, nodding his head. "We'll also take the *neopara* and the two workmen to help mark the track with *pangas*. It'll be a bit of a squeeze, but there's enough room for them in the Land Rover. I'll leave Unwa and the station wagon here."

We continue talking as we discuss the proposed route using a large-scale survey map with its detailed contours. Mac has marked a possible route, but we'll have to inspect it in case there are any unforeseen problems.

Folding the map, Mac puts it back in his briefcase, and says, "I'll be returning to Nairobi tomorrow after we've confirmed the route. I'll leave the rest to you. You can handle the *barazas* with Chief Jeremiah Miu and all the labour arrangements. The D.O. will provide an *askari* to take you to the chief's village." Grinning, he adds, "But you're used to that; you've done it all before. You can make your own terms, but keep within the department guidelines. I suppose you've brought your rifle?"

"Yeah," I say. "There's a game hunting area between the Chyulus and the Mombasa Road and the Tsavo National Park in the east. I've got an advantage over the DWA plantations. They pay a shilling a day to their workers, but in addition to the money, I provide the men with fresh meat two or three times a week. That should be incentive enough to attract a hundred *watu* (men) to work for us."

Mac laughs, "Christ, I remember all that meat you shot in the Olambwe Valley. The base camp looked like a bloody butcher shop." With a twinkle in his eyes, he pauses for effect, and then says, "Yeah, it was your fault that I had to have all my teeth pulled when I got back from Gemba. You, and your bloody game meat."

"Ah, come on Mac," I say, "you know that was pyorrhoea poisoning. My dad had the same thing."

Mac grins, "Not on your life, Mumford. 'Twas your bloody meat!"

✳✳✳

The rhythmic thump of the motor generator no longer disturbs the night. Old man Pearson's shut down the generator at 10:30 when the last guest vacated the bar. The silence is broken only by the high pitched hum and whine of crickets, and the occasional squeal from some small animal as it falls victim to a prowling predator, probably a dik-dik killed by a leopard or some other nocturnal animal. It brings back the memory of the leopard that had tracked me one night up to the site from the base camp. *Yes*, I think, *Mbwinzau is noted for its leopards*.

There's no ceiling to the *banda*, only rough-cut poles that support the thatched roof. Above me, a gecko slithers in the steep thatch, as I lie awake beneath the mosquito net, turning over the day's events in my mind.

Tomorrow after Mac leaves, I'll see John Hunter and let him know I'm hunting in his area. John Hunter is well known in the Kenya hunting community, and ranks as one of the old white hunters. I am eager to meet him, and wonder what he looks like.

Drifting between sleep and waking, my thoughts wander in a twilight world. Seen through my mosquito net, the moonlight shining through the window is dim. It shrouds the room with a diffused light, hiding the rafters in deep shadows. I see the beaches of Europe, and Joan with me on Capri. Then, I remember the look on Joan's face when she sees Billy waiting for us in Nairobi airport. I fall into a troubled sleep.

Marking the Land Rover Route up Mbwinzau

It was early when we left Makindu, and Mbwinzau was just a distant dark hump on the eastern horizon. Now it's eight-thirty, and the peak looms up ahead of us, thrusting two thousand feet above the flat plain. We've crossed to the north side of the Nairobi-Mombasa railroad tracks and are racing along beside the steep southern face of the ridge. Plainly visible, our former survey site is located high above us on a massive rock embedded deep into the ridge. As the Land Rover sweeps round the left-hand bend to climb over the eastern end of the range, its engine strains under the load of six men. The dirt road winds up the steep grades through thickening bush and forest, and then levels out as the Land Rover crests the rising land.

"Aye," says Mac, as the bush thins. "It's about here that Unwa and I got in behind Mbwinzau with the station wagon. Keep an eye out for an opening."

Slowing the Land Rover down, I can see an old path in the bush. "This'll do." I say, as I swing the steering wheel to the left. "Hold on; we're going *bundu* bashing."

As we turn off the road to the north, the Land Rover takes the soft soil ridge on the side of the road with ease. Picking our way across level land through bush and grass, we work our way round the back of the ridge in a sweeping half circle, until thick bush and rocks block our path. We've driven in about half a mile or so from the main road, and are two or three miles west of the village of Kibwezi.

Switching off the ignition, I get out to join Mac who is already scanning the slopes with his binoculars. "This should do," he says. "It's probably about as far as we can get in with the Land Rover. We'll leave Katumo to look after the vehicle." Turning, he calls to the *neopara* and the two labourers, who scramble out of the Land Rover and join us.

The range curves in an arc from the southeast to the northwest with the highest peak at the northern end. The bush is thick, and thorn trees are plentiful in the tangled undergrowth. Mac, the *neopara*, and I walk slowly forward, followed by the workers who blaze the trees with *pangas* to mark the way. Our immediate target is a gently sloping ridge, which angles in towards the main crest of the mountain, meeting it about half way to the top. Reaching a rocky outcrop on the lower edge, we stop to rest.

"Aye," says Mac, as we sit there and look back. "There are two or three dried-up *dongas* (riverbeds) that will need culverts, but there are no real problems so far. However, from this point to the top, it'll be tough going."

Near the top, a deep fissure in the ridge on the north side of the rock forces us to cross to the southern face. We pause for a moment to look down to where the Mombasa Road winds along the base of the range. To our right, the massive rock where we had carried out the survey tests straddles the ridge. Our proposed destination for the radio repeater station is on the opposite side of this rock, and farther up.

"It looks like we'll have to work our way along the frontal slope, Mac," I say, as we contemplate our next move. "There's a bit of a shoulder at the bottom of the rock, and the trees are holding the slope. It seems like that's the only way. We'll have to dig into the incline and throw out earth until we get to the cleft that we used last year."

Mac nods. "Yeah, that's what I was thinking. Let's have a look at it."

The vertical rock slab towers above us as we push through the bush and crumbly volcanic rock, until finally we break out into the open on the far side of the rock. Scrambling into the cleft, we are confronted by large boulders and loose shale, mixed with rock and earth. The path that we'd cut through here last year is now overgrown.

Using the tangled branches of a tree as a support, Mac climbs up the rock, while I follow close behind his lithe form. The back of his khaki shirt is soaked in sweat and now, disturbed by our passage through the bush, clouds of tiny sweat bees hover around our heads and irritate our eyes. Hauling our bodies up and over the edge of the rock slab, we stand on our old site. The flat barren surface brings back memories, and I smile when I see the cactus on the far edge. Clinging precariously to a narrow, earth-filled crack in the rock, it is still growing although it is no longer flowering.

The sun is high in the sky. We sit there, admiring the view of the game plains below and the distant rain forests covering the top of the Chyulu Hills. The long range of hills stretches from the Tsavo National Park in the east to the Nyiri Desert between Emali and Kiboko Drift.

Squinting up at the sun, Mac smiles. "We've done well, Mumford," he says. "That just about wraps it up. The rock in the cleft shouldn't be a problem and will provide a good base for the steel tower and radio station." He gets to his feet. "Let's go. I want to get back to Nairobi tonight. There's a meeting in the office tomorrow morning. Meanwhile, you can arrange to get men from the chief, and start on the road."

As we make our way back to the Land Rover, we re-check some points in the marked route. It's three o'clock when we reach the rest house, and, after settling his bill, Mac leaves. Pearson is standing by my side as I watch Mac go. The Ford station wagon moves down the drive, turns left onto the main road, and disappears in a dust cloud.

I turn and smile at the older man, "Another customer gone; it's just you and me tonight."

"Ah, he'll be back," Pearson says. "Safari types come and go." He looks at me and adds, "Aye, lad, when I was your age I worked for the Harbour Authorities in Mombasa as a diver. That was the life! 'Twas in the days when diving suits had those bloody metal helmets, and air was pumped down a hosepipe. After I gave that up, I went hunting in Uganda for a few years, before my missus and I started this business."

As we talk, I ask him where I can find John Hunter, the game warden. "Better than that, lad," he says. "My *shamba* boy can show you. Hunter has an office in the government *boma* on the outskirts of Makindu. It's not far, maybe half a mile."

John Hunter, the Game Warden

"Aye," says John Hunter, a burly man in his late fifties or early sixties, as he sits back in his office chair and pauses to light his pipe. "I've heard about your survey team and have met Mac Gregory." The soft Scots accent is reassuring and puts me at ease. He is one of the old white hunters of East Africa. He had been involved in the rhino culling operations that opened the Kitui area for African resettlement when he was a game control officer, as well as with many other projects and safaris before the war. "Weren't you up on Mbwinzau last year?" he adds. "I seem to remember there was a radio survey team testing there,"

"Yes" I say, "I've been up Mbwinzau several times. We want to build a Land Rover track to the site. Eventually we'll put a radio repeater station there."

Pausing for a moment, I add. "I've arranged a *baraza* with Chief Jeremiah Miu and the village elders tomorrow, and hope to employ a hundred local labourers on the road. As an incentive, I'd like to shoot game meat once or twice a week on my license. I understand that the Chyulu plains are open to hunting, but wanted to check with you first."

John nods, and takes the proffered permit. "That's no problem," he says as he glances at it and hands it back. "The office likes to keep us informed of hunters in the district. This is a general license that entitles you to shoot a variety of game; however, the Nairobi office will have told you that when they issued it."

A slight breeze from the overhead fan disturbs his greying hair, and, as he instinctively smooths it with his hand, he asks, "A hundred labourers?" He smiles, "The chief's going to like that, especially the meat. How long do you expect it will take to make the track?

"About three weeks," I reply, "though I hope to get a rough track to the top in sixteen days. After that, I'll have to put culverts in the *dongas*, so three weeks is a fair estimate. I plan to pay the men a shilling a day, plus game meat. I've a truck full of road building equipment at the rest house. We're tackling the road from the north side up to the ridge, because it's not so steep that way. Mac Gregory and I walked over the route this morning, and blazed trees to mark it."

"Look, it's getting near sundowner time," John says as he stands up. "How about coming to my house for a beer. I'm interested in the work you're doing, and I understand from the D.O. that you're putting repeaters on mountaintops from Uganda to the coast and on down into Tanganyika. Is that correct?"

The sun is setting over the Machakos range as I get up and follow him outside. "Yes," I say. "That's right. The emergency derailed our schedule a bit, but we're getting back on track now."

✳✳✳

There's a slight breeze, and it's pleasant sitting on the veranda where John has left me. As I sip from the glass of cold beer, I glance around at my surroundings. The house, a ranch-style bungalow, has been raised up off the ground on concrete columns about four feet high for coolness. It has a steep, thatched roof, and I can see the rafters above from where I sit. The veranda furniture has been made locally from interwoven, pliable boughs, using wooden boards, probably from packing crates, for the seats and table top. The rustic furniture enhances the informal appearance of the house.

"Sorry about that," says John as he returns. "I had to tell my houseboy something before I forgot it." He laughs, and then adds, "I must be getting old."

As we sit on the veranda, our conversation ranges from the emergency back to John's pet subject, hunting. "Those were the days of Karamoja Bell and John Boyes, King of the Kikuyu, around the turn of the century. I first met Boyes when I was a young lad out from Scotland," he says. Fascinated, I listen to his yarns, which range from tales of game culling operations and marauding elephants in Uganda, to clearing rhino in Kitui to provide areas for native settlements. It is late and night has fallen when I leave John's bungalow. His last words as I go down the veranda steps are, "Aye, lad, hunt on the plains near the Chyulus. You'll get zebra there as well as other game."

Plain but wholesome food is always the order of the day at Pearson's Rest House. The cook's repertoire is limited to meat, potatoes, and vegetables, with rice or a salad appearing occasionally on the menu. Tonight is no different. After dinner, coffee is served in the bar/lounge, but as I'm the only guest tonight I do not linger long, but go to my room. Tomorrow, I'm to see the chief and finalize the labour situation.

The Baraza with Chief Jeremiah Miu

"*Uko, bwana, uko*—there, *bwana*, there!" The *askari* sitting beside me in the Land Rover points to the small track leading off the main Nairobi-Mombasa Road.

"*Ndiyo, naona sasa*—yes, I see it now," I reply. The Land Rover jerks, its bodywork shaking violently, as I slow down to turn off the main road onto the bush track. Katumo clings to the vehicle's open sides as we bounce over the ridge of built-up murram (laterite) soil left on the edge of the road by the scraper. Smiling, I grip the wheel, controlling the wildly bucking vehicle, as we drive along the narrow footpath. "Hang on, Katumo," I yell, enjoying the sensation as the thorny branches, shoved apart by the force of our entry, spring back, scraping the sides of the vehicle.

For a mile, maybe two miles, we follow the track's winding course across the flat, bush-covered plains to the northwest of Mbwinzau. Then the Land Rover emerges from the thinning bush into more open terrain of dried-up grassland. On the edge of the plain, a cluster of round, conical huts merge into a background of trees.

"*Tumefika shamba* —we have reached the chief's village," says the *askari*. There's a sense of relief in his voice as we draw up beside a ten-foot high ant hill close to the open archway in the thorn tree fence encircling the huts.

Surrounded by curious African men, women and children, with a few pi-dogs yapping at our heels, we follow the *askari* as he leads the way to the chief's hut at the far end of the village. It is now mid-morning, and the cooking fires have been extinguished; only small piles of grey ash and blackened stones outside the huts mark their existence. By the time we arrive at the chief's hut, the gathering has swollen, and probably includes every man, woman and child.

Forewarned of our presence, Chief Jeremiah Miu stands outside his hut surrounded by the village elders. A short plump man in his late thirties or early forties, he is informally dressed in khaki shorts, shirt, and open sandals. On his head, he wears the traditional District Administration pith helmet with the lion emblem, which distinguishes him from the elders gathered around him. As we approach, the *askari* introduces us.

Barazas are typically, long drawn-out affairs, and I have a feeling this meeting will follow the normal pattern. The elders sit in a semicircle in front of the chief's hut, the traditional meeting place for the village and its council of elders. There is a large shady tree near the hut, and, as the guest of honour, I am given a chair near the chief. He takes his seat in front of his hut, and the meeting can now begin.

As we settle down to business, I address the chief and his elders: "*Mwaka jana* —last year I came here and employed many of your people as porters for the survey site on Mbwinzau. Now I have come again. This time, I am going to make a road up to the site on the ridge of the mountain. The work that I have to offer will bring money for the men and women of the Kibwezi district. I will need a hundred men to work on the road, and I have come to ask you for your help."

Many of the elders and villagers in the village cannot speak Swahili, and the chief gets up from his seat, holding up his hand for silence. Then as a hush falls on the meeting, he speaks to his people in the Wakamba language, telling them about the basic purpose of the repeater station on Mbwinzau, and my request for workers. A murmur surges through the villagers who are waiting and listening in the background as the elders talk amongst themselves.

The discussions about wages are long and drawn out. When each man finishes speaking, the chief translates for my benefit. One elder says, "DWA Plantations pay our young men a shilling a day for work on their sisal plantations. How long do you expect it will take to cut a road up Mbwinzau to the site?"

When I hear the name of the nearby sisal company mentioned, I already know what they're asking. As I listen to the chief's translation, my answer is ready. When the chief sits down, I reply, "The District Officer pays each labourer fifty cents a day. I will pay a shilling a day, the same as the DWA Plantations. In addition, I will shoot game meat twice a week for the workers to eat. I expect the work to take roughly sixteen days, and I will pay cash on the day that the work is finished."

An excited murmur runs through the waiting villagers and the elders as the chief translates my offer. Inwardly, I am smiling because I know that the offer of game meat will be the clincher with the elders and the chief. The meat will be shared out among the men, and brought back into the village. There is some haggling, but my price is firm.

The chief is smiling as he accepts the offer, and a date is settled for the labourers to start work on the road. "Aiyee," he says in Swahili "My people will start work one hour after sunrise the day after tomorrow at your camp."

The *baraza* is over and it is noon when I say goodbye to the chief and his elders, thanking them for their assistance. Accompanied by a small crowd of excited onlookers, we return to the Land Rover and drive down the dusty narrow bush track to the main Mombasa road.

At Makindu, we leave the *askari* at the D.O.'s office. The D.O. is a youngish man, possibly in his late twenties or early thirties. I stop in to let him know the results of the *baraza*. He asks, "Has Mac gone back to Nairobi?"

"Yes, he went yesterday," I say, "soon after we'd marked the route on the northern side of the range. There's a better gradient there for the heavy trucks we'll be using. Mac will be back, so no doubt you'll see him again."

"Yes, I expect so," he says. "There's still the building and towers to be erected, and equipment to be installed before it's complete. Will the repeater operate automatically?"

"For the most part, the repeater station runs itself." I say, explaining the maintenance routine. "There is a warning system that warns the terminal in Nairobi of a problem. The system indicates the type of fault so that the terminal station knows whether to send out a mechanic or a radio technician. Maintenance men will periodically visit the site to service the motor generators and top up the diesel oil in the holding tanks. The equipment is fully duplicated, and the motor generators automatically change over every forty-eight hours."

We talk on a while; then I take my leave and drive back to the rest house with Katumo. I'll be leaving Pearson's tomorrow morning. We've got to get the base camp prepared for the arrival of the labourers on the following day.

Road Construction: the Base Camp

Aye, lad, we'll be seeing you again soon." Old man Pearson smiles as he rings up my account on the cash register, and gives me the receipt. "'Tis lonely up there on Mbwinzau. If you want company, come over one evening for a beer. You've got the Land Rover, and you're only twenty miles away. John Hunter often drops in for a drink."

That was early this morning, and since then we've been busy on Mbwinzau setting up the base camp and getting ready for the workers who will arrive tomorrow morning. Chief Jeremiah Miu has put the call out for men, and they'll be here at first light.

Dusk is falling now, falling swiftly, and on the other side of the clearing, about fifty yards away, cooking fires are burning outside the three tents. Katumo has his own tent, Idi shares the second tent with Karanja, the *neopara*, while Munyao and Mungati, the two labourers, have the pup tent. When the men call out to each other, their voices carry across the clearing, and occasionally I can hear laughter. The sounds, however, are usually indistinct and merge with the night noises of the African bush.

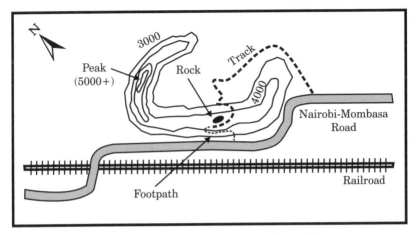

Figure 31. The Land Rover track up to the repeater site on Mbwinzau

Munyao and Mungati will keep the base camp supplied with firewood and water. They can collect deadwood for the campfires from the nearby bush, but the water source is some distance away. They'll fill the forty-four-gallon drums from a spring on the south side of the range, and Idi will bring the water drums back in the truck.

The base camp is submerged in darkness, and the long, high peaked ridge of Mbwinzau is no longer silhouetted against the western sky. The firelight illuminates the area cleared by the labourers this morning. Where the light does not reach, the thick bush seems to press in, and stunted trees and thorn bush are thrust into dark shadows where they assume grotesque and mysterious shapes.

With the coming of night, I light the pressure lamp hanging on the ridgepole of my tent's veranda section. Compared to kerosene lanterns, these lamps provide a far superior light. I still feel the wonder when comparing the lamps because, when I was growing up, the farmhouse where we lived in England had kerosene lamps, and my mother still uses them. I shake my head. *Nothing has changed there since Dad died in 'forty-two. When I left to come to Kenya in early 1949, we still didn't have electricity or flush toilets, although drinking water had been piped across from the adjacent golf course. Somehow, my family is still there, eking out a living.*

In some ways, my life on safari is just as basic. I smile as I look at the cans of steak and peas standing in a pan of boiling water on the Primus stove. "Aye," I mutter to myself, "I'm back on safari." Nothing keeps long in the bush; even bread goes mouldy after two or three days. On safari, we exist mainly on cans of meat and vegetables, occasionally buying potatoes and eggs from the nearest native market or country *duka*. We've no refrigerators; such luxuries belong to Nairobi, the big city.

My dinner's over, and, as I throw another log onto the burning embers, my campfire erupts in sparks. Across the clearing, the labourers and drivers are sitting around their campfire in a close-knit group. Listening to the murmur of their voices, a feeling of loneliness comes over me, but it is momentary. I occupy myself with other thoughts. *How many times have I been alone in the bush? Spread over the years, it must be months!* I smile, a sardonic forced smile.

At least, it's safe here in Wakamba country; there are only lions and elephant. If you don't bother them, they won't bother you. There's no Mau Mau here, thank God, so I can sleep easy at night. Another thought occurs to me. "Yeah," I mutter, "what if I'd been alone on Loldiani Mountain when that *Mau Mau* gang arrived demanding shelter. They'd have murdered me for sure."

As I sit in a camp chair watching the flames, the fire has a soporific effect. *It's either that or the beer!* Before leaving Nairobi, I'd bought several bottles of *Tusker* for my chop box. It's not that I'm a drinker. In fact, I seldom have more than one small bottle in the evening, and often I don't drink at all. Anyway, if I have more than one bottle, I begin to feel detached, the skin on my face feels strange, and I know that I've had enough.

My mind wanders, and new thoughts surface. *Why do we all like Mac Gregory?* I think. *The safari crews almost worship the guy to the point that when we're on safari, we all cultivate small Van Dyke beards, beards like his.* I laugh as another thought occurs to me. *It doesn't extend all that far. We all shave the beards off before we return to Nairobi.*

Unmarried and in his late thirties or early forties, Mac'll go anywhere. There's a strangeness about him, however, an invisible barrier that you can't break through. Rumour has it that during the war he was one of Britain's back room *boffins,* a member of the top echelon of engineers and scientists. He never addresses any of us by our first names, just our surnames—Mumford, Scales, Williams, or whatever. When someone else calls me Mumford, I find it demeaning. That's what the monks did when I was at school. But Mac's an odd one, and we all heed him regardless. He has a trait that makes men follow him. We're "Gregory's boys," an *elite* safari group. At least, that's what we think.

Now, looking across the clearing to where the small group of Africans sits beside their cooking fire, I realize that there's the same instinctive separation between whites and blacks, despite my own feelings. It's the disparity that worries me, the invisible barrier imposed by society. Maybe it's the natural pecking order of all life forms. I like the African men I work with, and I trust them. Since the advent of *Mau Mau*, however, it seems that "respect" for white people (for want of a better word)—or whatever has protected us as a minority and kept us in a privileged position—has worn thin amongst the Africans.

My mother, an ardent communist, would love the comparison. I can almost hear her talking to me. "Aye, love," she'd say, "it's the auld class system. You've got to be born in the upper class to be a part of the elite. It's the old school tie that counts, but that and colonialism will all disappear some day. You know what it feels like to be considered inferior here in England. Well, that should give you an inkling of how the African feels about you. Once the white man loses 'face,' or that facade of nobility, his days are numbered. His 'face' is the only thing that separates him from the Africans; once he loses that with all the pomp and ceremony of the British Crown, then it's all over."

I sigh wearily and get up off my chair and seek my bed. I can't alter the future. There's no doubt that we'll win the war against *Mau Mau* in the military sense, but the seeds of anti-colonialism have been sown. The world is changing, and I know in my heart that we'll have to change too, in order to survive.

Labourers, One Hundred Strong

As promised, the men recruited by Chief Jeremiah Miu come soon after dawn. I wake and dress to the sound of voices outside my tent as the crowd of labourers, accompanied by their wives and families, arrives, their numbers swelling by the minute. There are one hundred men, more if I want, because the wages are good.

"*Aiyee, watu wengi walikuja*—many people have come," Katumo says, his eyes wide with wonder as he surveys the gathering crowd.

"*Ndiyo*, they've heard that I provide *nyama* (meat)," I say with a grin as we stand together outside my tent. In upcountry Swahili—the lingua franca—the word *nyama* means both meat and animals. Swahili is actually a coastal language, and purists laugh at the crude Swahili in common use in other parts of Kenya. It's a bit like Pidgin English that way, but then, each tribe has its own language so it is no reflection on the local people.

Except for a hasty cup of coffee brewed on the Primus, I've foregone breakfast today. The chief has sent his headman and a tribal *askari* to keep order among the crowd of men, women, and children. To them, this is an event. As the lone white person, I am also an object of much curiosity and comment from the gathering.

A *mzungu* has come to the bush and brings work to their people. In this remote area, many of them, particularly the women and children, have never seen a white person before. It's like a holiday, and I am the showpiece.

Another attraction is the fact that I can provide them with fresh meat. The old way of hunting, using spears or bows and poisoned arrows, is a thing of the past. The Game Department now closely controls hunting throughout East Africa. Areas are set aside where animals can be shot under license, while game parks and animal reserves are off-limits to hunters. Hunting is permitted on the Chyulu plains, and is controlled from Makindu by John Hunter and his African game scouts.

There is a continuing war between the game wardens and the poachers, who hunt with dog packs, traps, and sometimes-illegal guns. As a rule, the African population can't get licences for guns or hunting, even if they could afford them. Occasionally, a chief who has been proven trustworthy may get a license and permission to hunt. Other exceptions include the tribal police, regular police *askari*s, and the army, but they don't hunt game.

There is work to be done. As we go about our business, I ignore the stares and the curious, wide-eyed children clinging to their mothers. A table is set up under the shade of the tent veranda, and I take my place there, with the headman sitting beside me.

The excited chatter of the crowd dies down in anticipation as the head man tells the *askari*, "*Mwambia watu yetu* —tell the people to form a line if they want to work for the *mzungu*."

The men, urged by the *askari* armed with a baton, hurriedly line up, and the first man nervously approaches to register.

"*Jina yako*—what's your name?" I ask, looking up at him with a smile, and trying to put him at ease.

"Kalenda, son of Makuna," he replies, glancing nervously at the headman who nods his head slightly. As I print the name in my book, the *askari* grabs the man's hand, extends the thumb, and presses it onto an ink pad. A sigh passes through the watching families as the man's thumbprint is transferred to the book next to his name. He walks away to disappear amongst a small group of relatives who examine his thumb with curiosity, and the next man in line takes his place. Our day has begun.

Over three hours pass before we finish. Each man's name and his thumbprint are recorded in the Miscellaneous Payments book, and the men are organized for work under the directions of Karanja, the *neopara*. Katumo and the headman translate for those tribesmen who cannot speak Swahili or English.

Experienced in roadwork, Karanja knows his job, and the labourers will work under his supervision. Quickly and efficiently, he organizes them into work gangs, and at the same time gains their confidence and cooperation. Satisfied, I stand to one side and watch. "*Okahaha*—come here," he says to the men, grinning, as he intentionally lapses into Kikuyu.

"*Sema Wakamba*—speak Wakamba," the men reply, laughing good-naturedly at his slip of the tongue.

The *neopara*'s grin widens. He can speak the Wakamba language fluently, for is he not a blood brother of the Wakamba? I smile at the exchange because I feel that Karanja has the people with him and they'll work well under his control.

The *neopara* knows our work plan, and, using a system that the men are familiar with, he will create an organized work force. "*Tutafanya kazi sawa sawa desturi yetu*—we will work piecework, as is our custom," Karanja says, addressing the men. "The bwana and I will mark out the track to be cleared each day, and, if you complete the work quickly and satisfactorily, then you can leave early. The normal working hours will be from eight o'clock in the morning, to three-thirty in the afternoon. As agreed with Chief Jeremiah Miu, every third day the bwana will hunt for *nyama* from three-thirty to six o'clock when night falls." Karanja, pauses, then adds with a grin. "I think you will get very fat, but I want you fit for work in the morning."

An excited murmur runs through the labourers and their families as they talk excitedly amongst themselves. Then there is silence as Karanja holds up his arm and makes a final point. "The bwana will want men to come with him in the truck to fetch back the meat on the day of the hunt." He looks around at the expectant faces, and says, "I don't think that will be a problem!" He smiles at the response from the crowd.

Turning to the men, the *neopara* then arranges them into work gangs, picking the strongest for the advance group who will clear the trees and thick bush with axes and *pangas*. A second group will follow them to clear the undergrowth and stumps with *pangas* and *jembes*—hoes. The next group of labourers will level and fill in the ground, using *karais* (large metal bowls) to carry the stones and earth. These bowls are balanced on their heads using a ring made from grass to protect the scalp. Periodically, culverts will be installed where the road alignment goes through streambeds to ensure that the road is not flooded in the rainy season.

✳✳✳

The quiet serenity of Mbwinzau echoes with the sound of axes biting into trees and the bustle and shouts of labourers who periodically burst into song as they perform their tasks. The first day has gone fast; the initial targets set down the previous day by Karanja and I have been accomplished. With the last workman disappearing into the bush, we go back over the track and plan the next day's piecework. The routine has been established, and now, as Karanja and I walk through the bush, we talk of the road and the people.

Like so many of the Africans employed by the post office, Karanja is an ex-army man. I like his frank, engaging manner and ready smile. "*Ndiyo*," he says, "I was a driver for a transport unit in North Africa, and later became a sergeant. After the war, I left to join the government." He smiles, his small, military-style moustache twitching as he speaks. "I was with the PWD—that's where I learned about road building— before coming into the building section of the post office. Now I'm here with my brothers, the Wakamba. It's a peaceful part of the country."

We continue to talk while we mark out the sections to be done the next day, and then wander back to the base camp. It is dusk by the time we get back, and the cooking fires are already alight. I'm hungry because I have not eaten all day.

The *neopara* has gone to his tent. I can see him and Idi moving around their cooking fire as they talk. I wonder whether Karanja is a Muslim; I know that Idi is, although I don't know what sect he belongs to. It's not that it really matters. As for myself, maybe I'm a pagan, or rather, just an agnostic. After experiencing war, there are many men like me, who have lost faith in religion, but then that's another story.

✳✳✳

Stripped to the waist with beads of sweat running off me, I work with the gangs, especially the lead work gang, toiling shoulder to shoulder in the broiling heat. I like the satisfying thud of an axe biting into a tree or the slash of a panga attacking some unfortunate bush. The Africans think I'm crazy. Maybe I am a bit, but I feel restless.

"Why do you work like an African?" they ask.

I laugh as I reply, "*Sababu napenda kazi namna hii*—because I like this work."

They shake their heads in disbelief. "Ah, bwana, we think your head is crazy."

I smile, but there is method in my madness. When I work with the men, it encourages them to greater efforts. They are competing with the bwana, because he is working like one of them.

Snakes, Bloody Snakes!

"*Nyoka* (snake)!" Echoing across the bush, the cry comes from the forward gang.

Hearing it, I hurry to the scene, swearing as I go, "Snakes, bloody snakes!"

We've hit a series of python nests on this, the third day of work on the track. Up until now, progress had been good, and we've cleared a half-mile of track through the bush. Now, we're encountering broken rock and thick thorn bush, an ideal location for reptiles. They nest in the undergrowth and in the rocks and crevices hidden by the thick tangled scrub.

I hate killing snakes. Most of them are harmless, even the python. Only ten percent of African snakes are poisonous, but most Africans, in common with many other people, are scared of them. You can't really blame them. After all, some of the deadliest snakes resemble harmless ones. It's difficult to tell the difference between the green tree snake and the green mamba, for example, when the main difference may be only the number of scales in a row. *Who has time to count the scales when they encounter a snake?*

"*Ah, bwana, nangopa nyoka* —I am afraid of the snake. He will eat me."

I glance around. It is the labourer whose panga uncovered the nest. "*Lakini, nyoka hii kidogo* —but the snake is small. It can't hurt you; because it is a constrictor." I say, "It squeezes its victim to death."

The man is not convinced. "Perhaps its mother is near, and she could be big," he says.

Unable to convince the labourers, there is no other course of action. I shoot one of the larger, slow moving snakes with my revolver. The shot blows its head off, and attracts the attention of the other work gangs. The men come running to see what all the fuss is about. Belatedly I realize that not only is shooting the snake a waste of good bullets, but it is also neither an efficient nor an economical method of solving the problem. I take up my *panga*, and, along with some more courageous labourers, attack the rest of the snakes, hacking them to pieces. The work is distasteful to me, but it has to be done because the labourers are afraid of any snake, poisonous or not.

As we view the mangled remains, the local men tell me that there is a thirty-foot python near the small spring on the other side of the ridge. "Ah, bwana," they say, "*nyoka uko inaweza kufa ngombe* —that snake can kill our cattle, so what can it do to a man?"

I shrug my shoulders and grin. "Well, maybe you're right. We have now killed all the ones here, so it is all over." I grab an axe and savagely sink it deep into a nearby tree." Having vented my frustrations on the stunted tree obstructing the road, I laugh as I call out to them, "*Iko kazi kufanya*—there is work to be done." The men laugh and join me. Swinging our axes and *pangas* with renewed vigour, we make the bush fall before our renewed onslaught.

✳✳✳

Chapter 8
Of Medicine and Meat

Bush Doctor

"*Bwana, bwana,*" It's Katumo's voice calling me. When I turn, I see Katumo assisting one of the labourers. The man is stumbling along with his face drawn and his right hand clutching his left hand, holding it to his mouth.

"*Nini alifanya*—what has he done, Katumo?" I ask anxiously as I hurry forward.

"*Nyoka, bwana*—snake, bwana, a bad snake," he replies.

Together we support the man between us as we hurry him into the tent. "*Nitajaribu dawa yangu*—I will try my medicine, but get the Land Rover ready, Katumo. You'll have to take him into the Makindu clinic. Take one of his friends with him."

While Katumo goes to get the Land Rover, I open our first aid box, and, as I search for the Fitzsimmons snakebite kit, I ask, "what sort of snake bit you?"

"*Sijui, bwana*—I don't know, but it was long and black. My hand hurts, and I've tried sucking at the wound."

Hurriedly, I wash the two puncture points where the snake's fangs struck his hand, slash the wound with a razor to draw a little blood, and then rub some permanganate of potash into the wound. "I cannot give you an injection because I do not know what type of snake bit you. Do you understand?"

The labourer nods, and I tie a small rope tourniquet around the arm. Katumo comes into the tent at that moment accompanied by the man's friend. Turning to them, I ask the friend to keep the tourniquet tight, but loosen it every few minutes so that the blood can flow. Within minutes the three of them are on their way, heading for the Makindu African clinic.

After putting the first aid things away, I wander back up the road past the gangs to where Karanja is working. I can do no more for the man. He's lucky that I carry permanganate of potash. That's the standard treatment for snakebite, and it should be effective for a few hours, sufficient time to get him to the clinic. From his description, the snake was certainly not a python.

The news of my medicine has spread around the neighbourhood, and I'm soon inundated with patients. Now I'm running a bush clinic, treating not just the cuts and wounds of my work crews, but the ailments of their wives and children. I feel a fraud because I have only a basic assortment of ointments, aspirin, bandages, and adhesive tape, in addition to the snakebite kit. I've talked it over with Karanja, and decide that I'll spend the first two hours of each day looking after the first aid box. I'll have to ask Katumo to get the Makindu clinic to help me out with medication next time he's there. If there are any difficult cases, I'll have Katumo drive them to the clinic.

The majority of ailments can be treated with my basic medical supplies, but some of the people lining up from the nearby villages are beyond my help. One day, an old man hobbles into camp. His matchstick thin legs are so badly ulcerated that the flesh is nearly wasted off the leg itself. "Can you help me?" the old man says, "*Mguu yangu mbaya—* my leg is bad."

The sight of his leg makes me nauseous. Wasted away and severely ulcerated, it is plastered with an obnoxious looking mixture of greenish brown dried-up paste. "*Hii dawa nini—*what is that ointment, *mzee*?" I ask him. Addressing him as *mzee—*elder or old man is a sign of respect.

"Ah," he says, "the witch doctor put it on. It's cow dung. He said it would help, but the leg has not healed."

Shaking my head, I say, "I am sorry, but I don't have medicine or ointment that will help you. I can have Katumo drive you to the clinic in Makindu.

"No," he says in Swahili, alarm in his voice, "No, if I go there, I will die." He turns away and hobbles off into the bush, back to his *mchawi* (witch doctor).

Helplessly, I shrug my shoulders. *What can I do?* Some of these cases are hopeless, and often native superstitions compound the medical problems. On the other hand, I have heard that cow dung is a good poultice and does draw out inflammation.

Then, a man brings in a young woman with her baby. "*Bwana,*" he says, "*Unaweza kusaidia—*can you help my wife's child?"

"*Nitajaribu*—I will try," I answer as I look at the young woman. "What has happened to the child?"

"She burned her heel," he says, as he beckons the woman forward. She is holding a young girl, about two or three years old, in her arms.

When she sees me, the child bursts into screams and buries her face in her mother's neck. I'm at a loss, and look quizzically at the man.

"The child is frightened of you," he says. "She thinks you are a strange animal, because she has never seen a white man before."

When the child calms down, she lets me look at her foot. With Katumo translating, they explain that the child's heel had been burned when she stepped onto hot, molten glass on the edge of the cooking fire that morning. The wound is beyond my abilities to treat, so the Land Rover is once more used as an ambulance to transport the child and her family to the Makindu clinic.

Game Hunting for the Pot

It's Sunday evening, September 13, 1953. Seated at the table under the tent veranda, I'm pouring over my camp diary and writing the departmental reports. The flickering light from the campfire is comforting, and, when I come to the end of the post office reports, I lean back in my chair. Relaxed, I watch the winking lights of fireflies that dart erratically in and out of the shadows cast by the pressure lamp. Only the game record remains to be done.

Yes, I think, *we did well today: two large impala*. There will be feasting and dancing in the bush villages tonight, with plenty of *pombe* (native beer). I can hear the drums beating in the distance; sound travels far in the African *bundu* (countryside). Already they are celebrating in the distant native *bomas*, where each large family unit is secure behind the ring of thorn bush hedges protecting their huts from wild animals.

We got back about three hours ago, just before sundown. As the huntsman, I've been given the choicest piece of meat, the loin, as my reward. Tonight, I barbecued it over the campfire. I plugged it with some bacon to take away the gamy taste, and it tasted good. I've put some of the cooked meat into the portable screened kitchen cupboard for tomorrow. I'm not sure whether the meat will keep, but at least the cupboard will keep the flies and ants away.

Returning to the paper work, I record the two *impala*, and then look back through the record. My hunting license sets limits for some species, but the allowance for common plains animals is large because the bush is teeming with game. *Aye*, I think, as I total them up, *I've been here roughly two weeks now, and I've hunted about four times, shooting eight animals, mainly Thomson gazelle and impala. The meat has been shared out among one hundred labourers and their families.* I straighten up in my chair and yawn, satisfied because I really don't want to kill too many animals. True, I like to hunt, but I don't do it for sport; I hunt to feed my workers.

Closing my record book, I wander over and sit by the fire. It's pleasant out here in the bush listening to the sounds of the night. I guess I'm a loner and a wanderer; the mountains and plains of East Africa and its varied tribes fascinate me.

My thoughts go back to an incident last Thursday. For some reason there were only three men, instead of the half dozen who normally accompany me. I left them in the truck with Idi near a small *koppie* (hillock) while I hunted in an area north of the base camp. This area was new to me, and I moved cautiously through the bush, periodically checking my direction with the compass and the sun, which was still high in the sky.

Stepping into a small clearing, I came face to face with an impala. For a split second the animal stood stock still, frozen, its muscles tensed, its head up with the horns flattening on its back, then it leapt away into the surrounding bush. There was no time to aim; I just pointed and fired. The heavy bullet struck its left shoulder, catching the animal in mid leap. As the impala lay writhing on the ground, I quickly dispatched it with a second bullet. Angry with myself, I shook my head. I prefer to kill quickly with the first shot; it's not wasting a bullet that annoys me, but the needless suffering.

As I waited beside the impala, I could hear the sound of bodies crashing through the bush and shouts of *"Bwana, bwana."* Answering their calls, I led them to my position. *"Kuja, kuja hapa*—come, come here, I am here, and there is meat."

"Aiyee, bwana," said the first labourer as he reached me, his face sweating from running in the bush, *"Umepata swara*—you have shot a large animal."

"Yes, an impala," I replied.

Wasting no time, the men quickly butchered the animal, cutting it into pieces, gutting it, and washing the intestines in the small pool of water. Curious, I sat there with my rifle across my knees, watching them go about their work. I was surprised when one man asked for matches. Shaking my head, I said, "I am sorry, but I don't have any."

"Haizuru, hakuna tabu—it doesn't matter," he said. Then, to my surprise, the three men ate the intestines raw. They grinned at my astonishment, and offered me some.

Thanking them, I declined the offer. "You must be hungry," I said.

Eating with obvious enjoyment, they nodded, *"Ndiyo, njaa sana—*

yes, very hungry." Then, their hasty meal finished, the men shouldered their loads of meat. As they marched through the bush in single file, I followed them back to the truck.

It was not eating the intestines raw that surprised me, but their request for matches. To me, it illustrated the impact of the modern world on primitive tribes. When I was in the NFD, the Africans there would light fires using a small crossbow to rotate a rod in a stone bowl filled with dry tinder. The old ways are rapidly being lost, and life is changing.

When we returned to the truck, Idi was waiting. Seeing that the animal's throat had been cut and the blood drained, he smiled. The Muslim ritual had been carried out, and he could eat the meat.

✳✳✳

Later that evening, I cleaned my rifle and checked the ammunition. Nowadays, I use soft-nosed, standard, lead-tipped bullets, which fragment when they hit, killing quickly. Unless they hit a vital organ, steel-headed bullets just pass right through, leaving the injured animal to suffer.

About a year ago, I was hunting on the north side of the Kavirondo Gulf when I shot a reedbuck. At the time, I didn't realize that the bullets I was using had steel tips. Although I shot three bullets into the animal, they simply whistled right through it. Badly wounded, the reedbuck lay on the ground, kicking wildly. As I was running out of ammunition, I had to use my hunting knife to finish it off. I got behind the animal and sprang at it, trying to stab it in the heart or cut its throat, then leaping away quickly to avoid its sharp hoofs. That's an experience I don't want to repeat, and I vowed I would never use steel-tipped bullets again.

The Track: Sixteen Days to the Top

We've completed the rough alignment of the track in just sixteen days, well within schedule, and Katumo and I have just driven the Land Rover to the top of the ridge. Now, standing under the large rock that formed our repeater test site, I feel a sense of achievement. A thousand feet below us, the cliff face runs sharply down to where the thin thread of the Mombasa Road snakes its way eastward across the game plains to Tsavo and into the rugged, lava surface of the Kibwezi area with its thick bush and stunted forests. To the north are the Yatta Plateau and the wilderness, bush, scrub and desert of the NFD.

"*Aiyee, bwana, tumefika juu*—we have reached the top," Katumo says, his soft voice reflecting an undercurrent of satisfaction. Like me, he has been working on Mbwinzau over a long period of time, and besides, it is also his tribal land.

There's still a lot to be done here, so we'll be working on Mbwinzau for a while yet, I think as I look back on the last sixteen days. The curves and bends in the track will have to be dug in and widened, culverts and drainage put in, and the track surface levelled.

Turning, I watch the work gangs, chanting as they haul away the rocks in the turning circle. The rock has to be broken up with sledgehammers and crowbars. Some rocks are difficult to smash, and we resort to the age-old method of building a bonfire on the rock surface, then dousing it with cold water. The sudden temperature change cracks the rock, and makes it easier to break.

"Yeah," I say to Karanja, the neopara. "We need a qualified blaster and explosives to split the rock."

"*Ndiyo*, bwana," he says. "Our building section has a man like that. Perhaps they will help!"

I smile and nod, "*Ndiyo, najua*—yes, I know, but our job is just to prove that the track is feasible. After we've done that, then the building section will take over. They will blast the foundations and any hard rock that we can't handle." I pause, gazing with unseeing eyes at the workers who are clearing the rubble and soft crumbling rocks, my thoughts elsewhere. "No," I say, "They won't send someone to blast out that rock just yet. We'll have to haul it out by hand, and break it with sledgehammers."

The sound of a shovel striking harder rock brings my thoughts back to the present, and I turn to Katumo. "Well," I say, "this won't do, Katumo. There's work to be done. Take our Land Rover below now. I'll stay here and help the *neopara* and the men to clear the rocks." Katumo nods and drives off in the Land Rover while I hang my bush jacket on a nearby bush and, sledgehammer in my hand, prepare to join the group of labourers.

As I stand in the cleft, I look up at the edge of the huge slab of rock lying across the ridge on the east side, about thirty feet above me. In the past, we had used the cleft to access the ridge, and had set up the survey tents on the top of the slab. Because I've seen the blueprints, I know what the future plans for this site are, and can visualize the work to be done. There is going to be a building erected on the west side of the huge rock to house the equipment and generators, and to provide overnight accommodation for any technician who comes to do maintenance.

It's going to be a big job, I think, *just hacking out enough room for that building and for a turning circle for trucks. The most that we can do is remove the loose boulders and mark out the area. It will then be up to the building section to level the site. Once that is done, a rigging crew will erect a hundred-foot mast. The mast will tower roughly seventy feet above the ridge, giving a clear optical view of the two repeater stations. The large antenna arrays on the mast will be aimed at the repeater site on Vuria to the east and the one on Kitindini to the west.*

Visitors from Headquarters

It's mid-afternoon the next day when we start widening the area for the turning circle. Like the men working with me, I've discarded my shirt, and the sweat is rolling off me. Chips and rubble fly off the softer rock as we slam our sledgehammers into the stone.

My naked shoulder brushes against the bare skin of the man working next to me, and I grunt in surprise. Our sweat is acidic, and my skin stings from the contact. I move away to give him more room to work, and continue my assault on the rocks.

Above the din of men chanting and steel clashing against stone, I hear someone calling, "Mumford." I recognize the voice, and grin. It's Mac. Turning around, I see Mac standing there, with a small group of men from head office. Laying down my sledgehammer, I pick my way across the rock and rubble to join them.

"Aye," Mac says as I approach. "I knew you'd be here with your men. You're right on target, sixteen days. It's bloody marvellous!" He pauses for a moment, nodding towards Messrs. Proud, Beresford, and Lilley, and says, "Well, you know everybody here."

"Yes," I say, as we shake hands all around. Then we all walk back together to the base camp, stopping periodically to examine the track.

✳✳✳

Over the years, I have worked under all of these men at one time or another. I'd met Lilley soon after I'd arrived in East Africa in 1949. When I transferred from the airport control tower to the NFD safaris, he'd been my boss. Proud is another of our senior engineers. Although I've known him for years, I've not had much personal contact with him. As one of "Gregory's boys," I regard him as just another Nairobi office *wallah*.

Don Beresford is a short, thickset man in his thirties with dark hair. He does freelance photography in his spare time, and is a friend of Karmali, a well-known local photographer. I can still remember the time in 1949 when Don and I carried out a routine inspection of a radio station at Oloitokitok in the foothills of Kilimanjaro. He brought a professional quality movie camera with him, hoping to get close-up photographs of charging rhino, so we returned to Nairobi via the Amboseli Game Reserve.

Our plan was simple. I was to drive the Land Rover close to the rhinos, provoking them to charge, while Don filmed them. As the rhinos charged towards us, I was to sit there, with the engine idling, waiting for Don's last minute signal before driving away. It was nerve-racking. A black rhino weighs well over a ton, and can reach thirty miles an hour in a charge. If the rhinos had hit us, they would have made short work of the vehicle and us. I never did see those pictures. Don and Karmali probably sold the film to some American company.

✳✳✳

"Well, Mumford," Mac says, as they prepare to leave, "it's a viable Land Rover track. It looks like you can cut down on the work force now. I'll send some large concrete pipes for the culverts; you'll have them in a couple of days. Just clean up the top section, get rid of loose rock where you're working, widen the bends that we indicated, and then leave it at that. The building section can take over the road; they have heavy road-laying equipment and men trained to work with explosive charges and blast rock. You should be finished here by the end of the month."

The light is failing as the engineers head back to Pearson's Rest House. The last I see of them is the dim shape of Mac's station wagon disappearing in a cloud of dust churned up by the wheels. As I stand watching, I hear the engine note change as Unwa, Mac's driver, shifts gear when they reach the main road.

Turning, I move back to my tent. The base camp seems strangely empty now that my visitors have departed. The workday, too, is over, and the labourers have left, disappearing into the bush. Karanja, Idi, Katumo, Munyao, and Mungati are seated around their cooking fires on the other side of the clearing. Alone with my thoughts, I light the pressure lamp outside my tent and hang it on the veranda ridgepole. It's time I made my evening meal.

Karanja, an Accident Waiting to Happen

The scream echoes in the rocky defile. Karanja's face is contorted with pain, and his hands are tangled in the thick, sisal rope. Startled, the labourers stop pulling in the midst of their chant. As the rope slackens, the *neopara's* hands are released, and he slumps to the ground, moaning. It has all happened in a split second.

The men had been attempting to move a large boulder, and had looped a heavy rope around it. Some of them pulled on the rope, while Karanja and others pushed the huge rock with their hands. Karanja had begun the chant, "*Aiyee, karamba, sema vuta!*" The twenty men, ten on either side, held the rope taut and tensed their muscles. On the word, *vuta* (pull) they had strained in unison. Somehow, the rope must have slackened momentarily and dropped over Karanja's hands before they began to pull it.

Kneeling beside Karanja, I wrap some cloth around his torn and mangled hands. He is in a state of shock, and can hardly walk. With two men on either side to support him, together we all stumble down the rough track to the base camp.

Seeing us approach, Katumo rushes up. "*Nini alifanya*—what happened?" he asks anxiously, "Is he hurt bad?"

"*Ndiyo*—yes, the rope caught his hand, and the flesh is torn badly. We must get him to the clinic right away, Katumo. Go get the Land Rover."

Clasping his hands tightly in the blood-soaked cloth, Karanja mutters through clenched teeth, "*Inauma sana, bwana*—it hurts very much."

"*Najua*, Karanja." I answer, as I thrust his hands into a bucket of water to clean off some of the dirt and grime. Carefully, I wipe his hands and disinfect the wounds, and then I bandage them and make a temporary sling. The initial shock is wearing off, and feeling is coming back into his hands. His face is drawn and haggard.

"*Ninasikitiki*—I am sorry, Karanja," I say, "but that's all I can do. Katumo will take you to the clinic in Makindu. They may send you to the hospital for X-rays. It's possible that some bones may be broken, and the doctor will have to set them."

Karanja nods, and sighs, "*Shauri ya Mungu*—it's an affair of God, bwana," he says. "If I'm not back today, then Ndutu Kilangu can take my place. He's a local man, but I trust him." He looks up at me and adds. "Katumo knows him."

Katumo comes in while Karanja is speaking. "*Ndiyo, bwana*," he says, "I know the man well. He is a good worker."

The Land Rover accelerates in a whirl of dust. Karanja is sitting beside Katumo, while one of the labourers is in the back of the vehicle. I like Karanja; he's a good man. We'll miss him, but by the look of his injuries, he won't be back today or even next week. He'll probably be sent to hospital in Nairobi. I've got to get back to the work gang, because the work has to go on. *Yes*, I think, *I'll get Ndutu Kilangu to take over from him.*

✳✳✳

Night has fallen, and with dinner over, I've time to relax. What with Karanja's accident and reorganizing the work crew under Ndutu, it's been quite a day. Voices float on the night air from the cooking fires across the clearing. I can see Idi and Katumo, the firelight flickering across their features, absorbed in conversation. Turning away, I am once more immersed in my own thoughts.

The clinic has done all they can for Karanja, and he is being sent back to Nairobi. *Aye*, I mutter to myself, *the train from Mombasa will pass through Makindu about four o'clock tomorrow morning. He'll get into Nairobi about nine o'clock, and then they'll take him to the hospital.*

Shaking my head, I go over the events again. Hauling rocks out of the way is a brute force, manual operation. Usually, we loop a strong, thick rope around the boulder, and then try to shift it by the sheer weight of a large number of people hauling on the rope. Several workers push the boulder, while others use crowbars to get it moving. The main force lies with the large number of men hauling on the rope. Having seen what happened to Karanja, the work crew was a lot more careful this afternoon.

Adding another log to the fire, I stir the embers into flame and watch while the wood is gradually consumed. The scene on the ridge keeps coming back to me. *It's ironic,* I think. *It's 1953, and we're still using manual labour to make a track up a bloody ridge. Imagine what we could do if we had a bulldozer and a few sticks of dynamite!* I have to grin at the thought. *I've never handled dynamite; I'd probably blow myself up. But a bulldozer, now, that's something else again.*

I stretch my arms above my head, and then reach for the coffee cup on the camp table beside me. *Not much chance of me getting a bulldozer.* The building section has them; they're the road construction experts. My job is just to prove that the track is feasible in the cheapest way possible. *Yes,* I think bitterly, *labour is cheap here in the bush and someone was bound to get hurt. It just happened to be Karanja. What's the shilling a day we pay for each labourer compared to the cost of using a bulldozer for a few hours? It might have saved Karanja's hands.*

The Zebra Hunt

It's several days now since the accident. Ndutu has taken over Karanja's duties as foreman, and we work well together. The turning circle at the top of the ridge is rough, but it's adequate to turn the Land Rover around. Now, the site is the responsibility of the post office building section. They've got the equipment to expand the site and to construct a road capable of handling heavy trucks. I've paid off some labourers, but I still have about fifty working here. Mac has sent some large concrete pipes to use for culverts in the *dongas*. The workmen are busy carting stones and soil to build up the road in places, as well as cutting into the curves to widen them.

"*Tunakwenda nyama*—are we going hunting today?" Idi asks. His expression is worried, as if he thinks I've forgotten. When I nod my head, the hint of a smile crosses his face.

"Yes, Idi," I say. "This is the third day. It will probably be our last hunt, because we'll be returning to Nairobi soon. We'll need some labourers to come with us."

Figure 32. Zebra herd, moving off.

Idi nods solemnly, "*Ndiyo, bwana, na fahamu*—I understand." He grins. "There are many men who want to come. They are waiting near the truck now, bwana."

"Okay, Idi," I say, glancing at my watch. "We've two hours before dark. We'll go now."

Idi hurries away to the truck to tell the waiting men, while I fetch my rifle. Opening the breech, I slide five bullets into the magazine. When I step outside my tent, Idi is there in the truck. There are at least fifteen men in the back. *Yes*, I think, *I'll have to shoot something bigger than an impala tonight.*

Then I remember something John Hunter told me. "If you want to shoot zebra," he'd said, "you'll find them in the foothills of the Chyulus. There are large herds there, and it's within easy reach of your camp."

"*Tunakwenda Chyulus*, Idi—we'll go to the Chyulus," I say as I climb into the passenger seat of the cab. "I have heard there are many zebra over there. Go towards Makindu, then turn left into the bush, and head for the foothills."

✳✳✳

The truck is parked on a *koppie* (a small rise in the ground), and I've left Idi and the labourers there. Earlier, I had sighted a zebra herd in a large clearing close to the foothills, and I've been tracking them ever since. Now, I'm about half a mile from the truck, lying on another small, grass-covered *koppie*, with the zebra grazing about one hundred and fifty yards away.

As usual, I'm wearing khaki drill shorts and a bush jacket, and I've had to crawl through the spear grass. The grass has found its way into the top of my leather leggings and army boots, and the small, sharp seeds itch. Every time I try to edge forward, the herd seems to sense that I'm here.

Either through my inexperience or just bad luck, I'm finding it difficult to get a rifle sight on the herd. The short-barrelled Mannlicher-Schroner doesn't have telescopic sights; instead there's an adjustable V-notch back sight and a ball bead front sight on the rifle barrel. Each time I think that I am within rifle range, somehow the zebra have managed to move off.

Cautiously worming my way forward on my belly, I keep downwind from the animals. *There's not much wind blowing, so it can't be my scent that's making them nervous.* Perhaps a wary member of the herd has caught some slight movement. Suddenly they are off again, following a young stallion's leadership.

The Kill, and the Bond between Animals

Frustration gets the better of me. I adjust the rifle sights to a range between one hundred and one hundred and fifty yards. Lying flat on the ground with my elbows digging into the dusty soil, I raise the loaded rifle and carefully aim at the lead stallion. Holding my breath, I gently squeeze the trigger. The stallion seems to somersault in the air, and collapses in a cloud of red dust. At the same time, the rifle slams back into my shoulder with the recoil.

The soft-nosed bullet has hit the stallion a stunning blow in the neck and throat. Somehow, the zebra manages to struggle to its feet, and heads for the shelter of the nearby forest and bush. To my astonishment, as if on a prearranged signal, the herd splits up. Half follow the young stallion, while the remaining animals follow another leader in the opposite direction.

Scrambling to my feet, I run after the herd, reloading the rifle as I move. When I reach the spot where the stallion had been hit, it is obvious from the amount of blood that the animal is mortally wounded, and can't travel far. I set off into the thick bush, moving in the general direction of the fleeing herd, because I want to put the poor creature out of its agony. As I follow the telltale blood drops, I suddenly come upon the remnants of the herd standing in a glade amongst the trees. It is as though they are waiting for me, knowing that I will come.

In all the time that I have hunted game, this is the strangest, most pathetic scene that I have experienced. A mere ten paces away, the stallion stands motionless, waiting. There is pain and expectation in his eyes as he looks at me, his executioner. Beside him, shoulder-to-shoulder, the mare is poised, prepared to die with her mate. Like spectators watching the drama unfold, the balance of the herd are bunched twenty paces back and partly hidden in the bush.

Filled with dismay, I know that I have to put the stallion out of his pain. Slowly, I raise the rifle, take careful aim at the heart, and squeeze the trigger. As the shot rings out in the confined space, there is instantaneous movement. Killed, the stallion slumps to the ground, while the female rears up and flees. The waiting herd springs to life, and crash through the bush as they take flight in fear and panic. The noise of their flight fades, and quiet again takes hold of the forest. Lowering the smoking rifle, I sit on the ground near the lifeless carcass, close to tears.

The sound of approaching voices calling to one another, along with the noise made by my labourers as they run through the bush, awakes me from my reverie. They had been observing the herd from a distant point near the truck. They had seen me shoot, and then follow the zebra into the bush. The sound of the second shot has brought them running, eager for the rewards of the hunt. But for me, it is a hollow victory. The whole episode has been heartbreaking, and I resolve never again to take such a risky shot in the hope of bringing an animal down.

"*Aiyee, bwana, nyama kubwa*—It's a large animal; it's a zebra. Do you want the head as a trophy?" one of the tribesmen asks. He appears to be their leader, as he takes command over the quartering of the animal and distribution of the meat.

Sickened by the whole affair, I shake my head. "No, I don't want the head, but I would like the hide."

Following Muslim tradition, the men slit the animal's throat to let the blood drain out into the ground, and then they skin the animal. The hide is a large one, and they carefully remove it along with any surplus fat, before folding it. One of the men will take the hide to the truck. Next, about ten men cut up the carcass using knives and *pangas*, while the remaining men portion out the loads. Soon the job is done, leaving only a few bones on the bloody grass for the gathering scavengers to pick over. The vultures are already hovering overhead as I join the long line of men staggering back to the truck, laden with meat and the hide.

Realization and Regret

Far from being the proud hunter, I feel dismayed. The stallion, the leader of the herd, is now nothing more than slabs of meat being carried on the backs and shoulders of these men. With my rifle slung over my shoulder, I bring up the rear of our little procession. There is a lump in my throat as I try to rationalize what has happened. I try to tell myself that this is the law of the jungle, that there are always lion and other carnivores lying in wait for the herd, and that many hungry people in the villages will be fed tonight.

Surrounded by the talk and laughter of the excited tribesmen, I reach the truck where Idi is waiting. *"Ah, bwana,"* he says, *"umepata nyama mingi leo*—you have got much meat today, there'll be feasting tonight. The chief will be pleased."

When we reach the base camp, I unroll the skin, and treat it with rock salt, which will protect it until it can be properly cured. The tribesmen have done an excellent job of removing all the surplus fat from the skin. Carefully, I fold the skin, wrap it in a sack, and place it in a carrying box that I have brought out from Nairobi specifically for skins collected from hunting.

Later that evening, the villagers present me with the choicest cut of meat, a large loin steak. I, too, in my way, join in the hunt celebrations, as I cook the meat in a frying pan over the fire, and listen to the distant drums. I've made the local villagers happy and native beer will prolong the dancing long into the night. The steak is cooked and my evening meal is ready when I reach for my last bottle of Tusker. I, too, will celebrate the zebra, but with a pang of regret. I can still see the look in its eyes and that of its mate.

In early October, just over five weeks since we left home, the road is completed and the labourers paid off. Loaded with tools and camping gear, the truck is ready for the return journey. Once more, with Katumo and I leading in the Land Rover, and Idi following in the truck with the two labourers in the back, our small convoy moves out from an abandoned base camp and heads for Nairobi.

Zimmerman and the Zebra Skin

Last night, when I got home from Mbwinzau, I'd checked the zebra skin, and it was still in good condition. Freshly salted and folded, it's now back in the carrying box, and locked in the trunk of the car, ready for transporting to a taxidermist.

Joan had remarked, "It looks a nice skin." Then she'd asked, "Where are you going to get it cured? Are you going back to Zimmerman?" I'd said "yes" at the time, but this morning, in hindsight, it occurred to me that I should ask one of the safari companies for their opinion.

The time's my own, and after reporting back to the office, I wandered down to Kerr and Downey Safari Ltd. in Saddler Street to ask their advice. The receptionist referred me to one of their directors, who recommended Zimmerman highly. "Yes," he said. "Zimmerman's the leading taxidermist here in Nairobi. He does an excellent job with all our clients' skins."

The director was interested in my safari work, and we chatted about the survey project and the zebra skin. Encouraged by his questions, I talked enthusiastically about my hunting experiences and related the story of the zebra hunt. When I finally left his office, he implied that if I wanted to work with them, there was a position for me.

Satisfied with their recommendation, I drove to Zimmerman's smallholding near the Tatu Sisal Estates in Kiambu.

***

Tucked away in the bush, Zimmerman's place is located on a small, side road, a little west of the Thika Road. The taxidermist himself comes out to greet me. He's an older man with white hair and a wizened look about him, but he's still very active. "Ah, *jong*," he says, "You've been here before. You brought a big crocodile skin you wanted to use for a pair of shoes for your wife. That must have been about a year ago, wasn't it?"

Despite my efforts, I can't help grinning a little ruefully. "Yes, that's right; it was a twelve footer." Shaking my head, I continue. "The scales were too large, and the skin was covered with warts. But this time, I've got something better. It's a zebra skin." Lifting the box out of the car, I set it down carefully on the grass.

"Well," Zimmerman says, "let's have a look." He motions to his assistant. "*Fungua sanduku*—open the box, Samuel," he says.

Samuel pries the lid off. As the skin is unwrapped, rock salt falls from the folds. He lays the hide, hair side down, on the grass. Then, crouched down on their haunches, the two men examine the skin while I watch anxiously.

Zimmerman looks up and smiles. "*Ja,*" he says, in a thick Afrikaans accent, "this is good, man." He feels the texture of the skin and smells the hide. "Aye, it's a lovely skin," he says. "Whoever skinned it knew his job. There's no surplus fat or nicks in the skin. Where did you say that you shot it? The Chyulus?"

When I nod in response, Zimmerman turns to Samuel and says, "*Wakamba walifanya*—it was the Wakamba people, your tribe, Samuel, that did this. It is good work."

Pleased at the indirect praise, Samuel grins as he lifts the skin and carries it into the workshop behind the barn.

Zimmerman's set-up is an interesting one, and he employs maybe fifteen or more Africans. His showroom is filled with mounted heads, horns, and rugs, while in the back are piles of hides and large vats of chemicals. As he shows me around, he explains something of the process. "*Ja*, man," he says, "some animals have fur, but antelope and zebra have hair with a hollow shaft. Hair breaks easily, so you can't use these hides on the floor. You've got to hang them on the wall or put them over the back of a chair. We also use a special process because we're not making leather. We need to keep the hair and fur on the hides."

From the showroom, we wander into the yard and watch his men work on a skin for another client. "They're softening up the skin," he says. "It's a boring job, but a necessary one. The softness and flexibility of the finished hide depends on the rubbing and working of saltpetre and alum into the skin."

Pausing briefly, Zimmerman scratches the back of his head, then continues, "*Ja, jong,* your zebra skin will need some scraping, but not too much. Many of the skins that come in still have a lot of residual fat left on them." Then he adds. "There's only one thing that's not right. You should have left the head skin on. The hide is not so valuable without the head."

"Yes," I say, "but at the time, I just didn't think. I had wounded the zebra badly, and had to put it out of its misery. You know, when I tracked it down, the stallion and its mate were standing together, shoulder to shoulder, just waiting for me. I probably could have killed them both, but I didn't. Having to kill the stallion was bad enough; it was all too traumatic. Somehow it seemed like they were devoted to each other, and the female was risking death to stay with her mate to the end. I've never seen anything like that before."

"*Ja,* I've seen it myself," Zimmerman says, "but that was long ago when I was young." As we walk together towards my car, we continue the conversation. When I take my leave, he shakes my hand and says, "It'll be about three weeks or so before I can finish the zebra, but I'll let you know when it's ready."

A Chance to be a White Hunter

It's four-thirty in the afternoon when I pick Joan up outside her office in Harding Street. "Well," she says, as she gets into the car, "I see the box has gone. You got to Zimmerman's then."

"Yeah, it's been quite a day," I say, with a grin. "First, I went to Kerr and Downey because I thought that I might as well get a second opinion on a taxidermist. They reckoned that Zimmerman is the best, both here and internationally. Most of their clients use him." I smile as I think back on my meeting with Zimmerman, and add, "You know, Zimmerman remembered that I'd taken him that crocodile. He even showed me around his workshop."

Joan nods, "When does he think it will be ready?"

"Oh, about three weeks," I say, and pause as I back the car out of the angle park. "But you'll never guess what happened at the safari company office this morning!" Unable to suppress my excitement, I continue, "They offered me a job." Out of the corner of my eye, I see Joan look at me.

"You're joking!" she says.

"No, I'm not. When I asked their advice on taxidermists and curing hides, the counter clerk took me to see one of the company directors. I must have talked to him for at least half an hour. He was very interested in my hunting experiences, and intimated that, if I wanted a change in employment, his company would be interested in taking me on as an apprentice white hunter. He asked me to think it over and let him know."

Joan's face is serious as she says softly, "Are you going to take him up on it?"

It's a loaded question, and one that I've been turning over in my mind all day. Automatically, I drive along Delamere Avenue, and turn right into Saddler Street. "I don't think so," I reply, "but it's nice to be offered a job out of the blue, isn't it! It does a lot for your ego."

"I guess it's a choice of staying with the department, or taking a chance with Kerr and Downey as a white hunter." Joan's face is thoughtful as she continues. "The trouble is that in a few years' time white hunters may be a thing of the past, and then what can you do? I know how much you like safari work and the bush, while I love the city and my job as a legal secretary. It's my life."

She pauses deep in thought, and then continues with a short sardonic laugh, "What happened to that young fellow I married back in 'forty-six," she says. "Life was easier when you were in the Merchant Navy. Of course, we were still in England, and I had my mother and relatives close at hand." Sighing, she looks at the jacaranda trees lining the road as we pass the Norfolk Hotel near the approaches to Ainsworth Bridge.

"We're settled in Nairobi now, and, although you're away on safari, I do have a job and friends here," she continues. "But there's no guarantee where you'll be stationed if you work for a safari company. Also, what are the prospects in the future?"

I keep my eyes firmly on the road ahead as I drive. "Yes, those are all good reasons for not taking up the offer. Granted I like working out in the bush, but any hunting I do there is strictly for the pot. Besides, all my life I've been in radio work, first in the Merchant Navy, and now here as an assistant engineer with the department." Pausing a moment, I turn the problem over in my mind. "It seems silly to throw away all that experience and my qualifications to change course and start all over again."

There is silence in the car, as we both mull over the choices before us. It is a long time since we've talked seriously about our future. We have been treating life as it comes, assuming that it will continue in the same privileged manner that it has in the past.

"Yes," Joan says, breaking the silence. "At least in the technical world, your prospects are brighter. Besides, you're away on safari long enough as it is. We're no longer kids, and I want some home life."

"That's just my point," I say. "Home life is important to me, too. That's one reason why I'm not considering the position seriously. There's also your career to think about, as well as mine. Anyway, the department safaris will be petering out when the radio routes are completed in the next year or so. Then, there'll be mainly maintenance work with just the occasional safari."

Joan nods and smiles. "Yes, we've made our own careers, and it's working out for us."

Tantalizing though the offer had been, I feel a sense of relief. Life is complicated enough and the decision to stay with the department seems the right one. I drive on to Westlands where I take the turn-off to Spring Valley and home.

Night Patrol in Spring Valley

Several days after arriving back off safari, I report to the controller at the Spring Valley Police Station for night patrol duty. "Aye, "he says, "I'm glad you called in. We still need as many men on our roster as possible. The patrols have been so successful that the incidents of arson in Nairobi have been almost eliminated. Crime statistics have dropped dramatically in the residential areas. The patrols are releasing our regular police for duties in reserves like Kariokor, Doonholm Road, and

---

HQ Riverside Drive
& P&T Dept

FORM POLICE 28

COLONY AND PROCTECTORATE OF KENYA

FORM OF APPOINTMENT OF SPECIAL POLICE OFFICER

TO *MUMFORD, J. G. K.* ....

ADDRESS *DAPHTON CT. BOX 5025 N6:* ....
RIVERSIDE DRIVE

You are hereby appointed a Special Police Officer, under section 57 of the Police

Ordinance, 1948, as from the date shown hereunder, until released by the Commissioner of

Police, within the *Kilelishwa* ....Police Station local area.

K.T.M. Holmes.
....
Assistant/Deputy/Commissioner of Police.

Dated at *Nairobi* ....this .... *Twenty Seventh* ...day of

October ....1952.

(To be completed in Duplicate)

Figure 33. Form issued to Special Police Officers (reproduction). These volunteers patrolled residential areas and generally assisted the police.

the Mathari Valley where they're urgently needed to combat oath taking and Mau Mau courts. It's no easy task."

He gives me a list of names in my sector and phone numbers for my contacts. Like the previous patrols that I have been on in Kileleshwa, I've drawn the midnight-to-two patrol. This time, I will have a new partner, John Bullard who lives a short distance away up the valley.

Slightly built, John is an ex-RAF pilot. As we patrol the lanes and side roads in the Spring Valley area, he talks about the bombing campaign by RAF (Royal Air Force) bombers in the Aberdares and Mount Kenya forests. "Aye," he says, "All this bombing of *Mau Mau* hideouts by RAF bombers that we read about in the newspapers is nonsense. They're still using the same old bombing techniques."

"It's a known fact that bombing is notoriously inaccurate; you're lucky if you get within five miles of the target. That's why we started pattern bombing German cities and industrial centres in the last war." After a short pause, he continues, "Most of my settler friends reckon they're killing more elephant and other animals than *Mau Mau*. It would be interesting if they gave known casualty figures, but they don't."

"Yeah," I say, "I've heard that point raised before. I don't think that I've come across anyone on the outlying farms who agrees with the bombing. Today's newspaper said that the *Mau Mau* forces are concentrating on building up their communications networks in the forests. Maybe the bombing is an attempt to disrupt their system, and scare them out of the forests, but I can't really see that working. The report also said that a whole division of British troops is trying to quell the uprising. That's a lot of men."

John nods, "Erskine is really using his brain with his 'villagization' system. He's forcing the bloody Kikuyu to move out of their scattered, smallholdings into protected villages. That's a good idea, because it segregates the African reserves from the forest fighters. He did that when he was the Commander-in-Chief in Malaya. It was very effective in cutting the guerrillas off from both food sources and support from the local people."

As we patrol the area, we continue talking quietly. Sometimes we stop to listen for movement in the bush or along the side lanes, and then speaking in whispers, we move on through the night. It is shortly after two and the end of our shift, when we part company near my apartment in Marlborough Road.

✳✳✳

Chapter 9
The Mombasa Coast

Kwale Repeater Site

It's early November 1953. The blue of the Indian Ocean reflects the cloudless sky in the early morning light as I stand outside the main tent, drinking a cup of coffee. Eric is sitting next to the radio transceiver in the veranda section. He's waiting for a scheduled radio call from Bungy in Vuria in the Teita Mountains, roughly a hundred miles inland to the west.

The Kwale repeater site is located on a hilltop in the Shimba Hills, a sable antelope reserve overlooking Mombasa and the Indian Ocean. We've been here two weeks now, and this is the last day of our radio propagation tests. When we arrived, we were able to drive straight onto the site, so there had been no need to hire porters. I remember saying to Eric, "If all the sites were as easy to get to as this one, it would have made a big difference."

He'd laughed and replied, "Yeah, Nasu Point in Uganda is the only other one."

***

Bungy's voice comes over the radio transceiver. "This will be our last transmission from Vuria," he says. "We've got thirty or forty locals waiting outside for loads to take down to the base camp. Did you get that? Over."

"Yes. Reading you *strength five,*" Eric says into the microphone. "When do you expect to be operational again?"

"Roughly three or four days. We'll leave Vuria this afternoon, and stay the night in Moshi. It's a good day's run down to Tanga via Korogwe, and we'll need another day to set up camp on the old repeater site.

Let's say it'll be Tuesday morning, November 10." Bungy chuckles as he adds, "That should give you and Gord lots of time for swimming in Mombasa."

While Eric has been talking to Bungy, I've been frying eggs and bacon. Now, as we eat breakfast, Eric talks between mouthfuls. "Yes," he says, "there's no reason to stay up here while Bungy and Geoff are moving their site."

The prospect of spending the weekend on the Mombasa beaches is hard to resist. As our eyes meet, we both grin. "You're on, Eric," I say. "We could do with more supplies, and we can leave the Podson in the Mombasa post office yard."

Manor Hotel, Mombasa

Less than two hours later we're on the way. We've disconnected the radio equipment and stored it in the Podson, and left Kamundu to look after the tents and site. Although the ocean is barely five miles from our camp as the crow flies, it's at least twelve miles by road from the site to the T-junction with the coastal road where Jardini and similar coastal resorts dot the palm-fringed beaches. Then it's another six miles north to the Likoni Ferry and Mombasa.

Although it is not readily apparent, Mombasa is actually located on an island that lies at the mouth of a system of creeks on the Kenya coast. On the west (or landward side), the Makupa Causeway links it to the mainland. At Port Tudor on the north side of the island, the Nyali Bridge, built on floating pontoons, spans a shallow creek that leads to the old *dhow* harbour. The deep-water Kilindini harbour lies on the south side of town. Here, a ferry transports vehicles and passengers across the harbour mouth to Likoni.

Eric is driving the Podson, and, when he sees the long line-up of cars and trucks at the Likoni ferry ramp, he swears. Slowing the Podson, he draws up behind the last truck. "To hell with it," he says. "Look at all these bloody trucks and cars. It will take us at least an hour before we can get across."

Shrugging my shoulders in resignation, I reply, "Probably, but it's Saturday and there's holiday traffic coming and going into Mombasa from the coastal hotels." I nod towards the ferry worker. "It looks like he's selecting three or four cars for every two trucks that he chooses for each crossing." After a long wait, we are finally at the head of the line of trucks, and are beckoned forward onto the ramp leading aboard the ferry.

It is almost noon when we finally arrive in downtown Mombasa. We book into the Manor Hotel near the junction of Salim and Kilindini Road, and leave our baggage in our hotel room. Then Eric drives the

Podson into the post office yard just a block or so down Kilindini Road.

"Come on, Gord," he says as he clambers down from the cab. "Let's see if Lew's still here." Glancing at his watch, Eric adds, "We'll have to hurry because they pack up for the weekend about one."

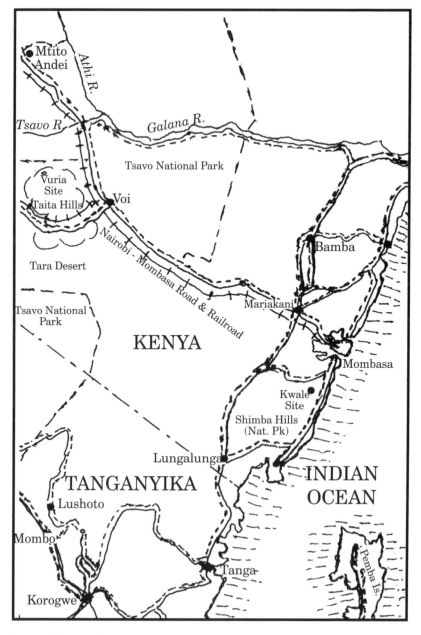

Figure 34. Map of Kenya & Tanganyika, showing Voi, Mombasa, and Tanga.

Lew's in charge of the carrier room, the nerve centre of the Mombasa long-distance backbone telephone routes. Here, local telephone circuits are terminated and fed into the VHF radio terminal equipment for transmission over the radio repeater routes.

As we push open the swing doors, we enter a long, air-conditioned room stacked with equipment racks. In the far corner, we see Lew, seated at his desk and surrounded by filing cabinets. About six foot two inches tall, he is in his early thirties, with a sharp, angular face and brushed back black hair. Lew is known to be a ladies' man, but despite many romantic affairs, he is still single.

Seeing us approach, Lew stands up and comes towards us. "Aye, we thought you two would be dropping in," he says, in a soft Welsh accent.

With a smile on my face, I answer, "Yeah, we just couldn't resist it, Lew."

"Ah, to be sure," he says, grinning. "'Twas the lure of the beach and the sea now. Actually, we heard Eric talking to Bungy about it over the radio this morning. Where are you two staying," he asks.

"Usual place, the Manor Hotel," Eric answers. "It's close to the post office yard and we can park the Podson here. We've got to be back on the Kwale site on Monday to test the Tanga route with Bungy."

Lew glances at his watch, and nods. "We'll be stopping for the weekend shortly," he says. "How about I pick you up at the hotel after lunch, and we'll go off to Nyali Beach for the afternoon?"

Nyali Beach and the Coral Reef

Constructed of wooden trestles supported on floating pontoons, the Nyali Bridge sways under the weight of traffic. Lew's car lurches onto the bridge, and then, reaching the far bank, it shudders as it climbs the potholed, tarred road. At the T-junction, the road to Mtwapa Ferry and Malindi is on our left, while the palm-lined, dirt road to Nyali is on our right.

Lew turns right, and we drive through Nyali, an exclusive white residential area where expatriate government officials and company men live. The driveways are edged with canna lilies, which thrive in the sandy coral soil. However, despite the efforts of the occupants to make lush, green lawns, only clumps of tired, sparse grass survive. Stunted, bright red flamboyant trees, frangipani, and vibrant bougainvillea grow in profusion among the palms in the gardens surrounding the houses.

Near English Point, the road veers away from the creek, and we have a brief glimpse of the old harbour with its picturesque dhows and Fort

Jesus standing guard at the entrance. The road bends and the harbour disappears from sight, as we head north towards the Nyali Beach Hotel.

***

A weird world surrounds me, a watery alien world filled with changing shapes and shadows. Lying motionless, face down in the sea, I breathe through a small snorkel attached to my goggles. Glancing to one side, I see Lew's body, strangely white in the water, as he floats on the surface, arms outstretched and feet slowly kicking. Just below me, the coral glistens in the sunlight that penetrates the shallow depths of the reef. Built up by the skeletal remains of fish over the passage of time, the colour of the coral varies with the growth and vegetation on its rough, grey, serrated surfaces.

The sun feels warm and reassuring on my back as I watch the teeming aquatic life in one of many large pools left behind by the receding tide. Intrigued, I can see the variety of small and large shoals of multicoloured tropical fish swimming in and out of the caves and fissures in the coral. Zebra fish, parrotfish, and angelfish, to name but a few, swim in these waters, while sharks roam the depths outside the reef, looking for prey. The water is crystal clear now, but in April and May, seasonal storms and tides bring in seaweed, making the water pale green, and greatly reduce visibility.

When the tide is low, it can be dangerous to snorkel on the main reef. Then, the full force of the Indian Ocean hits the exposed edge of the reef with a spectacular display of power. The long, ocean rollers dash head foremost against the reef, sending white plumes of spray high into the air, only to fall back in cascades of foam against the backdrop of the blue sky.

Periodically, I lift my head above the surface of the sea to check my position. It is then that I can hear the distant roar of breaking waves pounding and shattering against the edge of the coral reef in the background. Sometimes I try to imagine what it would be like to swim over the reef in these waves, but just the thought of being thrown against the sharp coral makes me shudder and my skin cringe.

Lew and I had waded up to our shoulders in the warm, seawater, sometimes swimming over channels in the coral, to reach the edge of the reef. Then, we turned back to seek safer areas to snorkel. We're both wearing rubber-soled canvas shoes to protect our feet from the razor-sharp coral. This underwater paradise has other hazards besides sharp coral. Sea urchins, which resemble spiky, black balls, can give you a painful sting if you step on one with bare feet. The stonefish, however, is even more deadly; it's a killer if stepped on. Fortunately they are rare, and encounters are few and far between.

Hearing Lew call my name, I lift my head and tread water. "Aye, Gord," he says, "It's time to wander back. Eric will think we've deserted him. Besides, it's nearly sundown, and I could do with a drink."

"Yeah, we've been out here about a couple of hours," I reply. Looking towards the beach, we can just see Eric who is sitting under our beach umbrella, talking to a hotel steward. "It looks like Eric has beaten us to it," I say, "but I doubt that's a soft drink he's ordering." Grinning, I say, "Let's go. It kinda makes you thirsty, doesn't it? Besides, we've also got to return the snorkels and goggles that we rented."

Turning our back on the reef, we start moving towards the shore where palm trees grow along the high water mark. Beyond the beach, we can just make out the red-tiled roofs of the whitewashed buildings, and the surrounding bougainvillea and frangipani. The sight is familiar because Joan and I come regularly to the coast on holiday, and Nyali Beach Hotel is one of Kenya's leading coastal hotels.

As we pick our way through the rough clumps of coral, wet sand and seaweed on the shallow, sloping seabed, Lew echoes my thoughts. "It's a pity Eric has to miss so much because of his leg. I don't see how he could reach the reef over this coral. At low tide, you sometimes have to walk one hundred and fifty to two hundred yards. Maybe he could use a boat to get out to water deep enough for him to swim."

"Yeah," I say. "He can do marvels with that artificial leg, but . . ." I shrug my shoulders leaving the sentence incomplete. "It's not that he can't swim. He's like a fish in water. He prides himself on doing just about anything. When we landed on Sigulu Island, he was with us in the water and reeds as we all struggled to hack out a landing place. The fresh water doesn't seem to harm the steel joints of his leg; but I don't think salt water would do them much good."

The surf's up to our knees as we near the beach, and we hear Eric's voice. "I thought you'd bloody well drowned," he says, putting his book down on the towel beside him. "It's sundowner time." His eyes are hidden behind the dark glasses he wears to ward off the glare of the sun from the dazzling white coral sand.

Sundowner Time

The sun is setting behind the tops of the palm trees and casts long shadows over the beach as we towel off. Wrapping a large bath towel around his waist, Lew changes into his underpants and shorts, then pulls on his shirt. Grinning, he says, "Let's go up on the patio. There's a bar there, and it's more comfortable. It's the weekend, and there'll be the usual Mombasa crowd out for the evening."

Removing his sunglasses, Eric glances at his watch. "Yeah, it'll be dark in half an hour. We might as well make a night of it,"

We move up from the beach, stopping for a moment at the small, *makuti* thatched beach shop to return the goggles and snorkelling

Figure 35. The patio at the Nyali Beach Hotel.

equipment. Then we walk up some concrete steps lined with canna lilies and shrubs to the hotel patio.

Low, whitewashed concrete walls edge the large oval patio and separate it from the beach. The far side of the patio merges into a long semicircular veranda, with wide, red steps between the colonnades. We sit down at a table, and give our orders to the wine steward. Lew nods towards the patio. "The patio is made of polished marble, and they use it for dancing," he says, "The band plays on the veranda. As you can see, the French doors of the dining room all open onto the veranda and dance floor." Pausing, Lew sighs, "Unfortunately, you've got to wear monkey suits in the evenings here, or at least a jacket, shirt and tie."

"That cuts us out," Eric grunts, "we're in safari gear. Got any ideas where we can go in Mombasa that's near the Manor?"

"Aye, but it's a bit of a joint on the road to Fort Jesus, quite close to your hotel. It's a nightclub called the Star Bar. Sorry, Gord," he says, "but it's a merchant seamen's hang-out and the liveliest place in town. It's an interesting dive, and the food is reasonable. Who knows," he continues jokingly in his singsong Welsh accent, "you might just meet some of your old seagoing friends there."

"That I doubt," I reply, "but strange things do happen. Back in 1945 when I was in Colombo, Ceylon, I met the Wilks twins; they'd gone to school with me in London. Then a few years later, I met John Newton, another friend from school, on the docks of Buenos Aires."

Eric laughs, "That settles it. Let's go and see if we can find any of Gord's mates. Sounds like some joint." I can see the amusement in

Eric's eyes as he subconsciously pushes back the black hair from his forehead and drinks his beer.

It's already dark when we get up to leave. The night is warm, and the tables are beginning to fill up on the patio. As I look out to sea, I can see the lights of a ship heading north up the coast twinkling in the still night air, and I wonder where it is going. *Aden probably or the Arab emirates. Who knows? It is a ship in the night.* My thoughts go back to those days when I used to stand on a ship's deck and look longingly at the lights on the shores of foreign countries and wonder who and what was behind those lights, and wish that I, too, were there.

The Star Bar

When we arrive at the Star Bar, the nightclub is swinging to a local dance band. We order their specialty, fish and chips with fried eggs. When I decline the bread rolls, I'm given a sad looking salad instead. Around us, the tables are littered with Tusker and Whitecap bottles, indicating that the clientele are more concerned with beer than food.

There's a Union Castle passenger ship in port, and some of the crewmen are here, including a couple of sailors seated at the next table. "'Ere, Lofty," we hear one say. "Just look at those two chicks over there on their own, man. Let's go 'n' ask 'em for a dance." The two men get up and wander across the dance floor. Their night has begun as they join the other couples dancing to a blues number.

Here in the Star Bar, as in similar, back street dives of most seaports, colour is forgotten as the races mix freely, even in class- and race-conscious Kenya. As I watch the dancers, who range from white to various shades of black and brown, the familiar scene brings back memories of the China coast.

As he eats, Eric nods towards the dance floor. "Does this remind you of your seafaring days, Gord?" he asks.

"Aye," I answer slowly, pondering the question, "especially after the war, in Southeast Asia or any other port for that matter. Merchant Navy men were and still are looked down upon by the population at large, so what can you expect? Aside from the *Mission to Seamen*, the only entertainment in port for them is the dives and dens of the dock areas. Most of them get no farther from the dock gates than the nearest pub. At least, this nightclub is on one of the main streets."

"That's true," Lew says, joining the conversation. "A wife in every port. You can't blame them. Here today, gone tomorrow, and some of these girls are really good-looking," he adds with a grin. We eat as we talk, and order another round of beer.

Later in the evening, when the atmosphere and the effect of beer encourage the exchange of confidences, Lew, tired of mild flirtations and dancing, talks of his current girlfriend. "Aye," he sighs, "other women are just not the same; I can't get Gwen out of my mind. She's been transferred to the Kampala office, and I've been thinking of transferring there, too. It's great here, but I feel unsettled, and the department's changing now. If I move, it's about the right time to do it."

Eric nods, "Yeah, that's understandable. They'll want carrier and radio technicians for the terminals and repeater station maintenance. We'll all be splitting up soon, anyway."

"Yes, I guess so," Lew says, his face thoughtful. "Now the surveys have reached the coast, there's only the links between Dar es Salaam, Zanzibar and Tanga to do. That route just needs the sites re-checking and new repeater stations built to house the equipment and generators. As you know that was one of the original prototypes of Marconi's links here in East Africa."

He looks towards me and adds, "That was before the Ngong to Nakuru experimental link." Lew pauses as he sips his drink, stretches his arms and legs, and then continues. "They completed the initial testing while you were on overseas leave using the existing site on Zanzibar. The testing was done with the cooperation of the Dar carrier room, and now the Zanzibar site is at the building stage. It's on a low hill, so you drive straight onto it, like you do at Kwale."

"Mac tells me that they're planning a new repeater route from Dar inland up to Dodoma," Eric says, "and they're going to split the teams into two groups. Some of us will be on the installation phase on the Kampala-coast route, while the rest will test the new Tanganyika route. It's a toss-up who goes where. Mac will need men experienced on the new equipment to do alignment adjustments before the routes can be put into service."

"Ah, well, it has to come," I say. "It's been obvious from the start that we'll be moving onto the installation stage. Once the building section has constructed the roads and repeater stations, we'll start to install the equipment and generators. The radio towers will probably be erected at the same time." Pausing, I eye Eric thoughtfully, "But I didn't realize they were planning another route in Tanganyika; that's news to me."

"Aye, I only heard about it myself just before we left Nairobi," Eric says. "It was an offhand remark, so I didn't pay much attention to it."

It is after midnight when we leave the nightclub and walk slowly down the darkened street to the junction of Salim and Kilindini Roads. Lew collects his car from the hotel parking lot, and we watch as he drives away. The rear lights of his car fade, and then disappear, as his car mingles with other traffic in Salim Road. Turning, we enter the

Figure 36. Local fishing boats on the beach at low tide.

hotel, and, after collecting our keys from the night clerk, mount the wide staircase.

"What a day," says Eric as he lies on his bed. "I enjoyed that even though I couldn't swim out to the reef. It's too difficult with one leg."

"Yes, I know. What with the coral and the sea urchins, it's impossible. The sea is too shallow for swimming until high tide." I hesitate for a moment, and then continue, "You know, there's a swimming pool on the edge of the cliff facing the sea. It's near the hospital and State House. How about going there tomorrow? We can have a lazy day by the pool, get some lunch there, then walk down to the African market in Salim Road."

Sleepily, Eric nods, "You're right. I know the pool you're talking about. I've been there before. We'll do it, but right now I've gotta sleep." Pulling the sheets over his head, he turns his face towards the wall.

Strange, but I can't sleep. There are too many thoughts racing through my mind. The Star Bar has awakened memories, long buried memories. I can hear Eric's rhythmic snoring, and eventually I, too, fall asleep.

The Broken Manhole Cover

It is Monday. We'd planned an early start back to Kwale, so we settled our account at the Manor Hotel first thing before we went over to the post office yard. That had been the plan, but today seems to be one of those days when things go wrong.

Sunday had gone off so well. We'd overslept, and nearly missed breakfast; however, we managed to drag ourselves to the hotel dining room just before it closed. Eric had enjoyed himself at the pool. Despite his handicap, he's a good swimmer. In fact, he's in his natural element in water, both diving and swimming.

We'd passed the hospital on our way back to the African handicraft market in Salim Road, and then headed for the Copper Kettle, a small coffee bar in Kilindini Road. Specializing in light meals and pastries, the Copper Kettle is popular with Mombasa residents and tourists alike. We'd had coffee and cakes there before returning to our hotel for dinner. Later in the evening, Lew had joined us in the Manor Hotel bar.

✳✳✳

This morning, I fell through a broken manhole cover in the post office yard, and cut my right leg just below the knee. Someone from the office bandaged my leg, and drove Eric and me to the hospital emergency.

Now, sitting in the emergency room, I don't feel so good. Eric's fussing about me like an old hen, and the accident has cast a cloud over the whole weekend. The incident is imprinted on my mind, and I can vividly recall the shock and pain of falling. The cut on my shinbone is deep, and will probably needs stitches.

The doctor, a kindly old man with white hair, says, "How'd you do that, son?" He removes the bandage and looks at the open lips of the wound.

"I stepped onto a cast iron manhole cover in the post office yard," I reply. "It was cracked, and I fell into the hole when it broke." Then I add, "The sharp edge of the cover gouged my leg."

"Hmm," the doctor says, as he examines the gash. "You'll need several stitches to close the wound, and you'll have a tetanus shot as well."

✳✳✳

It is almost noon before we eventually leave Mombasa. With my leg bandaged, I sit beside Eric who's driving the Podson. Soon Mombasa and the Likoni Ferry are behind us, and the Podson is labouring slowly up the escarpment.

"Aye," says Eric, "the beach made a good break. We need to get away from the camp once in a while. The bloody department gets their pound of flesh from us. When we're on safari, we work seven days a week, month after month." Driving with one hand on the wheel, he draws deeply on the inevitable cigarette. "Yeah," he continues, his voice softening, "and there is no overtime, just a lousy five-shillings-a-day subsistence allowance when we're in the bush. We must be daft."

"Well, you love it, Eric," I say with a grin. "You'd not like an office job any more than I would."

"That's true," Eric admits. "If I play my cards right, maybe I'll get a chance to work for the Marconi Company. They say that Marconi has contracts to put radio repeater links into South America. Now, that's where I'd like to go. I bet they pay their representatives a bloody sight better than this lot do."

✳✳✳

"*Aiyee, bwana*. What is the news of *Mombasa?*" Kamundu's face is wreathed in smiles as he greets us.

"Mombasa is a very fine place, Kamundu," I say, and then add, "The sea is warm to swim in and the beaches are beautiful, sparkling white."

As I get out of the Podson, Kamundu sees the bandage. "*Lakini, bwana*," he says, "but you have hurt your leg. What happened?"

His concerned expression changes to wonder when I tell him about the broken manhole cover, and he shakes his head. "*Bahati yako mbaya*—your luck is bad," he says.

As we talk, we unload the equipment from the Podson, and put it back in the bell section of the main tent. By sundown, the camp and repeater equipment are in place and checked out.

Eric is cooking tonight, and, as we chat together, he finishes peeling the potatoes, sprinkles a smidgen of salt over them, and puts the pot on the cooking fire. "We're back to the old routine," he says, as he punches holes in the tops of two cans. He then places the cans—one of steak and the other of peas—in the pot of boiling water on the Primus stove. "It may not compare to the Manor Hotel, but it feels more like home."

When the potatoes are ready, he drains them, and, after adding some of the milk that we bought in Mombasa along with some margarine, he busily mashes them. "Excellent," he says, after tasting them. "The best mashed potatoes west of Mombasa. You're going to enjoy your dinner tonight."

Kwale-Tanga Tests

Testing has started again. The Tanga site is on the air, and the test signals are good. Bungy made contact right on schedule. Now the story of how I fell down the manhole in the Mombasa yards is being spread amongst our group, becoming distorted with each telling. The survey group is a close-knit one. All our wives know each other, and inevitably safari news and gossip gets passed along until, in the end, the story bears little resemblance to the facts. Hopefully, by the time I get back to Nairobi, it will all be sorted out, or forgotten. But for the moment, the talk is about me.

When I bemoan the fact, Eric grins, "You can't do much without everyone finding out, but you know that. There are not that many whites in Nairobi, especially when compared to the Africans and Asians, and all there is to do is talk about each other." Nodding towards my leg, he asks, "How's the leg, anyway?"

"A bit sore, but the doctor gave me a tetanus shot so it should be all right in a day or two, provided it's kept clean. He also gave me some ointment and more bandages, but there's always the medical box in the Podson."

"Aye," Eric mutters. "We'll be here about three weeks, so it should be healed by the time we get back to Nairobi."

✳✳✳

Confined to the camp for the first week by my leg, and then by everyday routines, I find that the time passes slowly. The rhythmic chop of the Elliott recorder as it strikes the recording tape goes on incessantly, twenty-four hours a day, seven days a week, and gets on my nerves. Eric, however, seems impervious to the sound, and to the background noise made by the Yardley Wavis generator. Sitting in the shade under the tent veranda, absorbed in his book, he is in another world.

From our camp, we can see the ocean beyond the foothills. My thoughts wander as I watch a ship, hull down on the distant horizon, heading east away from the land. The sea looks calm and peaceful, but it is not always that way.

✳✳✳

The Indian Ocean had also been calm early in 1945. The small tanker had cut through the blue sea, sending frothing white waves rolling across the still water. Porpoises played in the bow waves, and Tommy, a young, fair-haired seaman, had talked to me excitedly. "Look, Sparks," he had said. "There's a waterspout; I've never seen one before."

Two days later, Tommy was dead; he was just seventeen. Late one night during the graveyard watch, a fierce monsoon storm came up. Tommy was on the for'ard deck, when a wave burst over the bow, and caught him. He was swept overboard and drowned. There was only the testimony of a broken guardrail chain, and that of the second mate to mark his passing. Remembering Tommy, I can feel a lump in my throat. *Yes*, I think, *the ocean is beautiful, but it's only a mask. It can turn on you in an instant, without warning.*

✳✳✳

The sound of Bungy's voice coming over the transceiver brings my thoughts back to the present. "Kwale, this is Tanga; do you read?"

Eric puts his book down to answer the call. It's a routine report, and I catch a sentence or two.

"We're experiencing fading signals," Bungy says. "Probably the heat of the day is affecting the propagation, but the signal is still well above the commercial level. Is your transmit signal steady?"

Eric replies in the affirmative.

While they continue to talk, I wander over to the Yardley Wavis engines to check the fuel levels in the tanks. It will be dark soon. At night, the temperature and humidity will fall slightly, and, because of this variation, the signal strength will rise.

Although we've been here three weeks, I've yet to see a sable antelope in the game reserve; however, the thick vegetation makes the valleys ideal places for concealment. The surrounding hilltops are relatively bare of bush, and the coastal rain forests are interspersed with open grasslands that are dry and yellow on the sunbaked land. A large variety of tropical birds inhabits the area, ranging from hornbills to weavers and bee-eaters. Kamundu assures me that he has been told by the local inhabitants that, although they are seldom seen, elephants, lions and even leopards move in and out of the park over the year on their migratory routes from the hinterland.

Nairobi Bound

It's December 3, 1953, and the Tanga site is being evacuated. Bungy and Geoff have closed it down, and are off the air. Their last message was: "See you both in Nairobi. Good luck on the road. Tanga signing off." Now our site is a hive of activity. Our radio transceiver and the test transmitters plus battery banks are dismantled, the antenna mast is taken down, and the tents are folded and packed. With the motor generator stowed in the Podson, we're ready to leave.

"Aye," says Eric, looking at his watch. It's just ten-thirty, not bad. We should make the Voi Hotel before dark, which will give us an easy run to Nairobi tomorrow. We'll be home for the weekend."

Kamundu is riding in the back of the Podson as I drive the vehicle down the track to the main Tanga-Mombasa Road. Turning left, I head north for the Likoni Ferry and Mombasa. The ferry line-up delays us, so it's past midday before we clear the outskirts of Mombasa and, heading west, rumble across the Makupa Causeway. The engine growls as I gear down to begin the long winding climb up to the plateau that runs along the Kenya coastal strip.

"Ah," sighs Eric, as we near the top of the escarpment, "take a last look at the coast for a while, Gord."

As we crest the last sloping climb, I glance back, and get a momentary glimpse of the distant streak of blue sea before the palms of a plantation obscure my view. "It won't be that long," I say. "Joan and I are coming to the coast over the Christmas holidays."

It's dusk when Voi appears out of the twilight. The Teita Mountains, stark and gaunt, are silhouetted against the setting sun. Now as we approach the outskirts, the lights are coming on in the railroad marshalling yards. Night has fallen when we arrive at the Voi Hotel.

After signing the register, Eric and I wander onto the veranda, and find two comfortable chairs at an empty table.

My hands and arm muscles can still feel the vibrations of the steering wheel, and my hands tremble slightly as I raise the glass to my lips. The taste of the cold beer refreshes me, and I smile at Eric. "God, I needed that, Eric," I say, adding, "I'm parched."

Relaxing, we watch the glittering lights below and the distant movement of goods trains in the marshalling yards. When the dinner gong sounds, we head for the dining room, along with the rest of the hotel guests.

After an early breakfast, we leave Voi, and, with Eric driving, head west on the main road, which goes through the Tsavo National Park. It's my turn to take it easy and sit back in the cab. Between the Tsavo Bridge and Mtito Andei, there is a wandering herd of elephants crossing the road. A huge bull elephant is standing guard in the middle of the road, and his large tusks and bulk are intimidating. Although he must weigh at least two or three tons, he can move fast if he feels like it. The Podson is big, but I'd hate to be in the way if that bull decides to charge. The metal doors would give way like paper when those tusks hit. Discretion is the order of the day, and we wait patiently for the elephants to cross before we attempt to drive by.

It is late in the afternoon when we top the rise near Lukenya, and can see and smell the small township of Athi River before us. In the distance, we can make out the Aberdares, while Nairobi is faintly visible in the folds of the foothills. The ford across the Athi River is almost dry. The short rains failed this year, and it's now the hot, dry season, which lasts from December to March, when the long rains are due.

When we arrive, the lights are on in the Marlborough Road apartment, and Joan comes out to greet us. Kamundu hands out my safari kit and luggage from the back of the Podson, and Samson, our servant, carries them up the outside stairway to the apartment while Eric and I talk to Joan.

"What's this about Gordon falling down a manhole, Eric?" Joan asks.

Eric grins at me as our eyes meet, and I laugh, "I told you so, Eric." Then, turning to Joan, I say, "It's a long story. I'll tell you about it later."

Eric has gone now. He will drop Kamundu off at the Post Office, and will keep the Podson at his place in Langata over the weekend. We watch from the veranda as he reaches Marlborough Road and heads up out of Spring Valley. Putting my arm around Joan's waist, I murmur, "It's good to be home Joan."

✳✳✳

Chapter 10
Mbwinzau Tower

Mac's Briefing

"The survey stage is over," Mac says, nervously pacing the floor of his Whitehouse Road office. Although expected, his words give rise to a feeling of regret in my mind, and a feeling of uncertainty about the future.

Glancing around at the small group of safari crew members gathered in Mac's office, I try to see how they're reacting. Eric is half leaning against a file cabinet, and Bungy sits on a bench, while Geoff Perrins and I are standing. All of us, however, are listening intently to Mac's words.

Mac has stopped pacing and stands in front of his desk. "Now that the survey teams have reached the coast at Mombasa and gone on to Dar es Salaam, the main survey has been completed," he says. "We're having to regroup." He pauses briefly, pondering his next words.

"There is still the Dar-Dodoma route to survey, but now we urgently need to get the Kampala-Mombasa route working and passing traffic. We've reached the construction stage, and I want you all to get experience in the installation and alignment of equipment, for both terminals and repeaters."

Turning to me, he says, "Mumford, you'll be going down to Mbwinzau with the riggers on Monday. They're expert at erecting the towers, but I want you to supervise them, especially when they are erecting the crossarm on top of the radio tower. It's your responsibility to assemble the multiple Yagi directional arrays and get them hoisted into position on the tower crossarm."

Looking around at the others, he continues. "We'll maintain contact with the radio transceiver links that we've used in the past. Williams and Scales will install the station electrical wiring and the engine room control equipment in Kitindini." After a short pause, he adds, "The Kitindini tower has already been erected."

The meeting is over, and a new phase in the backbone telecommunications route has begun. *Yes,* I think as I turn to leave the office with the rest of our group, *if I am to supervise the installation of the directional arrays, I will have to climb the tower.* The mere thought makes my stomach churn. I can still vividly recall how it felt when Eric and I connected the Yagi arrays on the Nairobi radio tower. I've no head for heights, but stubbornness got me to the top that time.

The mast on the Mbwinzau site is not on the top of a five-storey building, however, but well above the level of the rock where I used to camp. *That's a thousand foot ridge.* I shrug my shoulders helplessly and steel myself for the inevitable. *I'll just have to get used to heights, just like I had to get accustomed to motion sickness when I was at sea, and that lasted five years.*

The Mbwinzau Repeater Station

Dusk is falling as we unpack our personal belongings and camp beds from the truck. Then, with Yakub beside me, I unlock the main door, and together we explore the empty repeater station. The concrete walls are bare and uninviting.

"Ah," he says, "this is like the building at Kitindini. There's a main engine room, a storeroom, and a small room where the field maintenance man can sleep." Laughing, he adds, "but there's no toilet. We'll have to use the bush. Maybe they'll put in a long drop later."

"It's like the old safari days, Yakub," I say with a grin. "We'll simply have to use a *jembe* (hoe) and toilet paper. I'll get Mac to have a toilet installed; it should be in the plans."

We'd left Nairobi on schedule this morning, January 18, in the fully loaded, three-ton International truck, and we've made good time in clear weather and sunny skies. Tomorrow we'll start work, but right now it's time to settle in for the night. It's been a long day driving over potholed dirt roads, but it must have seemed even longer for the four men riding in the back of the open truck. Daudi and Dawoodi, along with two African labourers, had made themselves comfortable on top of the loads. They had hidden under the truck's tarpaulin, which protected them from the dust thrown up by the wheels.

I've known Yakub and his crew of Daudi and Dawoodi over the years on other projects, and get on well with them, Yakub is a stoutly built, middle-aged man, with dark, swarthy features and an ample paunch.

Of medium height, he is casually dressed in workman's clothes, usually a khaki open-necked shirt and long grey trousers with a broad belt, and wears sandals on his bare feet.

Dawoodi, on the other hand, is a snappy dresser, even in working clothes. Taller than Yakub, he's dark featured, thirtyish and good looking, with a preference for coloured shirts. I rather suspect he is a ladies' man. But the most unusual of the trio is Daudi. Smaller than average, he has a pock-marked face, jet black hair, and a dark brown complexion. Amazingly agile on the towers, he shows no fear of heights. Perhaps he gives the impression of being younger because he is small, but he is probably in his thirties, and normally dresses in khaki shorts and shirt.

Figure 37. Mbwinzau repeater station before the tower was erected (Photo was taken from the rock above).

It is getting late and the sun has set when I turn and leave Yakub. The riggers have already set up their camp beds in the storeroom, and the two labourers are busy collecting firewood. Katumo has put their things in the main equipment room, which he will share with them. He has also carried my bags, camp bed, chop box and safari kit from the truck and deposited them in the smallest room. This room is intended as sleeping quarters for the maintenance man.

The bare, clinical, cell-like atmosphere of this room makes me feel lost, but the feeling is momentary. However, I miss the familiar comfort and coziness of my safari tent. Placing the bi-Aladin lamp on an old packing case left behind by the last occupant, I pump up the pressure in the lamp and light the mantel.

The bright light reflects off the bare whitewashed walls, and projects its light out into the dark of the night. Like a beacon, it attracts a myriad of *dudus* (insects), including mosquitoes, which set up an incessant humming. Hastily shutting the door and window, I spray the room with insecticide. I had forgotten that Mbwinzau is cursed with *dudus* of all shapes and sizes when night falls, especially at this time of year.

When the room is closed, however, it soon becomes unbearably hot and stifling. In desperation, I abandon it to the *dudus,* and, taking my food, Primus stove and cooking utensils, I move out onto the concrete pathway. There, seated on my camp chair, I prepare my evening meal. Letting my thoughts wander, I search for a solution. *Yes,* I think, *it's a pity they didn't install a screen door, or possibly an air-conditioner. I'll suggest that to Mac when I get back. They'll listen to him.* It will definitely make life easier for the maintenance personnel

Sitting outside, relatively free from annoying *dudus*, I prepare my evening meal. The smell of curry carries to me. A short distance away, the riggers are sitting outside the storeroom. I can see Dawoodi's form, silhouetted against the light from their kerosene lantern that shines through the doorway. He is talking to Yakub and Daudi as he stirs the pot of curry boiling on their small, portable *kuni* (charcoal) stove. From custom and experience they have brought several bags of charcoal with them from Nairobi. Charcoal is cheap in Nairobi and widely used for cooking by the African and Asian communities. Like most of the survey safari crews, I prefer to use a Primus stove because it's cleaner; however, kerosene is more expensive than charcoal.

Low and indistinct, the murmur of voices drifts towards me against the background of night noises from the bush. The dim, flickering light given off by the burning charcoal throws shadows on their faces, distorting them. Their English is understandable, but usually they speak in Swahili, or use their own language when they talk to each other. I'm not sure whether they're speaking Gugerati, or Urdu, but the sound reminds me of the Bombay bazaars that I visited during the war.

I've worked with these riggers on and off for some time now, and we get on well together. They've all worked for the post office for years, and probably their fathers did so before them. There were many labourers brought from India in the early 1900s to work on the construction of the Kenya-Uganda railway. Today, the Asian community in Kenya is roughly three times larger than the European (white) population.

My thoughts wander back to the time that I and a hundred labourers had cut a Land Rover track through the virgin bush and rocks. *How the track has changed.* Now, a metal swing-gate bars the entry to the road up Mbwinzau. On the left-hand side, a large notice board states that this is a private road leading to the East African Posts and Telecommunications Repeater Station. I had opened the gate, and let the truck through. Then, for old times sake I took over the truck from Katumo, and drove up the smooth murram road.

As the road swept back in an arc towards Mbwinzau's long, rising ridge, I could see the shady trees and bush on the bend where I once camped. The road itself has a foundation of fine stone chips and rubble, cemented together with fresh murram soil and a sticky substance like oil or molasses, before being watered, rolled and flattened smooth by a steam roller. *Yes, the building section has done a good job on my road, laying tarmac on the steepest sections, grading the edges, and putting culverts in the gullies to drain away storm water.*

Changing into four-wheel drive to negotiate the steep slopes and curves, I'd nodded towards the road, and said to my companions, "*Sasa, wafikiri*—now what do you think? Our building section has done well. It's a distinct improvement on the Land Rover track."

Katumo laughed, "*Ndiyo, kweli*—yes, truly, bwana. This truck would not have made it up the old track. The bends have been widened, and there are culverts where we once drove through dried-up *dongas*."

We reached the top of the ridge, and the big flat-topped rock formation, where we camped during the original survey, towers above us. The road had been dug into the slope of the ridge using jack hammers to widen the passage along the base of the huge rock face. The old cleft, used to climb onto the top of the rock in the past, had been blasted and then enlarged on the west side of the track, and the area around it had been levelled. The builders had also constructed a concrete plinth in the centre of the turning circle. This plinth will form the base for the radio antenna tower, and tomorrow we will start to build it.

✳✳✳

A disturbance in the bush brings my thoughts back to the present, and I listen intently for a moment, but it's quiet again. I miss my campfire, miss looking into the flames, and miss the comfort of its light. *Yes*, I think, *tomorrow I'll get one of the labourers to collect some firewood for me.*

The moon has come up now, and the building is quiet and still; the riggers retired to their quarters some time ago. It's late when I wash my dinner plate and cooking utensils. The fires made by the riggers and the labourers are just thin layers of gleaming embers when I finally turn in.

The window of the rest room is fully open, but it's still hot inside. Protected from the multitude of insects by the mosquito netting covering my bed, I lie under a thin sheet, feeling restless and unsettled, until sleep finally claims me.

The weak rays of the sun shining through the window at an acute angle wake me early in the morning. I push aside the mosquito net and stroll outside. One of the labourers, probably Kamau, has brought a bucket of water and left it outside my door. Stripping to the waist, I wash.

Erecting the Tower

Yakub ticks off the last of the four angle-iron sections, as Dawoodi and Kamau lower it to the ground. The truck is empty now, and Yakub joins the others gathered near the concrete base. The tower will be erected here, using these twenty-foot galvanized steel sections as legs. Jutting two feet above the flat surface of the base are four anchoring points made of thick, steel angle-iron, buried deep in the concrete.

The riggers now check coded parts of the tower assembly and miscellaneous bags of steel nuts and bolts; triangular holding plates, crosspieces, and the crossarm girders of this gigantic Meccano set, and place them in separate piles. "*Ndiyo, bwana,*" says Yakub, "everything checks out okay. I'll get the riggers started."

Nodding, I turn away. "They're your team, Yakub. I can't be of much use to you until you're ready to erect the Yagi arrays on top of the crossarm. In the meantime, I'll get a temporary antenna erected for the radio transceiver, and get our communication system going. After I've made contact, I'll check back, and give you a hand."

***

With Katumo's help, the VHF rod antenna (commonly called a *bazooka* because of its shape) has been erected above the fuel tank located on the roof of the station. A long coaxial cable runs down the outside wall of the building and through the open window of my room, where it connects to the VHF communications radio transmitter-receiver (transceiver) sitting on a table.

A mobile Yardley-Wavis motor generator supplies electrical power to the equipment through a thick power cable leading from a small thatched lean-to that Kamau, our labourer, has built to protect the generator and batteries from the heat of the sun. As I connect the power cable to the transceiver, I glance at Katumo and ask. "Have you checked the petrol for the motor generator?"

Katumo nods, "*Ndiyo, bwana,* the tank is full."

The two-stroke motor that drives the generator bursts into life as I pull the lanyard, and the familiar rhythmic throb disturbs the quiet of the site. Now that the small radio transceiver has power, I return to my room, switch it on, and call Kitindini.

Eric answers on the first call. "Hello, Mbwinzau, Kitindini here, reading you loud and clear. Over." Our communications established, we talk for a few minutes before arranging a regular calling schedule.

***

By now, the rigging crew has completed the first stage of the tower. The four twenty-foot sections that form the legs of the hundred-foot tower are in place, and the horizontal sections are bolted into position.

Yakub has organized an improvised crane using two-inch diameter pipes and blocks and tackle to haul the heavy steel sections up the tower. Fascinated, I watch the riggers. They have been together for years, and work as a well-oiled team, sensing each other's needs instinctively.

Daudi climbs the bare steel sections with the ease of long familiarity. He handles the diagonal crosspieces with precision as he and Dawoodi manoeuvre the pieces into the pre-drilled slots, and then bolt them together.

I smile as I watch them, the short, the tall, and the fat. Dawoodi is not really that tall. He's about medium height, five foot nine or so, smooth-faced with heavy dark eyebrows and a shock of black hair. Thin and wiry, he is talkative, holding forth in a stream of singsong words in his native tongue as they work, while Daudi is shy and self-effacing.

Yakub is in his mid-forties, and already has threads of grey growing in his black hair. Laid back in his attitude, he simply smiles as he shifts from position to position on the steel tower, supervising, checking progress and helping his men.

Every now and then he raises his voice, giving orders to Kamau and Njerogi on the ground below, to bring more cross-sections and bolts from the piles of material scattered around the base of the tower.

The Yagi Antenna Arrays

While Yakub and his men work on the tower sections, my thoughts turn to the construction of two steel frames for the Yagi antenna arrays. These arrays will be mounted on the ends of the crossarm, which will be bolted across the top of the steel tower at its centre point, forming a large steel lattice structure like a "T".

With Katumo's help, I sort through the coded angle-iron pieces, and begin to assemble the frames. When they are ready, I will clamp four Yagi antennae on each frame in a square formation to form the array.

These arrays are designed to transmit or receive a narrow radio beam to and from the next repeater station, and will be mounted on the ends of the crossarm at the top of the radio tower. One array will be mounted on the west side of the tower to form the radio link to Kitindini in the Machakos Hills, while there will be a duplicate array on the east side to transmit and receive signals to and from Vuria in the east.

The arrays are completed a few days later, and ready to be hoisted up the tower. Yakub smiles as he looks at the assembled arrays. "*Hii mzuri sana*—it is very good, *bwana*," he says. "We will be ready for them in a day or two." He glances at Daudi and Dawoodi. "Once they are finished with the cross-arm, we'll rig up a derrick and hoist the arrays up the tower."

Figure 38. Yukub checks the framework with the arrays, before it is hoisted into position. The tower's shadow can be seen on the right of the photograph.

Aye, I think, *and then it will be my turn to climb up there. I don't relish the job, but I am committed.*

***

Almost two weeks have gone by, and the tower, having reached the one hundred foot mark, is almost completed, with only the crossarm to be fitted into position.

From the top of the tower, Dawoodi directs Kamau and Yakub as they pull the rope below. The improvised crane—a galvanized pipe boom and block and tackle—hauls the steel girders, swaying and jerking, up the side of the tower. Daudi assists Dawoodi to pull the girders over onto the flat top of the tower, and bolt them securely into position at their centre point to form the crossarm. By the time the riggers are finished, it is almost dark. Silhouetted against the sky, the tower, with the framework of girders lying across the top and jutting out ten feet either side, looks like a giant "T".

As I look up at the tower, I feel my stomach muscles tighten. Tomorrow will be my big day, the day when I go up the tower with the riggers to supervise the placement of the antennae arrays on both ends of that crossarm.

Aye, I think, *it's not just placing the arrays. I've also got to connect the armoured coaxial antenna cables for each array. My arms and legs feel like jelly.*

Trying to dismiss these thoughts from my mind, I concentrate on other things, like making dinner, but there's nothing exciting about my meals that could distract my thoughts.

When I sent Katumo into Kibwezi for supplies a couple of days ago, he came back with some cans of steak and kidney of doubtful age, a loaf of bread, potatoes, and a small can of condensed milk. The stock of fresh and canned foods that the local *duka* carries is evidently very limited.

A Time for Action

The sun is shining, glinting off the crossarm, and the two Yagi antennae arrays are ready. Standing at the base of the tower, I watch as Dawoodi and Kamau start hoisting the first one, pulling on the rope running through the block and tackle system. From the tower, Yakub is giving instructions to his crew, using English and Swahili with a little Urdu mixed in. "*Simama* (stop). Hold it," he shouts. The guideline ropes are stretched taut, but the array shakes unmercifully as it dangles some twenty feet off the ground. Yakub and Daudi are struggling to keep it from smashing against the side of the tower.

"Oh, no," I groan, as I watch the fragile Yagi antennae swinging perilously close to the tower. I can stand it no longer. Hurriedly fastening my safety belt tightly around my waist, I dash to the tower with the end of the belt flapping between my legs like a tail. "Katumo," I yell, "*saidia pamoja kamba*—help with the ropes. I'm going up the mast to try to keep the array from hitting the tower."

My fear of heights forgotten, I climb the ladder to the first horizontal crossbar, and then move along the beam to the tower leg. There is no ladder on the tower itself. Instead, on one tower leg, a series of thick, galvanized eight-inch steel bolts, threaded at one end, are bolted onto the outer face of the vertical L-shaped girders that form the leg sections of the tower.

Placed at right angles to each other and spaced one above the other about a foot apart, they are bolted on the outer side of the tower leg. The head of the bolts protrude six inches from the steel L-shaped girders, and provide hand and footholds for climbing the mast. This is a precarious operation for an inexperienced climber, who has to climb up the exposed side of the tower like a fly on a wall.

Grabbing one of these rungs, I begin to climb up towards the dangling load, coordinating the movements of my hands and feet. When I reach a point just above the load, I fasten the tail of my safety belt around a diagonal crosspiece, and then lean out, ready to take action if the array swings too close to the tower. Signalling to Yakub to resume pulling, I watch anxiously as, working under his direction, the riggers haul the array up past me.

Katumo has now taken over the guideline from Daudi. Climbing with the agility of a monkey, Daudi swings past me. Ignoring the rungs, he uses the cross-sections and diagonals to climb. Moving in tandem, the two of us work our way up the narrowing tower, while we fend off the array, thus preventing a potential collision. At the top, the tower legs, which were twenty feet away from each other at the base, are now barely three or four feet apart and form part of the crossarm.

So involved in this task am I, that I don't have time to think about the danger or my fear, until Daudi and I reach the top of the tower with the array. Then, as I fasten the leather safety belt around the crossarm, I realize where I am. Seated beside me on the crossarm, Daudi grins. "You're doing fine" he says, "We'll make a good rigger of you."

Laughing with relief, I reply, "that's impossible, Daudi. I am afraid of heights." Shaking my head, I add, *"Kazi yako ngumu*—your work is hard."

The large, cumbersome array dangles from the block and tackle, close to the end of the crossarm where it will be attached. By now, Dawoodi has joined us. From the security of the central section of the crossarm, I watch the riggers as they work. Oblivious to the height, the two men manhandle the array close to the swivel joints where the frame will fit and then lock it into position. Cautiously, I undo my safety belt and edge along the crossarm, moving away from my safe position and very conscious of the sheer drop below. Then, using the familiar shape of the Kitindini peak in the Mua Hills near Machakos to line up the Yagi antennae, I sight the array.

Once the first array has been sighted and locked into position, one after the other we squirm over the edge of the crossarm steel girders and feel for the rungs with our feet. Then we work our way down the tower, hand over hand, using the rods on the outer edge of the tower leg. My fear of heights has been somewhat blunted, but it is still there in the background. I'm relieved when I reach the bottom of the tower, and can once more stand on firm ground. This afternoon, however, we have to hoist the second array into position.

✳✳✳

Tired but satisfied, I sit on the crossarm behind the reflectors of the Yagi antennae array as I lock the assembly into position. "There,' I say to Dawoodi who is sitting beside me, "she's pointed dead on Vuria."

As he checks the compass, then looks east across the Chyulu plains and Tsavo National Park to the distant Teita Mountains, Dawoodi nods. *"Ndiyo,"* he says, "yes, I can see the peak. How far away is it?"

"About ninety-five miles in a straight line. A lot more if you go by road."

As we rest at the top of the tower, we talk for a while. With my safety belt securely fastened, I can relax, and I smile as I look down at the massive rock below. *We had to use rocks instead of tent pegs when we pitched the tents there. We started surveying this site in September 1951, about two years ago. Now there's a repeater station here on Mbwinzau. The same thing is happening all along the route. The regional building sections are busy.*

Dawoodi's voice breaks into my thoughts. "I'm going down now, bwana, *unataka kuenda*—do you want to go?"

"Yes, I was just thinking back to the surveys, when all this started. Now, it's coming to an end."

"Everything comes to an end, bwana," Dawoodi says. "That's why we're here."

Unfastening my safety belt, I follow him down the tower. "Yes, that's true," I say, "otherwise there would be no purpose to it at all. The survey was only one stage. We are now in the second phase, building stations and towers from the coast to Uganda."

Transfer to Vuria

Since that first day on the site, Kamau has brought firewood for me, and tonight is no different. When I sit and eat my dinner by the light of the campfire, it somehow seems to make closure to the workday. The fire is comforting, and the smoke keeps the mosquitoes away.

After dinner, I call Kitindini on schedule at eight o'clock, and talk to Eric. He and Bungy have finished the electrical wiring of the station, and are in the process of connecting the changeover cubicles for the motor generators.

"Aye," he says, on hearing my progress report. "I'll pass that back to headquarters. Don Beresford is planning to make some checks on the Vuria repeater. As you're nearly finished there, they may want you to go with him. When do you expect the riggers to leave, Wednesday the fourth?"

"Yes," I reply, after pressing the microphone switch. "We'll be finished sometime late tomorrow afternoon. There are just two antenna cables left to put up the tower, and the Yagi arrays to connect. Then we can pack up and load the truck. The riggers will be ready to leave Wednesday morning. I'll call you about this time tomorrow to get confirmation that Don Beresford is coming."

After we finish exchanging news, we sign off. As I put down the microphone, I wonder what the problem is at Vuria. An installation team from Mombasa has been working on the station, the building is completed, and the tower has been erected. I shrug my shoulders; I'll find out in due course.

✳✳✳

"Kitindini, this is Mbwinzau. Do you read? Over." As I call, there is a cup of freshly made coffee on the table beside me, next to my open diary. It's Tuesday, February 3, and our assignment has been completed. The two armoured feeder cables are clamped in place on the tower and terminated in the centre of the crossarm, close to the two Yagi arrays.

When Eric answers on my second call, I say, "We finished around five this afternoon, Eric. The feeder cables are up, the Yagi antenna links are in place, the joints are sealed, and the arrays are aligned on Kitindini and Vuria. Thank God, that's over. As you know, I never did like heights. Have you heard from Don Beresford?" Flipping the toggle switch to *receive*, I listen for his answer.

"Yes," he replies, "I sent your progress report to Mac who's working with Don over the network. Don will pick you up at Mbwinzau in the Land Rover about two or three tomorrow afternoon. You should be at the Voi Hotel tomorrow night. I guess your riggers and the truck will be off to Nairobi in the morning."

Settling back in my chair, I sip my coffee as Eric talks. Don is bringing two portable transceivers and test equipment with him to carry out some tests over the Vuria-Kwale link. They also suspect there is a fault in the antenna system, and want us to check it. Acknowledging receipt of the message, I sign off. Eric will forward my report to Mac, and confirm the meeting with Don.

✳✳✳

It's just gone two o'clock in the afternoon when I first see a vehicle on the plains, just a speck at the head of a fast-travelling dust cloud. As it approaches, then passes on the road far beneath me, I get up from my camp chair and move nearer to the edge of the ridge. It's a dark green Land Rover, and I can just make out the faint outline of the post office logo. "Yeah, that's got to be Don," I mutter, watching as the vehicle passes along the Mombasa Road, only to disappear from my sight where the road curves.

Shortly after ten this morning, the riggers and labourers left for Nairobi with Katumo driving the truck. Only my personal belongings, chop box, camp bed, and safari kit are left. All the rest—tables, tools, radio equipment, and generator—was loaded onto the truck and will be returned to Mac's store in Whitehouse Road.

Don will bring his own kit with him. Just in case he's forgotten to bring spares, I've kept sealing tapes and weatherproofing compounds, plus my safety belt. These will be essential in the event that the fault is in the Yagi connections on the Vuria tower.

As I wait at the front of the station with my baggage, I hear a faint roar of an engine approaching. As the noise increases, I see the Land Rover rounding the bend by the big rock. There is a grin on Don Beresford's round plump face as he pulls up beside me in a swirl of dust. "Hi, Gord," he says as he gets out of the Land Rover and comes over to shake hands. "Last time I saw you, you were working on that rock pile with your men. How's it going?"

"The tower and arrays are up," I say. "The riggers went off to Nairobi this morning. You probably passed their truck on your way here."

He nods, "I saw them going up the Mua Hills. Katumo was driving, wasn't he?"

As we talk, I take a look around the building, checking to make sure all the doors are locked. Because repeater sites operate automatically, they are designed to be secure, with heavy, solid metal doors and barred windows. There are air vents at ceiling height for ventilation, with large fans to draw in the air from outside, and circulate it around the engine and equipment rooms.

Security forces and local home guards are needed to protect the Loldiani repeater site, which is in a known *Mau Mau* area in the White Highlands. The emergency has, however, been confined to the Central Province and the Kikuyu tribal lands. Both the Mbwinzau and Kitindini sites are located in Wakamba country, a peaceful part of the country, so extra precautions are not needed.

After loading my baggage and safari kit into the Land Rover, we start off down the steep, winding road. Glancing back, I watch the tower and building disappear as we round the massive rock. Reaching the gate, Don looks at his watch before we turn onto the Mombasa Road and head east. "It's three o'clock," he says. "We should make Voi around six or seven. The road's been graded recently so it's fairly smooth, at least the part from Nairobi was." After a slight pause, he continues, "There's still that lousy bit through the scrub forest and lava ridges between Kibwezi and Mtito Andei."

As I think about that section, I smile. "Yes, but at least it's dry now," I say. "The rains are not due for another month. Those deep valleys and *dongas* can be a bitch in the rains. Watch out for elephants when we go through the Tsavo; they wander around at dusk. There are usually a lot of them in the bush going back and forth from the watering holes near Mudanda Rock."

The Voi Hotel

We are late getting into Voi. We were held up by elephant, but not in the Tsavo Park as I had expected. Instead it was in the thick bush and valleys just west of Mtito Andei that we encountered a large herd. Some elephants with their young were browsing in the bush on both sides of the road, while others, including one large male, meandered down the dirt road, swinging their heads back and forth as if daring us to pass.

As we slowed down and hesitated, a large National Parks truck came up behind us, and then passed us at speed. On the near side of the vehicle, a game warden was hanging out of the door of the cab, yelling and banging on the truck's body, while his driver, horn blaring, scattered the herd off the road. With the path cleared through the herd, Don swerved into the centre of the road and followed in their wake.

Figure 39. We encountered a large herd of elephant just west of Mtito Andei.

Looking at Don, I laughed. "Well, that's one way to get through a herd of elephant."

"Yeah," said Don, shaking his head. "That was a Park Warden's vehicle from Mtito Andei. He's in a hurry, and probably knows the herd. Elephants that stay in Tsavo are used to cars, and usually get out of the way, especially for a big truck." He paused, and then continued, "Trouble can occur when you meet migratory herds coming over the Yatta Plateau from the NFD. Those bloody things would probably charge. They weigh two or three tons. Just imagine what would happen if one sat on the Land Rover. They'd squash us flat, then play with the wreckage."

It's after seven-thirty when we arrive at Voi, and book into the hotel where we share a room in a *banda* with its own bathroom. Relaxing in a hot, soapy bath, I am daydreaming when I hear Don call me. "Come on, Gord," he says, "it's gone eight o'clock. We'll be late for dinner."

Hurriedly I get out of the tub, dry myself, and put on clean clothes. Then, I join Don in the dining room. "Ah," I say as I sit down and pick up the menu, "I feel like a new man. After two or three weeks in the bush, a hot bath is a real luxury."

"Yeah, I can believe that." Don grins, then adds, "The soup's good; it's mulligatawny. I'm having the fish, but there's broiled lamb chops."

I look at the menu, and, turning to the table steward, I order the soup and meat course.

The bath and dinner have taken their toll on my body, and as we sit in the lounge with our coffee, Don's voice turns into a blur. I must have fallen asleep for a moment, but I jerk awake when I feel his hand shake my shoulder. "You're tired, man," he says. "You're falling asleep."

As we walk up the gravel path to our *banda* at the back of the hotel, the cool of the evening wakes me. Once I crawl under the mosquito net and snuggle under the crisp white bedsheets, however, sleep is not long in coming.

⁂

Chapter 11
The Teita Mountains

The Road to Vuria

High in the mountains not far from the government boma in Wundanyi, the Land Rover takes the steep gradients easily, and, although I'm familiar with this narrow, winding road, the decreasing air pressure still takes me by surprise. Don glances at me as I swallow hard to relieve the pressure in my ears, and notes my pained expression.

"Yeah, the height really gets to you here. My ears popped, too," he says. Pausing, he shifts gears and then continues, "But we should expect it; we've climbed from three thousand feet at Voi to nearly six thousand feet at Wundanyi. That's quite a change in altitude."

Cut deep into the mountainside, the dirt track rises higher as we get nearer to the pass and the small village where our base camp was once located. Wundanyi is now behind us, and Vuria lies in the moorlands to the southwest of the pass.

We are probably within a mile of the village when I recognize the series of sharp bends and curves in the road. Seated in the passenger seat, I can see the deep ravine running down at a steep angle as the Land Rover's wheels churn up dust near the rocky edge. Little used, the track is just wide enough for single vehicles, so uphill traffic has the right-of-way. Oncoming traffic must stop in a lay-by (a wider section of the road) to let the other vehicle go by.

"This is where I nearly put the truck over the edge, Don," I say. As I talk, the memory is clear in my mind. "It was during a heavy rainstorm in October 1951, about ten o'clock at night. The road was churned-up mud with little rivulets running over it. The wheels got trapped in old, waterlogged ruts made by other vehicles, and we slid towards the edge."

Looking down into the ravine, I pause for a moment. "If she'd gone over, we'd have had it. Fortunately she stuck, teetering on the edge. Do you see that old tree stump over there on the slope of the cliff?" As I motion towards the right, Don nods. "I used thick manila ropes to anchor the truck to it, hoping that would stop the vehicle from going over the edge in the night."

"You were bloody lucky," says Don, shaking his head. "That was the old Dodge, wasn't it? I saw the photographs that you took the following morning." He gives a short, expressive laugh, and adds flatly, "If she'd gone over, that truck would've kept rolling right down to the bottom of the ravine. You couldn't have survived that!"

"Yeah, I know," I say. "The weather on this mountain range seems to have a pattern of its own. It was fine that night on the Tsavo game plains and in the foothills, but when we got here, a storm blew up out of nowhere and took us by surprise."

We drive on in companionable silence. As we round a bend in the road, the village appears, nestled in the midst of tall acacia trees, with

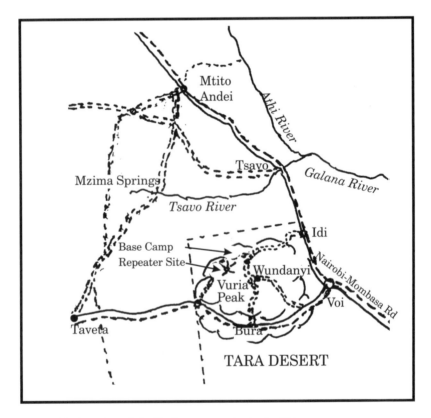

Figure 40. Location of the Vuria repeater site in the Teitas

the road to the repeater station close by. At the junction with the approach road, we draw up beside a swing gate, similar to the one at Mbwinzau. There is also a large wooden notice board, announcing that this is a private road, property of the East African Posts and Telecommunications Administration.

Vuria Repeater Station

Opening the gate, I glance up the long gravel road leading over the moorlands, mentally tracing its course to the distant peak. As I turn back to the Land Rover, I think about the past. *When the base camp used to be here, we employed sixty or more African porters, who trod this rough ground to the repeater site some five miles away, carrying loads on their* heads. *Now the Land Rover can cover the distance in a small fraction of that time.*

As we approach the site, we can see the steel tower. Placed a hundred feet up, the multi-quad Yagi arrays look like giant ears against the blue of the sky. Standing on the rounded peak, the tower dwarfs the sombre grey building at its base. The repeater site is surrounded by a half-finished, eight-foot-high security fence, made using concrete posts and thick, expanded wire mesh.

Constructed following the same plan used at all the repeater sites, the place has an air of bleakness about it. There's not a tree or shrub to relieve the desolation, just some half-dead clumps of coarse grass and small rocky outcrops. Don stops the Land Rover outside the main door of the building, and switches off the engine. As he steps out, he mutters, "Bloody hell, this is a bit barren."

"You could say that," I reply with a grin. "You should have lived here under canvas. It can get icy cold at night, and bloody hot in the day. There's nothing to break the wind when it comes up, so you need the storm guys on the tent. This is one of the highest peaks in the range. We're about four thousand feet above the Tsavo game plains."

"Well, I must say, the views are fantastic," he says, gazing at the distant horizon. He pauses, surveying the spectacular panoramic view of the Tsavo and surrounding mountains, and then continues, "It's no wonder Mac chose this place for a repeater site." He nods towards the west. "You get a good view of Kilimanjaro from here, and also Mount Kenya, farther over to the right. It's like being on top of the world."

"True," I say, "that's one of the fascinating things about the place. The view can change so suddenly, especially at night or in the rainy season, when the clouds close in like a dense fog on the peak. In the early morning, the clouds hover over the plains, and make you feel like you're on an island in an immense white sea." I pause a moment, remembering what it was like to step out of the tent into the cold morning air. "All you can see are Kili's twin peaks poking out of the cloud, as well as other mountain peaks surrounding us. As the sun grows stronger, the clouds rise up above the mountaintops, and the view changes again."

Fumbling with the keys, Don finds the right one, unlocks the main door, and we enter. The bases for the generators are in place, but the Pelapone Ricardo motor generators have not yet been installed. Instead, a mobile motor generator acts as a temporary supply of electrical power for the building.

"Ah, well," says Don, as he looks around, "we might as well get the Land Rover unloaded. We can't do too much until we get organized." Looking at his watch, he adds, "It's one o'clock, so let's get unpacked, and get something to eat. We'll likely be here for a few days because we've got to carry out some tests with Kwale and Mombasa."

Turning to me, he says, "I've got two mobile route transceivers, a communications transceiver, and a spectrum analyzer with me. The route transceivers have been modified to test both the receive and transmit paths from Kwale, and replace the normal repeater transceivers. It's a temporary hook-up to check out the system, and iron out any obvious bugs."

I nod, and say, "I guess one of the first things that we'll have to do is set up the VHF communications transceiver and contact Kwale to let them know we're here."

Don nods. "Yes, that's true. I telephoned the carrier room last night from Voi and talked to Lew. He'll be at the Kwale repeater site later, and will contact us about eight. That will give us time to check things over." Continuing our tour, we make our way to the staff room.

My eyes light up when I enter the room. Someone has obviously tried to make it more homelike. The walls have been painted a light yellow, which relieves the bareness, and there's a curtain on the window. There are two bunks, one above the other. Glancing back at Don, I say, "Well, at least we don't need our camp beds. There are two bunks here and a table."

Don looks around the room approvingly. "This one has been fixed up better than the one at Mbwinzau," he says. "I'll take the lower bunk; you're younger than I am."

We unload the Land Rover, and put the test equipment in the radio room. Once we start testing, we'll connect the transceivers to the two antenna feeder cables.

While we quickly sort out our personal effects, we talk. I put my sleeping bag and pillow on the top bunk together with odds and ends that will be looked at later. My mind, however, is on other things, and I broach the subject of communications. "You know, Don," I say, "we can fix the transceiver antenna on a pole, lash it to the ladder rungs on the roof, and then drop the cable through the window, like I did on Mbwinzau. That way, the transceiver is here, right by the bunks. If we have to, we can easily transfer the equipment and antenna cable into the equipment room."

Don nods, "Yeah, that's a good idea. But let's open our chop boxes, and get comfortable first." He glances at his watch, and says, "I don't know about you, Gord, but it's nearly one-thirty, and I'm hungry."

Soon the water for coffee is boiling on the Primus, and we're preparing a quick, cold lunch. We bought more supplies before we left Voi this morning—fresh bread, cans of

Figure 41. View looking towards Mombasa from Vuria Peak.

steak and kidney, corned beef, margarine, cheese, and jam, plus a variety of vegetables—more than enough for a week.

What a difference having a companion makes, I think, *someone who knows the people I know, and what's going on in the Nairobi crowd. It won't be so lonely this time, because there's someone to talk to.*

A Kindred Spirit

After lunch, we start the motor generator, so we've got electricity. *Yes*, I mutter to myself as we switch on the lights and check the power points, *we won't need the pressure lamps.*

The two test transmitters are connected to the coaxial feeder cable leading to the arrays, but we've not switched on the equipment yet. Using the same method that I used in Mbwinzau, we install the small communications radio transceiver in the staff room. Around dusk, we use it to call Kwale on the off-chance, but there's no answer. There are still two hours to go before the scheduled time.

Night has fallen on Vuria, and it's getting colder. We're using the Primus stoves indoors to prepare dinner. I'm mashing the potatoes when Don says, "You know, I can't climb that bloody tower. When I get up about ten feet, I'm terrified. I just cling there, like I'm frozen to the bloody rungs." He pauses and looks up at me, then continues, "That's one of the reasons why Mac suggested that you come with me. Another reason is that you're going to need to get experience on the signal analyzer and other test equipment."

Don hesitates a moment as he chooses his words, and then says, "Mombasa Region have asked Mac to help them out here with a test signal into Kwale because they're short of men. They think there's a problem in the Yagi array directed at Kwale." Don sighs, his shoulders sagging. "I suspect it's probably a short or an open circuit in one of the coaxial cable links in the array. I've brought two complete sets of links with me, as well as sealing cement and tape. With your experience with the riggers on the tower, Mac thought that you were his best bet. Eric's good, too, but he's in the middle of installation in Kitindini, so I'm afraid that the job's fallen to you."

"I don't mind," I say, as I add some margarine and a little milk to the potatoes. "In this job, you have to do just about everything, from road building to *barazas* with native chiefs. It also includes the technical side of things, and I don't know what else."

My thoughts go back to my childhood and Epping Forest as I say, "I can understand how you feel about heights, I fell down a tree when I was a kid and it scared the life out of me. That's how I got this," I say, holding up my scarred left hand. "My little finger got caught in a crack as I scrambled to find something to hold on to. It was the same a few months ago when I climbed the Post Office tower in Nairobi the first time. I was terrified. Just ask Eric; he knows. That guy's got only one good leg, but he can do just about anything."

There's a momentary silence as I look up at Don, and then continue, "I just followed Eric, keeping my eyes on his boots. I didn't dare look down. That tower is just about sheer; it's a hundred and twenty feet of pure terror. Yeah, I know how you feel," I say, "so don't worry. Climbing still bothers me, but I've got used to it." Shrugging my shoulders, I add, "It's all a part of the job now."

I like Don. He's honest about things, and he tells you straight out. He may not be able to climb towers, but he's got a lot of guts. *When we were in the Amboseli Game Reserve that time, he had me stop the Land Rover and not move until the last minute while he took movie films of the rhinos charging. It made me sweat. Thank God the engine didn't stall.*

Contact! It's good to hear Lew's voice again as I reply to his call over the communications transceiver. "Aye," he says, "so you've made it, Gord. How's Vuria?"

"A lot different since the last time I saw it. But then, so was Mbwinzau, what with the new roads up to the sites, and the buildings. Bit of a change from the old days under canvas. Hang on a moment; Don wants to speak to you."

Smiling, Don takes the microphone from me and speaks to Lew. "We'll be starting testing tomorrow with Kwale," he says. "We've got to check the arrays on site here for problems, so Gord will go up the tower. I'd like to keep this channel open in case I have to contact Mac in Nairobi. I've got two modified radio-transceivers here as well as this communications link and recorder units. We'll use them to check the signals between Vuria and Kwale. Mac wants some additional tests, so we'll be here a few days. Over."

Figure 42. Vuria repeater station and mast

Lew's voice comes back, "Yes, I've got all that. There's two of us here, and we're staying overnight to get an early start. The problem is probably in the antenna feeder cable or in the antenna coupling. We'll transmit test signals to you tonight."

As I listen, I grin and shake my head. *It looks like I've got a lot of climbing to do tomorrow until the fault is found and repaired.*

***

Don and I have been busy most of the morning checking and testing the equipment connected to the feeder cable. The incoming signal from Kwale is good and within its bandwidth specification, but they're not receiving our transmitted signal. Don's face is thoughtful. "There's a mismatch somewhere in the antenna, Gord," he says, looking at the output tuning meter for the transmitter section.

"Yes," I say, " The output won't tune. It looks like a short or an open circuit in the connecting link of the transmit array. You've got spare links, haven't you? I'll go up and replace the existing links with new ones. That should clear the trouble."

Don nods his head as he glances at his watch. "Yes, but we might as well have a break for lunch now before we start testing again. They'll probably want to take a lunch break as well. I'll radio Kwale and let them know the situation."

Looking at the sky, Don frowns. "I didn't think this was the rainy season," he says, "but there's cloud building up over the northern part of the range. Do you think it will rain? It'd be bloody nasty to get caught up on the top of the tower in a rainstorm."

"Well, it does some strange things here. As I said before, the mountain has a weather pattern of its own. I don't think it'll rain for an hour or so, but I'd better get up the tower now and change the Yagi links just in case."

"Yeah, maybe you're right," Don says. "We need to check them out."

The Icy Tower

The sun is hot on my back, but a cool breeze tempers the heat to a pleasant warmth as I sit behind the radiator elements of the array. Secured to the crossarm on the top of the mast by my safety belt, I change the interconnecting coaxial cables that feed the transmit frequencies into the stacked Yagi array from the feeder cable.

Absorbed in my work, I pay no heed to the clouds gathering over the range to the north, so I'm startled when I feel the first spots of rain. As I look up, I can feel the force of the rising wind tugging at my body. The rapid change in the weather is unexpected, and numbing cold rain starts beating on my face and body.

My heart is pounding in my chest as I work frantically, quickly replacing the last three-foot length of flexible cable with a spare link. While I am sealing the two end-connections in their respective sockets, the rain, driven by the force of a following wind, soaks my thin clothing and chills my body. My hands quickly finish sealing the joints.

Holding my breath, I undo the safety belt from the crossarm, and, clinging to the wet, slippery metal, I work my way towards the centre point. As I move, the trailing end of the safety belt whips about in the wind. Reaching the place where the crossarm joins the tower, I pause. My breath is now coming in half-sobbing gasps of fright.

The ground below is partly obscured by the swirling cloud and rain, but I catch a glimpse of Don, a blurred vision of his upturned face and open mouth, which seems suspended in time. The only sounds that I hear are the wind and the rapid thumping of my heart.

My hands are numb from the cold rain and colder steel, but I cling desperately to the steel cross-section of the crossbeam. Suppressing my fear, I ease my body onto my stomach, and reach with my feet into the void below, feeling for a foothold on the bolt. A surge of hope and relief momentarily warms my body as my foot finds it.

Cautiously, I lower myself over the parallel beam onto the bolts that protrude six inches from the steep tower leg. For a moment, I shut my eyes, attempting to calm myself; then slowly, testing each bolt with my feet and hands, I begin the long, slow climb down.

Half-blinded by the rain running down my face, I am acutely aware of the depths below me. I dare not look down as I descend backwards. Protruding at right angles, the thick, galvanized bolts are spaced down the outer edge of the tower leg, and make a very precarious ladder.

White with cold, my fingers feel frozen. I have difficulty gripping the bolts. I've suffered from poor circulation all my life, and now it seems like my hands and feet are reduced to unfeeling lumps of ice. Periodically I halt and huddle against the tower, cuddling the metal leg with my arms, while I try to blow warmth and mobility into my fingers.

After what seems an eternity, there is firm ground under my feet, but I feel dazed as I stumble through the rain to the building. Don has been watching from the doorway to the staff room, and, when I reach him, he says, "Christ, Gord, I thought at times that you weren't going to make it. You're soaked, man. You've got to get out of those clothes because they're sodden."

In comparison with the rain-drenched outdoors, the room is warm. Don has the Primus on and has made coffee. I've towelled myself off, changed into dry clothes, and put on a sweater. Now as I talk to Don, I sip from a mug of steaming coffee, wrapping my fingers around it so that the heat from the mug can soak into them.

"I just managed to get the last link changed and sealed when that bloody downpour started," I say. "God, that rain was cold, man, especially as I'd just a thin shirt and shorts on. I never expected the rain would come so fast. It took me completely by surprise."

"Yeah," Don says, "that was a real downpour. I felt helpless down here. Those steel sections must have been bloody slippery. I'll get on with the tests while you finish your coffee."

During the rainy season, the earth gives off a pungent, humid odour, which is peculiar to Africa. It's a pleasant, spicy smell that I've come to love. Now, as the rainstorm passes, I sniff this wet, earthy smell as I walk along to the equipment room where Don is carrying out tests.

As I enter, he glances up. "Well, Gord," he says, "you evidently cured the antennae problem because we can load the transmitter into the antenna now, and they're getting our signal. Kwale has finished setting up the radio repeater equipment and the big motor generators. They're aligning the equipment on the Mombasa terminal signals. They'll be ready for us to start a series of tests with them tomorrow morning. "

***

For the last four days, we've been busy carrying out tests with the Kwale repeater site and the Mombasa terminal. Noon on Tuesday,

February 9, marks the end of the tests. "Well, that's that," says Don, as he puts down the microphone and grins. "We're finished here. The Kwale crew is packing up. All we have to do is load our equipment on the Land Rover, and take an easy ride down to Voi. We'll be back in Nairobi tomorrow night."

By mid-afternoon, the Land Rover is packed and we're on our way. Don's driving, and he's in a hurry. He's decided to bypass Wundanyi, and takes the shorter route via Bura instead. This is a steep, treacherous, and rough road, which tees into the main Taveta-Voi road at Bura, a small mission station and settlement.

Hanging onto the dashboard, I smile as I think about Don's words. *An easy drive back to Voi,* he'd said, but this is a jolting, bone-jarring route. Although I've been on this road before, it's one that we usually avoided because it's nearly impassable for trucks in the rains.

Today the sun is shining, and the road is dry but rough, with deep ruts and potholes. Since coming to Kenya, however, I've been on even rougher roads. I've learned to drive on all kinds of roads, both sand and mud, and in fair and foul weather.

We reach Voi as the sun goes down, and book into the hotel where we share a room with its own bathroom. Having a couple of hours to wait before dinner, we sit on the hotel veranda and order cold beer from the bar.

Later that evening when I go to the toilet after dinner, I notice that there is blood in my stool. Agitated and feeling a bit uncertain about the possible cause, I call Don. "Don," I say, "do you mind coming here for a minute. I must be bleeding; because there's blood in the toilet."

When Don comes, he says, "It could be one of several things, Gord. You're out in the bush a fair bit, however, so it's possibly amoebic dysentery. When we get back to Nairobi, you'd better see a doctor, because that can be pretty serious. How'd you feel?"

"I feel okay, but I wondered whether it was an internal hemorrhage."

Don shakes his head. "No, I don't think so because there's not that much blood. But the doctor will have to get tests done. It will be late by the time we get in tomorrow night, but go to the doctor first thing on Thursday morning. I'll let Mac know what's happened."

***

Chapter 12
End of an Era

Hospitalized

The hospital is located in State House Road, which is lined with eucalyptus trees and blue gums. It is set back on a hill, near where the road curves over the crest not far from Government House. The Infectious Diseases Ward is light and airy, with large windows that look out onto lawns and shrubs. As I lie in bed, my view of the opposite end of the valley is screened off by a row of jacaranda trees.

Yesterday the government doctor examined me, and then arranged for me to be admitted today. "It's a pity that you didn't think to take a sample," he said. "This could be an internal hemorrhage from being shaken about on the rough roads in the Land Rover, or it could possibly be the early stages of amoebic dysentery." Deep in thought, he frowned, and then continued, "I'd rather be on the safe side, so I'll arrange for you to be admitted to hospital tomorrow. They'll put you through a series of tests; then we'll take it from there."

This morning, Joan drove me to the hospital where I was shown to a bed in the men's ward. A dozen beds stretched in orderly rows along both sides of the long, rectangular room. After I've put on the hospital gown and climbed into bed, the nurse came to record my temperature and blood pressure, a procedure that seems automatic in these places. After looking at the doctor's scribbled instructions, she gave me an injection. As she left the room, she said, "The operating room staff will come for you soon. Your tests are scheduled for eleven o'clock."

***

"What are you in for, mate?" asks the older man in the next bed, turning his head to look at me.

"Suspected amoebic dysentery," I say. "But they're going to carry out tests to make sure."

He nods, "Yes, they'll use a rectoscope to examine you. It's routine."

Another man, an Afrikaner from his accent, chimes in. "*Ja, jong*, if you're not sick now, you soon will be once they stick that up you." He laughs as he says, "Aye, lad, that bloody thing's big, and them nurses are tough. No use struggling when they hold you down. There's six of them, ain't there, Joe," he says turning to the first man.

"Shut up, Johan, and let the lad be," Joe says. "You're just a bloody *plaas japie* (country yokel) from the boondocks." Turning back to me, he says, "Pay no attention to him; he's just kidding you. The nurses here are very good to us."

Listening to the friendly banter exchanged between the two, a British settler and an Afrikaner, I grin.

✳✳✳

I didn't feel sick when I came into hospital, but now I feel like death warmed up. I can't lift my head above the pillow without being sick. All I remember is being wheeled into the operating room, and seeing the face of the anaesthetist leaning over me. He'd put a syringe needle into my arm, and within seconds I knew no more until I woke to find myself back in the ward. Time passes in a haze, and I don't remember how many times that Joan has been to see me. The vomiting continues for three days, and I am kept under medication. Gradually the nausea wanes, and finally I can lift my head without feeling queasy.

Three weeks have gone by, and, no longer confined to my bed, I walk around the ward. I've got to know both Joe and Johan. An Afrikaner, Johan loves to kid around. He farms up near Eldoret in Western Kenya; his family came here from South Africa in the early 'twenties. Joe, too, is a farmer, but he's from the Kipipiri area in the foothills of the Aberdares near the Elephant's Head. As it's one of the areas where I installed emergency radios, we often talk about the emergency and the area in general.

It's strange how uncommunicative doctors can be on their periodic visits. They simply ask you how you are, then look at the record sheets, and possibly prescribe some medication. It is when I'm being released from hospital, that I finally learn that the tests were inconclusive; however, they decided to give me the full course of treatment in case the bleeding or symptoms come back.

Riggers Ambushed

It's the morning of March 5 when I'm discharged. Joan collects me, and takes me home. It is only when we've had lunch that she finally tells me about the ambush.

"Yakub, Dawoodi and Daudi were attacked about a month ago when they were going to work," she says. "It was soon after they returned from Mbwinzau. Your riggers were amongst a group of Asians who were ambushed. Gloria told me, but I didn't tell you because you were in hospital. A *Mau Mau* bicycle gang, armed with revolvers and other weapons, opened fire on them at the corner of River and Government Roads. You know, by the Khoja Mosque."

"Oh, no," I say, a prickly feeling passing through me as her words sink in. "Are they all right?"

"Dawoodi and Daudi are okay; but Yakub was shot three times, in the hand, foot and stomach. Several of the Asian men were killed, but apart from some cuts and bruises, Dawoodi and Daudi escaped without injury."

"That's good," I say, "but what about Yakub? Are his wounds serious?"

"They're mainly flesh wounds, but the one in the stomach was more serious. The bullet passed right through him without touching any vital organs. I understand he is out of hospital and recovering at home."

"Thank God for that," I say. A sense of relief shudders through my body, and I feel my muscles relax. Then I add, "Did the gang get away?"

"Yes," Joan says. "According to the newspaper, it was all over in a few seconds. There was just enough time for the attackers to pedal up on their bicycles, fire their guns into the group, and then disappear down the back alleys of River Road."

She looks up at me. "They presumably backtracked into the shanty-towns of Doonholm Road and Kariokor. It all happened so quickly. People were in too much of a panic to stop them."

The Tide Turns

Swiftly and without warning, early in April 1954, the security forces move at dawn to seal off the city of Nairobi and the locations. At first, most residents of Nairobi are unaware of what is happening. On our way to work that morning, both Eric and I sense that something big could be going on when we see the large number of roadblocks and army and police trucks.

Rumours abound when the military hastily erects barbed wire around a large, open area of land near the main Nairobi Post Office, cordoning it off. Standing at our office windows, we watch the arrival of police and army trucks, their backs resembling gigantic cages, which are crammed with large numbers of Africans. One after another, the trucks roll up to disgorge their prisoners into this holding area. Straggling lines of people, dressed in a motley assortment of ragged clothing, disembark under armed guard, and then squat cross-legged on the dusty, sunbaked ground while they await interrogation.

Brushing his hair back from his forehead with his hand, Eric says, "There's got to be hundreds of them. It looks like they're cracking down on the criminals here and in the locations." He pauses for a moment, and then continues, "They're probably screening them before they take them to interrogation camps." He sighs, "It's about bloody time, too. The gangs were taking over the streets."

As we watch, some prisoners, who are being off-loaded from an army truck stopped just outside the barbed wire enclosure, make a break for freedom. The scene is chaotic as police *askaris* contain the area. Swinging their rifles by the barrels, they use them as clubs to hit indiscriminately at the men, knocking them down. Order is soon restored, however, and the men are dragged into the barbed wire enclosure.

I glance at Eric. "Does that remind you of those two prisoners we took to Homa Bay?"

Eric nods, "Yeah, those *askaris* certainly didn't use kid gloves, and neither do these. It doesn't seem to matter that it's black against black." He shakes his head. "Christ, you'd think that blows like that would cave a man's head in. They must have bloody thick skulls."

Later that day, the Forces Broadcasting Station announces that the army and police have launched Operation Anvil. A vast net is being cast in an attempt to disrupt and end the *Mau Mau* Central Committee and its organization, both in Nairobi and the surrounding locations. No further details are released, except that the operation is ongoing.

In the coming weeks, we gradually learn more about this combined operation. Systematically police and army units comb through hot beds of terrorism as they move through the African locations, suburbs, and streets of the crime-riddled city. Working to a pattern, they search house-by-house, and street-by-street, moving from the shanty-towns of corrugated iron and cardboard boxes in the Mathari Valley, Kariokor, and Doonholm Road to Eastleigh and more affluent areas of the city.

Anyone found illegally in the Nairobi area is taken prisoner. Army trucks are crammed with suspects who are then taken to screening camps and interrogation centres in and around the city. By the end of the month, twenty-seven thousand Kikuyu men and women have been rounded up, screened, and sent into detention camps. Most of the detainees are sent to Manyani, a large internment camp in a remote area between the Tsavo River and Ndi.

Earlier this year, the capture of General China had dealt a major blow to *Mau Mau*. Now, as a result of Operation Anvil, further terrorist attacks have been prevented in the Nairobi area. The terrorists in the forest are cut off from their supply sources, and are becoming desperate. Daily they are being further isolated by General Erskine's tactics, and are constantly harassed by army units with orders to search-and-destroy.

In one stroke, Operation Anvil has effectively destroyed both the Central Committee of *Mau Mau* and its entire organization in Nairobi. News of its success spreads like wildfire throughout Kenya, reviving the flagging spirits of the white settlers.

Capture of General China

I remember well the capture of General China, leader of the Mount Kenya *Mau Mau* forest gangs, who boasted that he could field an army of a thousand men at any one time in the forests of Mount Kenya. His capture had been announced January 1st, 1954, on the Forces Broadcasting Station, shortly after we arrived home. We'd been on holiday at the coast, and had celebrated New Year's Eve at Mac's Inn. Now Kenya had another reason to celebrate.

Billy's voice was strained with excitement, his face flushed and tense. "I don't believe it," he said, as he turned up the radio volume. "They've captured General China."

Joan was busy in the kitchen helping Samson, our house servant, to prepare a meal, but hearing the radio, she walked quietly into the living room.

We listened as the voice of the announcer came over the radio: "Today, during a firefight with the armed forces in the Mount Kenya forests, Waruhiu Itote, known as General China, was wounded and captured. Details of his capture are not known at present, and the military forces have released no further news. We will bring you more news bulletins when information is made available to the public." As the broadcast ended, Billy turned the radio off.

When the broadcast started, I had been kneeling on the floor, unpacking our bags, and sorting out dirty clothes for Samson to wash the next morning. The laundry was forgotten as my mind turned over this new situation in the fight against *Mau Mau*. The capture of General China was the break that both the white settlers and the African loyalists have been waiting for, and the news of his arrest spread throughout the colony.

Samson, who followed Joan out of the kitchen, asked, "*Habari gani—* what's the news, bwana? I heard General China's name. Is he dead?"

"No," I said, shaking my head, "he's been wounded and captured, but the army have not released any further details."

Samson, a Maragoli tribesman, smiles, and then says solemnly, "Why didn't the soldiers kill him? He is a very bad man."

Shrugging my shoulders, I replied, "*Sijui, lakini—*I don't know, but perhaps the soldiers did not want to kill him. He is more useful alive, because he can tell them many things about his army and how it operates."

His face serious, Samson considered the point, then his eyes brighten. "*Ndiyo*," he said, "*Ah, nafahamu*—I understand." He turned, and, with a smile on his face, returned to the kitchen. As the door opened, then closed behind him, we could smell onions cooking.

Joan and Samson had prepared a quick, hurried meal of liver and onions, mashed potatoes, vegetables and gravy. "Aye," said Billy as he speared a piece of liver, "this'll be a turning point in the *Mau Mau* fortunes, just like losing the fight for the Othalo Police Post was, but this time it'll be even worse."

As he chewed the meat, he was silent for a moment, and then continued speaking. "I'd hate to be in China's shoes. From what I've seen, the *Mau Mau* interrogation units are anything but pleasant. He'll be under great pressure to give information on *Mau Mau* units and locations."

Billy shook his head. "Yeah, sooner him than me. But I'm not sorry for him, when you consider what those bastards do to their victims and to their own people. Anyway, he'll probably make a deal to escape hanging. That's his only option."

It was late when Paddy, Billy's brother, picked him up and drove him home. We watched them leave from the apartment veranda. Tomorrow was Saturday, and on the Monday Billy had to be back with his KPR unit in Gilgil. The car's headlights swept up the opposite side of the valley and then they were gone, hidden by the acacia trees lining the stream that winds past our building.

"Why do holidays always seem to fly by?" I said, putting my arms around Joan. Jokingly, I added, "You don't really like sleeping in a tent, do you?"

She wrinkled her nose and shook her head, "No, I'm not the outdoors type. A tent's too cramped and uncomfortable." She laughed, "The next time, you and Billy can sleep in a tent if you want to, but I'm going to a hotel."

A grin spread across my face. "Well, at least you did give it a try. It's not really a holiday as far as I'm concerned because I'm out under canvas most of the year. I like the coast, and it made a break to get away from work for a while." I paused a moment. "The next time, we'll either go to a hotel or hire a *banda*. What about the Sinbad in Malindi, or Seafarers in Turtle Bay? Come to that, we can go anywhere, as long as we don't stay in a tent."

"Or we could take a ship down the coast to Durban." Laughing, Joan added. "Remember the Lloyd Triestino Line and the *Gerusalemme*."

Her words brought back memories of our holiday in 1951. "Yes," I said wistfully. "I remember Durban and its beaches, and the Valley of a Thousand Hills in the Zulu Reserve. How could I ever forget?" Glancing up at her, I smile. "Remember Beira? It was so hot and sweaty that we were glad to get back to the ship!"

The Last Assignment

It is Monday morning, July 5, 1954. The cold season is upon us, and the average temperature in Nairobi hovers around fifty degrees Fahrenheit. The long rains ended in May so at least it's not raining.

Over the last two months, Eric, Bungy, and I have been busy installing the repeater station electrical wiring and VHF radio equipment in both the Kitindini and Mbwinzau repeater sites. The building section has installed the large Pelapone Ricardo motor generators on their plinths, and we've wired up the control cabinets for the generators on the two repeater sites. With the repeater stations now operational, all that remains to be done is to align and check the overall system.

Eric greets me as I enter Mac's office. "Well, Gord," he whispers as I stand next to him. "Think old Mac'll tell us who's going on the Dar-Dodoma survey?"

"No, I doubt it. They'll keep their options open." I nod towards the door as Mac comes in from the back office. "We'll soon know."

✳✳✳

Mac is wearing an old, open-neck shirt, grey trousers, grey socks, and worn, brown shoes. His rumpled brown cardigan has leather patches on the elbows. Informal in both appearance and manner, he leans against the table. "Well, we're all here by the look of it," he says. "As you know, we're on the last phase before commissioning the routes from Nairobi to Mombasa and on to Dar es Salaam. The western route is completed and was operational by the end of April in time for the Queen's broadcast from Jinja when she opened the Owen Falls Dam."

He pauses briefly, and then continues, "Once the present routes are completed, the teams will be split up; this will be the last safari on the Nairobi-Dar route. We need trained people to maintain the terminal and repeater stations, so that means that the department will transfer some of you to the exchange carrier rooms."

Looking around the small group, he grins, then says, "As you are probably aware, only the Dar es Salaam to Dodoma repeater route remains to be surveyed. I will be concentrating on the survey side, while Mr. Proud, our senior engineer, and Mr. Lilley, our administration officer, will be directly involved in the changeover of staff. They will be responsible for all decisions on your future roles and assignments once the coastal route to Dar es Salaam is completed and in service."

Smiling, Mac says, "We've one last job to do now, and that's the alignment stage." He looks across at Eric and me. "Dar es Salaam Region wants staff to help them align the new equipment on the Zanzibar and Tanga repeaters. Scales and Mumford will take the Land Rover to Dar with test equipment, and then go to Zanzibar Island where they will carry out tests with both the terminal in Dar and the Tanga repeater."

Turning to Bungy and Geoff, he adds, "Williams and Perrins will man the Tanga repeater, working into Zanzibar and Mombasa." After discussing the testing procedures and equipment to be used, Mac closes the meeting by asking if there are any further questions.

"Not really," Eric says. He shakes his head as he glances at me for confirmation. "When do you want us to leave?"

"Soon as you've loaded your vehicles, and are ready to go," Mac says. "Tomorrow, if you like, but Wednesday at the latest. That'll give you time to arrange personal matters and pack your gear."

The Usambara Mountains

It's Wednesday, July 7, and after we packed the Land Rover with test equipment and our personal baggage, Eric and I had left Nairobi as scheduled at eight thirty this morning, with Eric driving.

It's almost three months since the long rains stopped in early April. No longer green, the Kapiti plains are dried up and the grass is yellowing. Slowly migrating to more fertile areas, the plains animals are scattered far and wide in their search for grass.

We've been on the road about an hour now, and Kajiado lies just ahead of us on the Nairobi-Namanga Road. Clustered around the railroad station, the small settlement consists of a few huts and a couple of wooden buildings, while a solitary Indian *duka* caters to the wandering Masai tribesmen with their herds of cattle.

Kajiado is a lonely whistle stop on the Magadi-Konza railroad track to Lake Magadi, a soda lake close to the Tanganyika border. As we speed by a lone Masai seated by the roadside, he waves. Soon, he and the settlement are lost in our dust.

Eric grips the steering wheel, his face set and his eyes thoughtful as he concentrates on the rough, potholed dirt road. "Aye, Gord," he says, "it looks like we'll be split up. This may well be our last safari together."

"Yes, it could be," The drum of the wheels on the dirt road fills the silence as I grope for words to express my feelings. "I suppose it's inevitable. But I love safari work. "It's a part of my life that I don't want to end. I'd hate to become another Nairobi desk *wallah*."

Eric swerves to avoid a pothole in the road. "You'll never be that," he laughs. "You're not the type, any more than I am." Shaking his head, he says, "No, you won't fit in there, Gord. All those office *wallahs* are hide-bound and ruled by regulations and red tape. After all these years in the bush, you're just not the type."

He continues. "Once my contract's up, I'm applying for a job with the Marconi Company, like Gaul and Mellon have. When these routes are finished, they're off to South America to do the same thing over there." He smiles and adds, "I reckon Marconi will need experienced men for those teams."

Absorbed in our thoughts, we talk on as we cross the Kapiti plains, heading south towards the rolling rocky landscape of the Ingito Hills and the foothills of Kilimanjaro. Further on, the mountain is clear of cloud and the snowcap of Kibo glistens in the rays of the morning sun.

The Tanganyika border crossing at Namanga is close as we enter the small township with its solitary petrol station, flanked by corrugated iron-roofed *dukas* and fruit stalls. A freshly painted sign indicates the turn-off to the Namanga River Hotel. Nodding towards the sign, Eric says, "Fancy a coffee, Gord?"

"Yeah, that's a thought," I glance at my watch. "It's just eleven o'clock. We've covered the hundred miles from Nairobi in good time. That's not bad, considering the road."

The old, colonial-style hotel is located on the lower slopes of the Ingito Hills. Parking the vehicle, we sit at a nearby table on the outside patio. "Ah," says Eric, stretching his arms and legs, "this is the life." He sips his coffee, then lights a cigarette. As he exhales, the smoke curls into the still air. "Think we'll make Mombo tonight?" he asks.

"Yeah," I say, adding, "Once we get past Arusha and Moshi, it's straight forward. Mombo is about two hundred and fifty miles from here. Then it's about another twenty miles from the Mombo turn-off to the Lushoto Hotel in the Usambara Mountains."

We drink our coffee, and continue talking. Then we pay our bill and stroll back to the Land Rover. I take over the driving, and, settling back in the seat, drive through the small border settlement to the Tanganyikan border on its outskirts.

A simple bar across the road marks the border. One end is weighted and pivots on a metal post, while the other end of the bar hooks onto a second post on the far side of the road. As I draw up to the barrier, an *askari* approaches the Land Rover from a nearby cluster of huts. Both countries come under British rule, so there are no real formalities at the border.

"*Jambo, bwana,*" says the border guard, as he hands me the record book. "*Andika kitabu yangu*—please sign the book, sir." Indicating the logo on the Land Rover door, the *askari* adds, "Ah, you work for the *serakali* (government)."

"*Ndiyo*," I answer as I hand the book back, "yes, we are going to Dar es Salaam."

Putting the Land Rover in gear, I wait for him to raise the barrier, and then drive off down the gravel road leading to Arusha. Cresting the long ridge of hills, we head south into Tanganyika and, turning southeast, bypass Arusha to skirt the southern foothills of Kilimanjaro to Moshi.

Lying in the shadow of Kilimanjaro, the small township of Moshi was named after the billowing smoke given off by the coal- and wood-burning steam locomotives. It used to be the railroad junction for the Tanga railroad when Tanganyika was still a German Colony. Now the town is an important junction linking the Arusha-Tanga railroad with Voi on the Nairobi-Mombasa route to Uganda.

Leaving Moshi behind us, I drive southeast along the edges of the North and South Pare Mountains, keeping the plains of the flat, dried-up Masai steppe on our right. It is getting late in the afternoon when we finally approach Mombo. At the intersection, a weathered wooden sign points the way to Lushoto via the Soni Falls.

"This is it, Eric," I say, with a sense of satisfaction. "The Lushoto Hotel is roughly twenty miles along it. Joan and I stopped here once when we were going to Dar. It's a nice, old-fashioned country hotel."

The tires squeal and kick up dust as I turn the wheel to the left, and then head north along the steep and winding dirt road cut into the mountainside. Glancing back and down, I can see the great plains of the Masai Steppe falling away behind us.

Splashed across the arid yellow of the steppe, a broad swathe of green outlines the plantations below. The sisal plants are laid out in long, straight, symmetrical lines, and the thick, fibrous leaves stand out against the stark countryside. The view is so spectacular that I pull off the road where the Land Rover tops the ridge of the first range.

We stand there on the ridge for several minutes, watching the setting sun as it glints off the long, thin, wispy cirrus clouds. Below us, the game plains of the Masai Steppe stretch flat to the horizon, broken here and there by small conical hills. A long plume of dust rises behind a fast travelling dot on the barely visible road below as it threads its way across the plains.

"Bloody marvellous," I hear Eric mutter as we resume our journey. The light is fading fast now, so we don't stop to look at the Soni Falls. Lushoto is close, only ten miles away.

The Lushoto Hotel

Refreshed by a hot bath and a change of clothing, we enter the dining room just before eight. There are only four other guests. An elderly couple is seated at a table near the door, while two men—the older one bearded and the other clean-shaven—have a table near the window.

Basically, the Lushoto Hotel is a bush hotel; it's neat and clean with a limited menu. Dinner is a set meal, consisting of soup, roast beef, mashed potatoes, and vegetables followed by a steamed pudding, traditional British fare. After all, Tanganyika has been a British protectorate since the end of the First World War.

As customary, coffee is served in the lounge after dinner. Here, mounted heads of deer and antelope hang on the walls. At one end of the large room, flames dance and flicker in the grate of a large, stone fireplace. It is cold here; we're high in the Usambaras, where the cool season lasts from June until the end of August. Like clockwork, the prevailing winds reverse direction in May or June, and the *Kusi* (southerly monsoon) blows up the coast from the southwest taking the dhows back to Arabia.

My thoughts are elsewhere. Absent-mindedly, I stir my coffee, spilling a little into the saucer. "Have you been to Zanzibar before?" I ask.

Eric shakes his head, "No, I never did get over to the island. When we get into Dar tomorrow, we'll stay at a hotel. We can check out the location of the repeater with the Regional Office. Mac just marked an X on the map of the island, so I suppose we can find it. Anyway, we've got to check in with the carrier room to let them know we've arrived and are ready to start testing. The Regional Office has installed the new equipment on both the Tanga and Zanzibar sites."

We order beer from the waiting steward, and talk on long into the night until the bar closes. The effect of the beer is relaxing and soothing, and we reminisce about the past, exchanging confidences and tales of bygone years. It is late when we leave, and I feel light on my feet as we stumble along the stony path to our chalet.

There is a mosquito net over the bed, suspended from a large, round, metal ring. Tucking the hanging ends of the net under the edges of the mattress, I slide between the bedsheets. They feel soft and comforting as my body relaxes, and I lay back on the pillow. Looming above me in the darkness, the dim shape of the sheer netting spreads out in a circle. Halfway between sleep and waking, my mind conjures up the ridiculous image of a nineteenth century dress held out by a hoop or crinoline, and I laugh softly at the thought.

How many drinks did I have tonight? Was it two or three? I can't remember. The skin of my face feels detached, so it must be at least two.

The moon throws a beam of light across the room from the latched and barred window. Shadows play tricks on my imagination, and, dismissing them, I turn over in bed and fall asleep. The last thing I remember is Eric snoring, and the white conical-shaped mosquito netting around his bed.

Sunlight fills the room when I wake to a knock on the door. Pushing aside the net, I scramble out of the bed and fumble with the door lock. When I open the door, I see the room steward standing there with a tray, and his face breaks into a wide grin. "*Jambo, bwana*," he says, "*Iko chai*—I have brought you tea." As he puts the tray down on the side table, and turns to leave, he adds, "Breakfast is ready."

Eric sits up in bed, and looks at his watch. "God, is it that time already?" he grumbles. "It's bloody near seven o'clock."

As we walk down the path from our chalet to the dining room, the mountain air feels fresh on my face. It's early, so there is still dew on the grass, but it will have dried by the time we have finished breakfast. In the distance, the heat thermals are forming on the Masai Steppe below us. The altitude here is roughly six or seven thousand feet, and the steppes are on average about one thousand feet above sea level.

The Road to Dar es Salaam

We leave at half past eight, with Eric driving, retracing our route to the main road. By the time we reach the northern outskirts of Mombo, the steep gradients and tight mountain bends have levelled out. Turning left at the T-junction, we head east towards the coast.

Once clear of the town, Eric accelerates and, picking up speed, makes up for lost time, driving southeast for Korogwe in light local traffic. "Dar's two hundred miles, give or take a few," he says

The spread-out town of Korogwe has disappeared in our dust trail as Eric drives the Land Rover at speed over the rough corrugated dirt surface of the Korogwe-Morogoro road. The T-junction with the Morogoro-Dar es Salaam road lies eighty miles south across the flat plains of the Masai steppes. Only the occasional village along the road's sparsely populated route relieves the monotony of the African scrub, with its thorn trees, yellowing clumps of grass and towering ant hills.

"Miles and miles of bloody Africa," Eric grumbles as the Land Rover settles down to a steady speed of sixty plus miles an hour. The drum of the wheels has changed to a steady hum as the speed passes its critical point of forty-five miles an hour, skimming across the ridges of the corrugations.

Occasionally there is a dried-up riverbed or perhaps a small village like Makata. Dignified by a name on the map, these obscure places inevitably turn out to be two or three small huts scattered around a rural crossroads, which may, or may not, lead to a distant bush village.

We've passed the Wami River, and are approaching the village of Msata, when a road sign catches my eye. "Look, Eric," I say, "that's the turn-off to Bagamoyo. Now, that's a place I'd like to see some day."

Eric grins, "Yes, me too, especially the old slave market and harbour. But I understand the road between Bagamoyo and Dar has been washed out for some time."

Despite the open windows, it's hot inside the Land Rover. Even the rush of hot air created by our steady speed of sixty miles an hour gives little relief. To add to our discomfort, the back draft sucks dust into the vehicle through every minute crack and seam. Shutting the sliding windows keeps the dust out, but it increases the heat inside the vehicle; either way, you can't win. The heat is debilitating, and I feel my eyelids grow heavy. The constant drumming of the wheels on the corrugated and potholed dirt roads is also soporific. As the miles go by, I doze in the passenger seat.

The Msata turn-off is far behind us now, and we're approaching the main road to Dar es Salaam when Eric's voice wakes me. "Wakey-wakey, Gord," he says with a laugh.

Sitting up, I stretch my arms, and then settle back in my seat. "I just closed my eyes for a moment," I say. "The heat and sitting here really gets to me. How about letting me take over the wheel. It'll keep me awake, and give you a rest?"

Eric, nods, "Yeah, that's a good idea. I could do with a break. How far is it to the main road?"

"It must be about ten miles. We passed the village of Mazizi just before I dozed off." Pausing, I look at the map. "There's a village called Lugoba a little farther on. Take the left fork there; it leads to the main Morogoro-Dar Road. I'll take over from there."

✳✳✳

The tarred road has degenerated into a lace-curtain road, a Kenya euphemism for a hardtop road that is badly potholed. *Main road? The bloody dirt road was better than this. If you hit the sharp, hard edges of the potholes at speed, they can cut into the tires and jar the alignment of the vehicle's framework. It's no wonder a set of tires lasts only a year.*

Biting my lip, I slow the Land Rover as we hit a series of potholes. The suspension bottoms, and jolted awake, Eric grabs hold of the bar on top of the dashboard. The canvas top of the Land Rover flaps and jerks, creating a racket of noise. Slowing down, I turn the vehicle onto the soft earth at the side of the road where the ride is easier.

Figure 43. Policeman directing traffic in Dar es Salaam.

"Did you say it was seventy bloody miles to Dar?" Eric shakes his head. "This must be the arse end of all roads."

"Yes," I say, "it could well be, but at least it's not raining. Remember the mud and rain in the Teitas? And the track across the Bue plains? It took Mellon and me three days to cross twenty miles of swamp, and then we needed the help of Smit's tractor."

Eric smiles as I slow down, picking my way through the worn and broken patches of road where heavily laden trucks have destroyed the paved surface. "Yes, "that's true." Settling down again in his seat, Eric closes his eyes, and tilts his black bush hat over his face.

We're driving through the fertile coastal areas, and have left the arid sparse semi-desert conditions of the plains and the Masai Steppe behind. Plantations of palm trees, fields of mealies, and thick bush interspersed with stunted trees are commonplace as we near Dar es Salaam. There are also more people—mainly native women with baskets of food and vegetables on their heads—walking along the sides of the road, probably on their way to the market. Dejected and ugly mud-and-wattle-huts with rusting corrugated iron roofs stand alongside rondavels with *makuti* roofs and fruit stalls, as the Land Rover passes through the shanty-town suburbs and into the city of Dar es Salaam.

Dar Carrier Room

"We've arrived, Eric," I say. "Now we need to find the post office yard. Do you have any suggestions?"

"Aye," he says, "make for the harbour. That's where the main administration buildings are. We can get our bearings from there." He rummages through the papers underneath the dashboard, looking for the city map, while I drive to the harbour. There are no traffic lights, but then none of the cities or towns in East Africa has traffic lights.

However, at the main road junctions, there are raised white boxes where an *askari* stands to direct traffic. Here in Dar, these officials wear white gloves, a red fez, khaki shirt, and shorts, with navy blue puttees and black boots.

We park the Land Rover under the shade of an acacia tree near the harbour wall, while Eric studies the map of the city. "Humph," grunts Eric, scratching his head. "Damned if I can find the bloody post office yard. The main post office is not far from here, but we're looking for the telephone exchange." Closing the map, he says, "Let's ask at the post office. Someone there should be able to tell us where the yard is. You know," he says ruefully, "when I came here before, someone picked me up at the airport; I'm damned if I can remember the goddamned road now." Looking at me, he grins, "You're not much better. You came here with Joan on holiday, so you don't have a bloody clue."

Amused, I say, "You're right. That's the last thing I'd be interested in on a holiday. But look on the bright side. We've found the harbour, which is the centre of attraction. It's a natural anchorage and it's really beautiful. Just look around you." I nod toward the sweep of the inner harbour. The deep-water berths stretch up the creek and a palm-fringed road runs parallel to the beach from the harbour mouth to the shipping berths. "And don't forget the church and the old government building behind us in the park land. They both date back to when Tanganyika was known as German East Africa, a German colony, before World War One."

Figure 44. Historic government buildings near the harbour date from the 1900s when Tanganyika was German East Africa

Eric lifts his head, looking skywards in mock despair. "Yes, Gord, it is beautiful, but we've still got to find the bloody yard."

Grinning, I get into the Land Rover, and settle behind the wheel

✳✳✳

"Bernard," I can't contain my surprise as I greet an old friend. "I didn't realize you were posted down here." Bernard Stow is in his forties, a short, stocky man with thinning hair. He used to be in the Nairobi carrier room, but I had lost track of him. Now he is in charge of the Dar carrier room.

"I've been here about a year," he says. "Mac Gregory told us that you and Eric were coming down to test the repeater link alignment on the Zanzibar repeater with Tanga and us. Who's on the Tanga end?"

"Bungy and Geoff Perrins," Eric says. "They should be there by now. When do you want to start testing?"

Bernard laughs. "Not tonight," he says, adding, "There is a car ferry to Zanzibar you can catch tomorrow morning at ten o'clock."

It was when we were discussing the break-up of the survey team crews that Bernard told us about his experiences in the Nairobi carrier room. "Aye," he said, "There's too many self-opinionated engineers in headquarters and too much red tape. That's why I applied for a transfer here." He smiled and went on to say, "It's peaceful at the coast. There's no backbiting or political squabbling from people trying to climb the social ladder. I can get on with my job in peace. I'm glad to be away from Nairobi."

We talk on for a while with Bernard who briefs us on the Zanzibar repeater, and eventually leave at four o'clock to drive to a nearby hotel. Tomorrow we'll cross on the ferry to Zanzibar.

On to Zanzibar

Government vehicles get priority on the ferry. When we drive the Land Rover up to the ramp, the officer in charge of loading signals us on board. Promptly at ten o'clock, the ferry pulls away from the dock.

"What speed do you think this old tub will do, Gord?" Eric says. We are leaning against the ship's bulwark, watching the harbour entrance slide by.

"At a rough guess, somewhere between ten and fourteen knots," I reply. "It's an old ship, but fairly large, so it's hard to say. During the war, the average cargo ship did about eight or ten knots at the most, while some old rust buckets could only do about six knots. Bigger ships like tankers could push it to twelve or more."

Eric nods, his face thoughtful while he works out our probable time of arrival. "Aye," he says, "it's about fifty miles to Zanzibar town, so I reckon we'll be there about one-thirty or two o'clock."

"That sounds about right," I say, "but if you want to confirm it, the ferry schedule is posted in the ship's lounge."

He shakes his head. "It was just idle curiosity."

Behind us, the mainland fades into the distance as the dim outline of the southern section of Zanzibar Island takes shape on our starboard bow. Roughly sixty miles in length from north to south, the main town and port, also called Zanzibar, lies at the halfway point. As the ship moves through the ocean between the mainland and the island, it creates its own light breeze.

It's two in the afternoon when the ferry arrives, and pulls into its docking area. Eric drives the Land Rover

Figure 45. Hotel in the old town of Zanzibar.

down the off-ramp onto the dock, and takes the main road through the town of Zanzibar. Seated beside him, I've got Bernard's directions in my hand.

"Bloody hell," Eric grumbles, squeezing past an oncoming car, "these streets are damned narrow."

"If you think these are narrow, just look at the side streets," I say. "They're impossible."

"Humph," grunts Eric, as the road opens up into a square where there's a hotel. Tall, white pillars support the balconies of the two-storey building, and flank the main entrance. "That must be the hotel Bernard was talking about. We might as well spend tonight here, and get some food supplies. We'll need them on the repeater site."

"Yes, that's true," I reply thoughtfully. "It'll also give us time to see a little of the town as well." Glancing at the road map, I add, "The repeater site is several miles outside of town, near the main road to Ndava in the northern part of the island."

Eric finds a space, and parks the dust-covered Land Rover. We walk through the tall, carved Arab doors of the hotel and enter a spacious reception area. At the desk, a smartly dressed Arab clerk greets us. "One or two rooms, sir?" he says.

"We'll have a double room with two beds," says Eric. "We'll be leaving tomorrow morning right after breakfast." Handing us the keys, the clerk calls a nearby attendant to take our luggage upstairs.

Our room has a balcony overlooking the square. When we step outside, we catch a glimpse of a nearby mosque, its dome partly hidden by the roofs of neighbouring buildings. To one side, a large acacia tree spreads its shade over a wooden bench in the courtyard. Glancing at his watch, Eric says, "There's still a few hours before sunset. Fancy having a look at the town?"

The Suk (Market)

Before leaving the hotel, we move the Land Rover to the hotel's parking lot at the back of the building under the care of their security guard. Locking the vehicle, we wander along the narrow, twisting streets, mingling freely with the local Arab and African population.

To counter the heat, men wear loose-fitting, colourful robes, and *kanzus* (ankle-length white or yellow embroidered cotton gowns, gathered at the waist with cummerbunds and buttoned at the neck), or wrap themselves in *kikois* (wrap around skirts that also serve as loincloths). The women are veiled and draped in the voluminous, black *buibui* (covering robes), their heads and faces veiled.

Islam is in evidence everywhere, and there are numerous, picturesque mosques. From their minarets, the *muezzins*—Mohammedan criers— proclaim the hours of prayer five times daily, calling the faithful to prayer with cries of "*Allah Akbar—God is great.*"

Attracted by the smell of incense and other, less identifiable smells, we amble down a narrow street between the rows of open-fronted *dukas* that line both sides of the street. It is a hive of activity. They're selling spices, yams, mustard seeds, paprika, pepper, and less exotic wares, such as bananas, bunches of dried onions, tomatoes and rice. As we pass by the various storefronts, the voices of the vendors try to entice us inside to buy.

As we roam deeper into the town's market section, the cloying smell of burning joss sticks hangs in the air. "Christ, Gord," says Eric. "I hate the smell of joss sticks; let's get the hell out of here."

Certain streets seem to be reserved for various trades; the money lenders and jewellery shops are all together, while in the next street, every shop seems to sell nothing but African and Arab carvings. Some streets are so narrow that opposite awnings almost touch, which discourages the bright sunlight from penetrating the depths below.

Dusk is falling when we decide to start back to the hotel. Here and there, lamps are lit and gleam in the windows facing the street, while lanterns hang at the front of many shops. "How's your sense of direction, Gord?" asks Eric.

I laugh, and then add, "We'll soon find out. The main road through town runs north and south. If we head east, we should come to it. Once we get there, we'll head north, and just keep walking until we get to the hotel."

Eric's not convinced. "In this maze of streets, it's hard to keep track of your direction." He jerks his head towards the fast dying sun, "The sun's almost gone, and then we won't know what's east or west."

"Stop worrying, Eric. Don't forget that all these little side streets eventually lead to the main road. We can always go into one of the *dukas* and ask. For a few coins, any young kid will act as a guide."

When we eventually get back to the hotel, it is dark. An enterprising shopkeeper had sold us a map for a shilling, and pointed out the way. Wandering about at night in the Arab quarter is not the most enjoyable experience. The sight of the square and well-lit hotel are most welcoming. I must admit that I was relieved to see them.

The Zanzibar Repeater Site

Shortly after breakfast the next morning, we leave the hotel, and, with Bernard's map as a guide, head north towards the village of Selem where we stock up with food supplies. Zanzibar Island is mainly low-lying coral. The eastern side is covered with scattered bush and grass plains, but the western side is fertile. The coastal road runs through coconut and clove plantations, but there are also fields of corn, cassava, and other crops. The western side also has ridges—some rising up about two hundred feet above sea level—and, on one of these ridges, we find the repeater site.

The galvanized steel tower, with its multi-quad directional Yagi arrays on top, is

Figure 46. The repeater station and tower on Zanzibar Island.

unmistakable. The access road to the site passes through a clove and palm tree plantation to the bush beyond where the tower stands. At one hundred and twenty feet, the mast is taller than most of the repeater masts, but the building is identical to those on other sites. A high wire mesh fence, topped with barbed wire, surrounds the building and tower.

When we reach the gate, Eric stops the Land Rover, and I get out to unlock the padlock, open the gate, and motion him in.

Tilting his hat back on his head, Eric climbs out of the driver's seat. "Well," he says, "We've arrived."

"Yeah," I smile, adding, "Three days isn't bad time, considering the roads." I nod towards the building. "One thing's for sure. Once you've seen one repeater site, you've seen them all. Same pattern, size, and shape." Looking up, I say, "Except the tower is higher here."

✳✳✳

The thick walls of the engine room mute the sound of the generator. Connected to a large bank of heavy-duty batteries, it started without any problem. The power control cabinet has also been set to changeover the duplicated engines every forty-eight hours, so we're operational. Eric smiles as we check the racks of radio equipment in the adjacent room. "The power's on, and the circuit breakers are still in, Gord," he says. "We'll let them settle down while we have lunch. Then we'll contact Bernard and start the testing sequences. I wonder if Bungy's got to Tanga yet?"

Figure 47. Dar es Salaam at dusk.

Our safari kits are unloaded, and the water is soon boiling on the Primus stove. While I put the coffee mugs on the camp table, Eric is rummaging in the chop-box. He's put out the fresh bread and margarine, plus an assortment of jams that we bought at an Indian *duka* this morning, and now he's looking for the cheese. "It's got to be here," he says. "We only bought the bloody stuff this morning. Perhaps someone's nicked it out of the Land Rover." In the end, he finds it hiding in a corner of the box.

The system alignment tests have started, and are going along smoothly as we work through the system, stage by stage. We match our hours to the working hours of the Dar carrier room staff, and work late into the night only when the daily tests are incomplete.

Three weeks have gone by, three weeks of testing and adjusting. Eric puts the communication channel handset down on its cradle. "Well, we're finished, Gord," he says. "I've already talked to Bernard in Dar, and that was Mac from Nairobi. The whole system is operational." A grin twists his face as he gets up from the test desk. "We'll be off home in the morning."

A Memorable Day

August 2nd 1954 marks the completion of the VHF radio repeater routes from Nairobi to Dar es Salaam that started back in April 1951 in Uganda.

The back of the Land Rover is loaded with our personal baggage, safari equipment, and the sensitive test equipment, which we've replaced into their original, shock-absorbent boxes. We've left the equipment running and have set the monitoring alarms. As I watch from the driver's seat, Eric locks the station door. This repeater station is now the responsibility of the Dar terminal and their maintenance staff.

"Okay, Gord," Eric says, climbing into the passenger seat, "Let's go." As we travel down the dusty track, the tower, standing high above the clove trees, is still visible long after the station building has disappeared from view. Back at the main road, we turn south, heading for Zanzibar town and the ferry terminal.

The ferry ploughs through the calm blue ocean towards Dar es Salaam, referred to by the slave traders as the *Haven of Peace*. Behind us lies the island of cloves and copra, mosques, palm trees, and quaint narrow streets. It's mid afternoon when the ferry approaches the mainland, and turns into the narrow channel. The long curve of Oyster Bay with its backdrop of palm trees and whitewashed houses, partly obscured by bougainvillea and frangipani, slides by on the northern bank.

Motioning towards the beach, I say, "Now, that's what I call living, just lying on the beach, soaking up the sun. By the time we've got off the ferry and taken the keys back to Bernard, it'll be late. We might as well stay the night in Dar. Once we leave here, the nearest decent hotel is in Morogoro, but that's well off our route."

"Yeah, that's what I was thinking," Eric says. "We've still got bloody near six hundred miles across those bush roads. To hell with it. We can stay at that hotel near the post office exchange." When he laughs, the crows' feet in the corners of his eyes crinkle. "We might even get to the beach for an hour or so."

It's early the next morning when we leave Dar es Salaam, and by midday, we are well on our way. The Dar-Morogoro Road is far behind us as we head across the Masai Steppes, followed by a trail of dust. When we reach the Mombo turn-off to Lushoto, it is still early in the afternoon, so we continue on the main road to Moshi, where we spend the night.

The last leg of what will probably be the last safari that we make together is a leisurely one. We skirt the foothills of Kilimanjaro and cross the border into Kenya shortly after noon. As we approach Athi River, the familiar stink of the abattoir greets us. It's soon gone, however, because we are driving fast. It's three-thirty when we reach the post office yard. Joan is still at the Harding Street office, so I phone her and arrange to be picked up after four-thirty. It is August 5, 1954.

✳✳✳

With the completion of the radio repeater routes from Uganda to the coast and on to Dar es Salaam comes the successful end of a pioneering era in East Africa that has created the backbone VHF radio telecommunications routes throughout the colony and territories. The men of the radio survey safari crews have played a vital role in the development of communications in East Africa that has brought the people of this land into contact with the outside world via the VHF radio repeater, multi-channel telephone and telecommunication systems. The safari crews have helped to lay the foundations for future African States of Uganda, Kenya and Tanganyika.

Now that the route is completed, the safari crew members are transferred to different sections. Eric has got his wish and is assigned to the new Dar-Dodoma survey team, along with Bungy and Geoff. As for me, I am posted to the Nairobi carrier room, where I'll be responsible for the maintenance and service of the VHF terminal and Kitindini and Mbwinzau repeater stations.

August 1954 also sees the waning power of *Mau Mau* and the beginnings of peace for the war weary land and its people. Eventually the war fought by the British government and the white settlers will be won, but they will lose the peace and power in the political struggle that ends with the Lancaster House agreement. The time of the white settlers and overseas governments has passed, and Africa is on the move towards *uhuru*—independence.

✳✳✳

End of Second Book of Trilogy

Author's Note

Drums of Rebellion is not intended to be a history of Mau Mau in Kenya, but to show a slice of life of Africa in chaos through the eyes of an expatriate living in Kenya and caught up in this turbulent period. The emergency declared in October 1952 was limited to the Central Province of Kenya, and ended, for all intents and purposes, in August 1954. Officially, it ended with the capture of Dedan Kimathi in 1956.

All photographs were taken in the 1950s, many on a small box camera, although I started taking colour slides sometime in 1952. I have made sketch maps to show roads and locations in East Africa as they were in the 1950s, because many place names were changed later.

✳✳✳

Bibliography

Anderson, David. *Histories of the Hanged: the Dirty War in Kenya and the End of Empire*. New York, W.W. Norton & Company, 2005.

Edgerton, Robert B. *Mau Mau: an African Cruicible*. New York, Ballantine Books, 1989.

Great Britain. Colonial Office. *Historical Survey of the Origins and Growth of Mau Mau* (Corfield Report). London, H.M.S.O., 1960.

Henderson, Ian and P. Goodheart. *The Hunt for Kimathi*. [London], 1958.

Mau Mau: a Pictorial Record. 2nd edition. Nairobi, English Press, circa 1954.

Mau Mau Ceremonies and Oaths (includes confessions and statements made to South Kinangop Screening Team and others). Mimeographed copy circulated to government offices in Kenya (circa 1954) and reputed to be a copy of a report being submitted to the British Houses of Parliament.

Books by J. Gordon Mumford

The Black Pit ...and Beyond, GSPH, 2000. (ISBN 1894263197).
"a fascinating personal account [that] provides an excellent
insight into what war actually means for the ordinary
participant." (A. D. Gregor, University of Manitoba, in *CM*.
List price   Cdn $19.95

The Sampan Girl, GSPH, 2001. (ISBN 1894263405). "A moving
story of life, love, and loss." (G. Watson, in *Canadian Book
Review Annual*).
List price   Cdn $24.95

White Man's Drum, Zebra Publishing House, 2004.
(ISBN 0973629703). "Attention to detail, solid research,
vivid description, and creative use of dialogue ...an
interesting glimpse into Kenya life and history during the
country's emergence from colonialism to independence."
List price   Cdn $24.95

Drums of Rebellion, Zebra Publishing House, 2005.
(ISBN 0973629711)
List price   Cdn $24.95

In Fate's Footsteps and *Tales of the NFD*. (Publication dates to
be announced)

Additional reviews are available on the author's website.
http://www.gordonmumford.com

Books are available through your local bookseller, on-line
bookstores (including amazon.com), or from the publisher:

ZEBRA PUBLISHING HOUSE
#413 - 3 Rialto Court
New Westminster, BC, Canada, V3M 6P2
Phone: 604-520-1487 - Fax: 604-520-1497
E-mail: zebrapage@shaw.ca.

Credit card payments are accepted on the website. For
information on bulk order discounts or overseas orders, please
contact us at the above address or by e-mail. Our website is
http://www.zebrapublishinghouse.com